P9-AFZ-993

OXFORD LECTURES ON LITERATURE, 1907-1920

TEN VOLUMES IN ONE

VOL. 1. THE CENTENARY OF TENNYSON, 1809-1909, by T. Herbert Warren. 1909.

VOL. 2. OXFORD AND POETRY IN 1911, by T. Herbert Warren. 1911.

VOL. 3. ROBERT BRIDGES, POET LAUREATE; READINGS FROM HIS POEMS, by T. Herbert Warren. 1913.

VOL. 4. HENRY BIRKHEAD AND THE FOUNDATION OF THE OXFORD CHAIR OF POETRY, by J. W. Mackail. 1908.

VOL. 5. SAMUEL JOHNSON, by Walter Raleigh. 1907.

VOL. 6. PROSE RHYTHM IN ENGLISH, by Albert C. Clark. 1913.

VOL. 7. THE ART OF POETRY, by William Paton Ker. 1920.

VOL. 8. DANTE GABRIEL ROSSETTI AND GERMAN LITERATURE, by L. A. Willoughby. 1912.

VOL. 9. THE STUDY OF ANGLO-NORMAN, by Paul Studer. 1920.

VOL. 10. MALHERBE AND THE CLASSICAL REACTION IN THE SEVENTEENTH CENTURY, by Edmund Gosse. 1920.

Essay Index Reprint Series

BOOKS FOR LIBRARIES PRESS
FREEPORT, NEW YORK

First Published 1924
Reprinted 1968

(General title page added for this reprint edition)

INTERNATIONAL STANDARD BOOK NUMBER:
0-8369-0762-0

LIBRARY OF CONGRESS CATALOG CARD NUMBER:
68-55866

PRINTED IN THE UNITED STATES OF AMERICA
BY
NEW WORLD BOOK MANUFACTURING CO., INC.
HALLANDALE, FLORIDA 33009

THE CENTENARY
OF TENNYSON

1809 — 1909

A LECTURE

GIVEN

TO THE UNIVERSITY EXTENSION STUDENTS
IN THE SHELDONIAN THEATRE

ON

AUGUST 6, 1909

BY

T. HERBERT WARREN, M.A., Hon. D.C.L.

PRESIDENT OF MAGDALEN COLLEGE
AND
VICE-CHANCELLOR OF THE UNIVERSITY

NOTE

I HAVE to thank my friend Dr. George Macmillan and his House for their kind permission to print in full, for the purposes of this Lecture, the poem 'Parnassus' by Lord Tennyson, from 'Demeter and other Poems', published by them in 1889. I have made too, as will be seen, special use of the 'Life' by Hallam Lord Tennyson and the Annotated edition of the Poems, in the Eversley Series. both published by them.

T. H. W.

THE CENTENARY OF TENNYSON

1809–1909

MEN, my brothers, men the workers, ever reaping something
  new :
That which they have done but earnest of the things that they
  shall do :

For I dipt into the future, far as human eye could see,
Saw the Vision of the world, and all the wonder that would be ;

Saw the heavens fill with commerce, argosies of magic sails,
Pilots of the purple twilight, dropping down with costly bales ;

Heard the heavens fill with shouting, and there rain'd a ghastly
  dew
From the nations' airy navies grappling in the central blue ;

Far along the world-wide whisper of the south-wind rushing
  warm,
With the standards of the peoples plunging thro' the thunder-
  storm ;

Till the war-drum throbb'd no longer, and the battle-flags were
  furl'd
In the Parliament of man, the Federation of the world.
  'Locksley Hall' (*written about* 1830, *publishea* 1842).

  Slav, Teuton, Kelt, I count them all
    My friends and brother souls,
  With all the peoples, great and small,
    That wheel between the poles.
  Epilogue to 'Charge of the Heavy Brigade' (*published* 1885).

IN attempting, no easy task, to render due tribute to
the great name and shining memory of the poet who
wrote these lines, on this, the hundredth anniversary of
his birthday, I count myself very fortunate that I am
permitted to speak to this audience and in this place,
for both are singularly appropriate, and I feel that, by
their fitness at least, this Commemoration will be in

some measure adequately and happily honoured. Let me first remind you that Tennyson, as his son records, ' especially approved of the University Extension Movement, for spreading higher education throughout local centres in Great Britain.' Still more, I feel assured, would he have applauded that further development which carries this teaching yet wider, and brings students to the old Universities from every portion of the civilized world. Your gathering represents, I believe, almost every land and language in which Western literature is cherished, and poetry akin to our own has been, and is, written and read. We shall have to-day, we of England, I feel sure, the warm and close sympathy of those of other lands, in our commemoration of our great and representative national genius and poet of the Age which has just closed. For Tennyson was—you will honour him none the less for it—pre-eminently an English poet. No poet, not even Shakespeare, has better depicted for its own sons, and others, the English country, or struck the English note more truly, or celebrated and encouraged in more heart-stirring songs the English achievements by land and sea. He was, too, for the Victorian Age, in its later phase, a poet of Empire, even as Shakespeare was a poet of Elizabethan expansion, triumph, and adventure. But has he not written—

That man's the best Cosmopolite who loves his native country
    best?

Tennyson was genuinely cosmopolitan. His sympathies from the first were with all the world, for its liberty and well-being. As a lad he burned to go to Greece and take part in the War of Independence of 1827. As a young man, he actually went, at the risk of his life, with his bosom friend, Arthur Hallam, to the Pyrenees, to assist the cause, as he believed it, of freedom for Spain. Nursed in classic Cambridge, he studied for himself the language and literature of France,

Germany, and Italy. And except Shakespeare, and in some ways Byron, there is, I suppose, no English poet so generally known to foreign readers. If translation be any test, there are translations of some or other of his poems into French, German, Italian, Spanish, Dutch, Norwegian, Hungarian, and Czech. Of several of the poems there are many. Of 'Enoch Arden', the most popular, there are at least six or eight into French, and even more into German. In France, the land of distinguished and distinguishing criticism, he has been the subject of a continuous stream of notices and reviews, extending from those of Taine and Filon down to the admirable renderings of M. Morel and the fine and sympathetic article of M. Faguet in the 'Quarterly Review' of last April.

From Germany, the home of thorough scholarship and sympathetic translation, he received perhaps his earliest continental recognition. Ferdinand Freiligrath hailed Tennyson as a true poet in 1842, and himself rendered some of his poems into German. A few years ago an indefatigable Polish scholar, Dyboski, lavished on him the erudite labour usually bestowed only upon authors long canonized by antiquity, and collected the results from a number of learned periodicals into a capacious tome worthy of a critic of Homer or Aeschylus. Within the bounds of the English-speaking race, it is worth noting that his 1842 volume found immediate recognition in the United States of America, from Hawthorne and Emerson, above all from his contemporary Edgar Allan Poe, who, with youthful enthusiasm, boldly placed him at once among the foremost poets of all time, while the earliest commentaries of merit came from Canada—the study of the 'Princess' by Dr. S. E. Dawson having a high and special value—and from Anglo-India.

But Tennyson has a still more individual claim on this audience. Your course this year is on Italy, her place in the world's history, her contribution to the thought, the knowledge, the art of the world. What could more fitly form an interlude in this course than that you should turn aside—if it is aside—for an hour to honour Tennyson? From his earliest days he loved Italy, her land, her language, her learning, her art. He began his study when a lad with his brothers and sisters and that friend who was more than a brother, who indeed introduced them all to things Italian.

> O bliss, when all in circle drawn
> About him, heart and ear were fed
> To hear him, as he lay and read
> The Tuscan poets on the lawn.

He travelled often to Italy. Of all his dainty and delicious and musical pieces there is none which better deserves these epithets than one, the outcome and the record of such travel, 'The Daisy,' beginning:

> O Love, what hours were thine and mine,
> In lands of palm and southern pine;
> In lands of palm, of orange-blossom,
> Of olive, aloe, and maize and vine.

His entertainment of Garibaldi is historic. He drew from Italy the subject of one of his plays, he has rendered the tribute of life-long love and admiration to the greatest of her ancient even as to the greatest of her modern poets, to Catullus and Horace and Virgil, and to Dante; and he has found among Italian men of letters, such as Paolo Bellezza, Saladino Saladini Pilastri, or Gaetano Negri, warm and discriminating admiration.

Your presence then aids me, and I am aided too by the thought of the place in which I stand. We are in Oxford, and in the Sheldonian Theatre. It was in this very building, and from this seat, that, fifty-four years ago, Oxford, by the hands of her Chancellor, Lord Derby, himself orator, scholar, and poet, bestowed upon a singularly illustrious band the highest honour in her power, the Honorary D.C.L. Degree. It was done with acclaim, indeed with 'tumult of acclaim'. The year was one of the years of the Crimean War, and the poet came in company with some of the heroes of that conflict. It was an exciting occasion. His son's Life tells us somewhat of the story. I will add a line or two from other sources. The undergraduates of those days were very vociferous. Even before Tennyson entered the Theatre he could hear from afar their shouts, which, he said, were like those of the Roman mob, crying *Christianos ad leones*, and when he came in 'he felt', as he told Max Müller, 'all the time as if he were standing on the shingles of the sea-shore, the storm howling and the spray covering him right and left.'

A friend of mine, Sir Charles Cave, has told me that he still remembers how an undergraduate shouted from the gallery amid general merriment, ' Did your mother call you early, Mr. Tennyson ? '

Then, says the Life, ' in the evening at Magdalen the poet had long talks with Gladstone and Montalembert.' I naturally had the curiosity, when I read this record, to know what was the theme of this converse held in my College by this great trio, a veritable Dialogue of Plato, and I had the audacity to write to Mr. Gladstone and inquire. The answer, if not what I hoped for, was interesting. Mr. Gladstone wrote :—

I am grieved to send you a disappointing answer. But reference to a very arid journal, containing little but dry bones, shows me that on the day in question (June 20, 1855) I saw Mr. Tennyson, then almost a stranger to me, but not in such a way as to give occasion for any serious record of the interview. Public life is cruelly absorbing. I doubt whether in any individual case it has been more absorbing than in mine. One of the serious results is, the risk of knowing nobody outside the pathways of politics. A book like the ' Life of Tennyson' makes me feel how fearful have been my losses in this matter.

But I must attack my main subject and ask you to go back with me, not only fifty, but a hundred years, and looking over the century which has run its course, to consider what are the place and part, which he filled and played, in whose name we are met.

Tennyson was born, then, on August 6, 1809, a hundred years ago to-day. A hundred years ago! So far and yet so near—so near and yet so far! So near —there are certainly some men and women who were living then who are still living now. If they cannot go back in memory quite to that year, there are many, the grand-parents, or it may be the parents, of some of us, who remember the epoch, some even the decade to which it belongs. Alfred Tennyson was the fourth son in a long and long-lived family. Of his brothers all have passed away, but of his sisters, the youngest, born eight years after himself, Cecilia, the lady whose wedding is celebrated in the Epilogue to 'In Memoriam', died only this spring, and one, a year nearer himself in age, still survives. When I myself first entered Magdalen as a young Fellow, the Senior Fellow of the College was a genial, sporting old Doctor of Divinity, who had been born in that very year and only three weeks after Lord Tennyson. He only died in 1896. He was a boy at Eton, an undergraduate at Oxford, with Mr. Gladstone, and had moved step by step with the generation to which both poet and statesman belonged. He remembered Disraeli as an audacious youngster canvassing the electors of High Wycombe. He used to describe the Oxford of old days, and in particular how the coaches came and went from the famed old Angel Inn, which occupied the ground upon which the Examination Schools, where most of your work is being done, now stand. I always thought that he enjoyed some of the remarkable vigour of those born in that remarkable year, 1809. For indeed it was an *annus mirabilis*. Aristotle tells us that there are good and bad crops in the human generation as there are in the products of the soil. 1809 was the birth year in England, as 1909 is reminding us, of Darwin and Tennyson and Gladstone, of FitzGerald and Lord

Houghton: in Germany of Mendelssohn, in America
of Abraham Lincoln and Edgar Allan Poe and Oliver
Wendell Holmes. It was a good year in which to be
born. It did not seem so at the time. Let us put ourselves back, in imagination, in Oxford in 1809, and at
the time of Tennyson's birth. It is a year of melancholy
moment for Oxford, and England, and Europe.

> Not a drum was heard, not a funeral note,
>   As his corpse to the rampart we hurried:
> Not a soldier discharged his farewell shot
>   O'er the grave where our hero we buried.

The poem indeed is not yet written. The young
Irish student whose passport, slight but sufficient, to
immortality it is to form, will only enter this year at
Trinity College, Dublin ; but the sad event is fresh in our
memory. Sir John Moore has fallen at Corunna in the
opening days of the year. Napoleon himself has indeed
left Spain, but after regaining Madrid. The English
have been driven to the sea. Saragossa has been taken.
We have to begin all over again. The Peninsular War
still lies before us. We are not in fear for our own island,
for it is only four years since Nelson fell in triumph on
the deck of the 'Victory' at Trafalgar, and purchased us
immunity from invasion. But beyond the seas we
are everywhere in disaster. Even the rising star of
Sir Arthur Wellesley is for a moment obscured. He
has just won the battle of Talavera and become Lord
Wellington, but has been obliged to retire into Portugal.
The Earl of Chatham and Sir Richard Strachan have
waited on each other too long, and the Walcheren
Expedition has ended in ignominious collapse. The
victory of Wagram has been followed by the Treaty of
Vienna. Andreas Hofer—*der treue Hofer*—the hero of
Tyrol, has been shot at Mantua as a rebel. The Pope
is in prison and the Papacy in abeyance. The fortunes
of freedom seem everywhere to have touched their *nadir*.
Yet England is a queer place. (At home England then

must have been not unlike England now.) Amid all these foreign distractions time is found not only to imprison Sir Francis Burdett in the Tower for en- deavouring to bring about Reform, but also to watch Captain Barclay walking a thousand miles in a thousand hours. And if we could only look forward over the hundred years which are to follow, how different would our feelings be! So near and yet so far. Everything that belongs to our lives, that makes the modern world, seems to have happened between now and then. To go back; Byron has left Cambridge, he has come of age, has taken his seat in the House of Lords, has published his 'English Bards and Scotch Reviewers', which has already run into a second edition, and has just set off with Hobhouse on Childe Harold's Pilgrim- age. Landor, who is to live till 1864 and to receive then the tribute of that youngest and last of the Victorian poets, who died a few months ago, 'the eldest from the youngest singer that England bore,' has left Oxford some years, but Shelley has yet to come and go. He will not arrive till next year from Eton, an awkward, shy, girlish freshman, genteel yet untidy, with his little head, freckled face, and crop of bushy brown hair crowning his tall, swaying form, as his brother freshman, Hogg, describes him, to depart again before the year is out. Eight years still must elapse before another budding poet, a vivacious, pugnacious youngster, not much more than five feet high, with thickly clustering gold-brown hair and hazel eyes, liquid-flashing, forcible, inspired—so the painter Haydon portrays for us the poet Keats—will be seen in Oxford, and near the new Schools, spending a few delightful weeks just over the way in Magdalen Hall, scribbling 'Endymion' while his friend Bailey studies the classics for the examinations which have just been instituted, or jumping into his boat and 'skimming into a bed of rushes and thereby becoming naturalized river folks'. Times far away, yet so near to us, for the Head of Magdalen Hall of that day did not die till 1868, only two years before I myself, as a schoolboy, first saw Oxford. Why, the Head of my own College in 1809, old Dr. Routh, could go back in memory another fifty years to the days of Johnson and Gibbon and Gray, and yet he lived till 1854!

But the real 'era' of the poet is not his first, but his twenty-first, birthday, when he has reached years of discretion, and has passed through the impressions of childhood into those of adolescence and early manhood. Let us move on to Tennyson's coming of age and to 1830. This is indeed a notable year for him. He is now at Cambridge, has been there two years, has found his friends there, that wonderful set whom we all know, for all the world came to know them. He has gained the prize for a Prize Poem on the amazing subject 'Timbuctoo'. What is far more, he has published his own first volume, the 'Poems chiefly Lyrical', he has won his place and the priceless friendship of Arthur Hallam. He has paid his first visit to the Continent, made his journey with Hallam to the Pyrenees and formed impressions which will colour all his after life and writings. In the interval between 1809 and 1830 the poets of his youth whom we mentioned have passed away, all young, all tragically: Keats, the first, by disease in 1820, then Shelley, drowned in 1821, and then Byron, in war, though not indeed in battle, and falling for a noble cause, in 1824. When Byron died, Tennyson and his friends felt as if the world was ending. In 1830 they felt as if it was just beginning, and indeed this and the next three years were of immense and intense moment to them and to the world. For these years, too, were truly the real beginning of the England which we know. In 1830 the first railway was opened. 1831-2 were the years of the battle and victory of Reform. 1833 abolished Slavery in the British dominions. Here, in Oxford, we may remember that it saw the birth of the Oxford Movement. It was in June, 1833, that

Newman on his way home from Sicily and from death's door, wrote, in the Straits of Bonifacio, the verses which, as he modestly says, 'afterwards became well known', 'Lead, kindly Light'. He reached Oxford in July, just in time to hear Mr. Keble preach that Assize Sermon in the University Pulpit on 'National Apostasy' which, as he wrote, 'he always considered and kept as the birthday of the Movement.' A month later Tennyson was taking what he did not then know to be his last farewell of 'his friend, the brother of his soul', Arthur Hallam. Hallam died on September 15, 1833, at Vienna. Just at the close of 1832 Tennyson had published his second volume, his 'Poems', dated 1833, but really given to the world at the end of the previous year. The time then, was for him, one full of event, spiritual and intellectual, moral and material, political and personal. For the moment the personal prevailed. Tennyson was crushed, but the world went on. In 1837 Queen Victoria came to the throne and the Victorian Age began. Since then we have seen the introduction of the steamship and the railway, electricity made the servant of sight and sound and communication, photography, the spectroscope, a hundred, a thousand other inventions; wars that have reconstructed the world, revolutions and reforms sometimes stormy, sometimes peaceful; the final establishment of the American and French Republics, the Unification of Germany, of Italy, of Canada, of Australia, of South Africa, the disappearance of the 'Temporal power', the introduction of parliamentary institutions into Russia and into Turkey. The movements of the mind and the material development of the world have been not less notable. In the same term and at the same age as Tennyson, another undergraduate entered Cambridge, whose name and thoughts have filled the world and whose work she has just been celebrating, Charles Darwin. When Tennyson was a young man he seemed to anticipate these great movements.

Ev'n now we hear with inward strife
    A motion toiling in the gloom—
    The Spirit of the years to come
Yearning to mix himself with Life.

A slow-develop'd strength awaits
    Completion in a painful school;
    Phantoms of other forms of rule,
New Majesties of mighty States—

The warders of the growing hour,
    But vague in vapour, hard to mark;
    And round them sea and air are dark
With great contrivances of Power.

So he wrote in the beautiful piece beginning 'Love thou thy land', the date of which we now know to have been about 1833, though it was not published till 1842. Another piece, less well known, belongs to the same period, 'Mechanophilus,' published only in his last volume at the end of his life, but written, as we are told, 'in the time of the first railways.' By an interesting symmetry of coincidence Tennyson's long life exactly fills the space, with the exception of a narrow margin at either end, of the nineteenth century. Born nine years after it had begun, he died eight years before its close. Its central year, 1850, was the central year of his own life, the year in which he married, in which he became Poet Laureate, in which he published 'In Memoriam'. He reflected, his poems reflect, the evolution of this long and eventful period. At first and for long he was before his time. As Mr. Romanes said, and Mr. Andrew Lang has demonstrated, he anticipated much of the main ideas of Darwin. Then, as younger generations came up, he remained abreast of his time. Perhaps towards the end of his day, perhaps still more since his day, he may appear to some to have fallen behind. Yet even now there are some of his words which seem even truer than when they were written. The 'nations' airy navies', 'pilots of the purple twilight', and all the rest, are just beginning to appear in sight and to be realized, those visions of the world and the future,

which he saw first in 1830, and wrote of in the earlier
'Locksley Hall'. His language about the Empire in
the same way is only now receiving its full realization,
so that to-day he stands side by side with the far
younger Rudyard Kipling as the English poet of
Empire.[1] He may not, at this moment, have the
credit for his originality, and for the very reason that
much that he discovered and revealed has become
so much of a truism and a commonplace and that he
himself is, as the French say, *connu*, and has taken his
place as a classic of the schoolroom and the University
Lecture. As Mr. G. K. Chesterton said a few years
ago so acutely, he may have disappeared from our
consciousness because he has so thoroughly conquered
us, and filled our thought, that we are unaware of the
process. But to-night, looking back over this great
century, let us render him his large meed of desert.
It may be that we are at an awkward distance, just
too far to feel his living influence, not far enough to
estimate it as part of the history of the world. But if
the latter be true we have some compensations—we
are still near enough to recover something of that
reality which has so recently passed away by the aid
of a tradition yet living.

What was he like then, this poet who would have
been a hundred years old to-day had he been living
with us now, who could thus reflect so much of the
century upon which we look back ? His poems tell us
best, and next to his poems the admirable classic life of
him written by his son, and the annotations, mainly the
poet's own, which his son has added to the poems.
Those who knew him and are still with us can tell
us something more. The portraits, drawn, painted,
sculptured, or photographed, may help us. If you will

---

[1] I have received only as this Lecture is passing through the
press, a letter from Dr. S. E. Dawson in Canada, emphasizing, what
I entirely endorse, that the 'Princess' has a yet unexhausted
message for the present moment on the true position of woman.

go to the delightful, refined, select Centenary Exhibition still open at 148 New Bond Street, and spend there a quiet hour or two, you may learn much.

First of all, he was throughout his life a splendid specimen of the human race. 'As a young man he was singularly fine looking, a sort of Hyperion,' said his contemporary FitzGerald: 'Apollo and Hercules in one,' as he wrote elsewhere, tall, six feet in height, broad-chested, strong-limbed, large-handed, with waving hair, dark, like one of southern race, of great physical strength. I myself only knew him when he was quite old. I well remember, I shall never forget, the first impression he made on me. *Qualis artifex!* were the words which rose to my lips, 'a great poet is a great artist.' Sensitiveness, imagination, discrimination, the critical, the creative spirit, seemed to breathe from his mien and face. Something of the same impression I received when I first saw Watts, and indeed they had not a little in common, these two friends and brother artists. It was only later that I came to see how strong he was, even in his extreme old age ; how magnificently strong he must have been in his prime. This union of strength and sensitiveness must always have been his. You see it in the portraits. Some of them show the one quality more than the other. The best show both. Samuel Lawrence's noble portrait of him as a young man shows, I think, both. The sensitive and the intellectual perhaps predominate in the very interesting early drawing, the earliest known portrait, that by Mrs. Weld. Woolner's two busts display more of the strength. It is perhaps more natural for sculpture to do so, but in the beardless one the sensitiveness is not wanting. Of Watts's fine portraits, some I think give less than the strength. The sensitiveness amounts to a troubled, almost vacillating sensitiveness. This may have been true in certain epochs, or at certain moments, of his life. Palgrave writes of his first impressions in 1849 : 'He had the look of one who had suffered greatly : strength

c

and sensitiveness blended.' The last portraits by Watts—the Trinity, Cambridge, portrait, for instance— seem to me truer to the poet's noble yet sensitive strength. For this was the man. He could not have been either the man he was, or the poet he was, without both. His friends found his portrait in the lines meant to be a Prologue to the ' Gardener's Daughter', but his son tells us it was not his intention that they should give such a portrait, and though they have some general characteristics of his, they do not satisfy me as individual enough. 'Tall and broad-shouldered as a son of Anak, with hair, beard, and eyes of southern darkness ; some- thing in the lofty brow and aquiline nose suggests Dante, but such a deep, mellow, chest voice never could have come from Italian lungs,' so Bayard Taylor described him in 1857.

Carlyle's somewhat earlier descriptions are well known. 'A Lifeguardsman spoiled by writing poetry.' 'One of the finest-looking men in the world ; a great shock of rough, dark, hair ; bright, laughing, hazel eyes ; a massive, aquiline face, most massive yet most delicate ' ; ' bronzed ' ; ' almost Indian looking ' ; ' his voice musical, metallic, fit for loud laughter and piercing wail, and all that may lie between.' Such are some of the touches by which at different times he described him about 1840.

His old friend Professor Cowell (who taught Fitz- Gerald to read Omar) wrote in a letter to Dr. Rouse : ' He was, as you say, a really great man. He looked one and he was one.'

Sidney Dobell said finely : ' If you had been told that that man had written the " Iliad " you would not have been surprised ' ; while Henry Reeve, who had known him from youth, spoke of his 'imposing appearance', when he was nearly 70, at his son Lionel's wedding in Westminster Abbey : ' He looked round the Abbey as if he felt the Immortals were his compeers.'

Perhaps after his early sorrows and anxieties had passed away, after he had married, and ' the peace of God had passed into his heart', the troubled expression may also have passed, but the same combination of strength and sensitiveness, the 'most massive yet most delicate' of Carlyle, I think always remained, and I think too it was characteristic of the man.   Independent, standing in his own strength, fearless, candid as a child, he was yet, as he said himself, 'a shy beast loving his own burrow,' and sensitive.   Long after his world-wide fame had been firmly established he was still sensitive to criticism, even when he knew it was wrong.   I remember one of his own characteristic utterances in which he put this himself in his own way.   We had walked out from Farringford in the direction of the Needles.   On our outward journey we had talked of fame, and I remember thinking how strange it was to be thus walking and talking with one whose thoughts and words would affect the world and whose memory would be preserved like the memory of the great of old, like that of Sophocles or Virgil, perhaps many thousand years hence.   It was like being in a little boat towed for a short time by a great ship that is about to sail to the ends of the world.   As we turned back in our walk our converse fell upon Plato and the Tenth Book of the 'Republic', of which he was very fond, with the 'Metempsychosis' as it is called, that famous idea that the souls of the dead, when their time comes to return from the other world to a renewed life in this, are allowed to choose what lives they will have, and how men then chose the lives of beasts and birds, while birds and beasts chose the lives of men ; how the King Agamemnon chose the life of an eagle; and Ajax, the strong hero, the life of a lion ; and the scurrilous jester, Thersites, the life of a monkey ; and the shrewd, world-worn, famous Ulysses, the life of a private man with no cares.

'If I had to choose life over again,' said Tennyson, in his deep voice, half humorously, 'I wouldn't be a poet, I'd be a pachyderm.'   Then, seeing me smiling, 'I don't mean a hippopotamus,' he went on, 'I mean I'd choose to be a thick-skinned fellow with no nerves.'   A few years later I was reminded of this when another great artist and man of letters, George Meredith, was talking to me of Tennyson and his relations with him in his own younger days. I had strolled down Box Hill, on the top of which I was staying, one sunny Sunday afternoon in September, about fifteen years ago, to see the old novelist. I found him lurching round and round his garden in the sun. The paralytic lameness which later on crippled him so sadly had already begun, but there was no lameness in his mind. He talked with the most delightful brilliancy on a number of subjects. We touched for a few minutes on Tennyson. He told me that when he was a young man he had a great admiration for the early poems of Tennyson, and he sent him, in some trepidation, his first volume.

This came out, it may be remembered, in the year 1851. Tennyson wrote back a very pretty letter, saying that there was one poem in the book which he had been going up and down stairs repeating, and that he had told his wife he wished he had written it. This, I gathered, from something Tennyson had told me, was 'Love in the Valley'.

Tennyson then asked him to come and stay the night with him at Twickenham, where he was living at that time. Next morning, as they walked out towards the Thames, Tennyson began, 'Apollodorus says I am not a great poet.' Apollodorus was the 'gifted Gilfillan', as he was called, a Scotch Minister and critic, author of a 'Gallery of Literary Portraits' published in 1845, who took himself, and was taken in those days, with a seriousness now forgotten. 'I said,' quoth Meredith, 'Why should you mind what such a man says?' To which Tennyson replied, 'I mind what *everybody* says.' Swinburne told him, Meredith went on, that Tennyson once said to him that a review in a halfpenny newspaper had caused him a sleepless night.

Meredith proceeded to make the criticism that Tennyson always, when he was praised, repeated his performance; thus he wrote a sequel to the 'May Queen', and he wrote ultimately a second 'Locksley

Hall '. To this I replied, ' Very ultimately, after sixty years,' and Meredith with a laugh admitted that this was so. As to the criticism, I do not know that it amounts to much. It seems a very natural and innocent thing to follow up a success, and there appears to be no reason in the nature of things why *encores* should be confined to music or to sung poems. If it is a fault, Meredith himself fell into it, for he took the original ' Love in the Valley' which Tennyson liked so much, and which consisted of eleven stanzas, and quite rewrote it, adding fifteen more. It is amusing to think that Tennyson told me that by so doing Meredith had spoilt it. The fact is, as every one knows who has had to do with real original artists, no two see alike. They would not be the individual geniuses they are, if they did. Tennyson was before all things a critical artist. If he was critical of others, he was far more critical of himself. This went with, and was part of, his sensitiveness. No poet probably ever deferred more to what he thought was good criticism, and he was very modest. But he was so often blamed and so often praised too for the *wrong* thing, and he found the praise perhaps even more trying than the blame.

> You did late review my lays,

as he once wrote to ' Crusty Christopher '.

> You did mingle blame and praise ;
> When I learnt from whom it came,
> I forgave you all the blame,
> I could not forgive the praise.

My first talk with him, I remember, was about criticism. He came into the room with the ' Spectator' in his hand; the organ in those days of his friend and one of his best critics, as he himself thought, the late Mr. R. H. Hutton. He began saying something about criticism. I mentioned the name of the late Mr. John Addington Symonds, who had encouraged me to write to him. He said, ' Do you think Symonds a good critic?' I replied that in many ways I did, but that I would rather hear whom he thought a good critic than suggest any myself. He replied, 'I don't know. I sometimes think a good critic's very rare, rarer than a good poet. I used to think that Goethe was one of the best critics. He always tried to see all the good he could in a man.' Something of these ideas he embodies in the little poem entitled 'Poets and Critics', when written I know not, but first published in his last volume, in 1892. It always seems to me in tone and form very like Goethe. How good and kindly his criticisms were may be seen from those scattered up and down throughout his son's Life, specially concentrated in certain chapters. He was aided by an admirable memory which enabled him to illustrate his judgements most delightfully.

His genius for criticism is shown in the very first of his letters preserved, written when he was only twelve years old. It was cultivated all through his life, for he was a real scholar. I remember well how when I was an undergraduate, Browning's 'Aristophanes' Apology' came out, and I and my friends were greatly impressed, as indeed we had reason to be, by the poet's erudition, in particular by his acquaintance with the fragments and the *scholia* of the Greek drama, and I said to Mr. Jowett, then the Master of my College, in the way young men do, 'I think, Sir, you know Mr. Browning. Isn't he a great Greek scholar?' 'A very home-spun scholar,' the Master replied. I think perhaps he may have done less than justice to his friend, but I have come to see what he meant. He thought and spoke very differently of Tennyson or of Swinburne.

What he thought of Tennyson he has recorded in the most interesting 'Personal Recollection'. But I doubt whether, in his preference for literary scholarship, the Master has quite done justice to Tennyson's learning. In the period after he left Cambridge he evidently read not only widely but deeply, and shows an acquaintance with authors generally known only to professional scholars.

The fact is, justice has hardly been done to Tennyson's intellectual force. Because he was so much of an artist, because he fulfils so amply in his poetry Milton's canon, that poetry should be 'simple, sensuous, and passionate', because his intuitions were so strong, because he was so obviously the *vates sacer*, the 'inspired seer', because he clung to the old and respected traditions and forms, while looking himself below and beyond them, his powers as a critical scholar and a scientific thinker and a metaphysical philosopher have been underrated. Matthew Arnold underrated him because he was not a bookish 'higher critic', and he has been compared unfavourably with Browning because he is not difficult in the way that Browning is difficult, but there is as much 'fundamental brain-work', as it is called, underneath his poetry as underneath that of Browning or of any poet of the century. He was not indeed an *esprit fort*, and the *esprits forts* are too fond of claiming the monopoly of intellect, but he certainly 'saw life steadily and saw it whole'. Thackeray, it may be remembered, called him the wisest man he knew. If he did not see it more whole than Mat Arnold, at any rate his poetry reflects a far more various and complete view. It is indeed this breadth of view, this sanity and this variety which constitute to some minds Tennyson's weakness, but in reality, I think, his strength. Poetry should be passionate, and the most obvious passions are love and hate, and the most intense at certain moments in life are personal love and hate. There are other loves and hates—love of country, political animosities. These too may fire the poet, and there are loves and hates, intellectual and spiritual, which may again speak in poetry. But these are naturally more long-lived and more diffused over life than the personal and individual emotions. Thus poets who have felt and have dealt specially with one or two seem in some ways to be more poetic. Sappho, Catullus, Villon, Heine, Burns, Poe; they seem essentially poetic. The poets of a more balanced and various disposition, in whom these feelings are more mixed and diffused, do not sting us with such fiery compulsion. Thus Catullus, in whom the personal *odi* and *amo* are so intense, or Lucretius, whose intellectual passion is so trenchant and tremendous, appeal to some minds more than Horace and even Virgil. This intense passion is to be found in Tennyson here and there. You will find it in 'Fatima', with its echo of Sappho and Catullus. You will find it in the incomparable love-lyric 'Come into the garden, Maud'. The intellectual passion of Lucretius may be paralleled out of the 'Two Voices', or 'In Memoriam', or in 'Lucretius' itself. But these are only a part of Tennyson. It is his variety that has made him so popular. Love of his country, of home and friends, his political, worldly wisdom, his humour, these have gained him other friends and followers. I have noticed that those critics who incline to underrate Tennyson almost always make some qualification and confess themselves surprised at his excellence in some one exceptional way. Swinburne— not indeed that he thought little of Tennyson, for he was an avowed and attached admirer—was carried off his feet, rapt into his most superlative rhapsodies, by 'Rizpah'. George Meredith, after telling me that he ranked Tennyson with Tasso, in the second order of poets, went on to say that he 'thought there was no poet with whose writings he was acquainted who had painted so many "inimitable vignettes"'. Professor Oliver Elton speaks of the handful of unassailable songs which place Tennyson for several instants near Shakespeare; and FitzGerald, who thought poorly of the later poems of Tennyson, coming suddenly on the 'Northern Farmer', found himself to his surprise crying over the 'old brute', as he called him, touched by the 'truth and tragedy' of the description.

There are many legends current about the poet's
'roughness and gruffness', as it is called. There always
are such legends about the personal peculiarities of
genius. Some are mere gossip, some amusing and
harmless, whether true or not, some not overkind nor
overtrue. 'There never yet,' as he sang himself,

> Was noble man, but made ignoble talk.

As I have said, he was shy, he was sensitive, he disliked being lionized or run after. Poets differ like
other people. Horace enjoyed being pointed out as he
walked along the street. Virgil ran into the nearest
shop to hide himself. Tennyson was like Virgil.
An amusing story, and one which may be taken as
typical, is the well-known one about Mrs. Cameron,
his very old friend, who took many licences, and one
day sprung, as she often did, a party upon him, and
when he did not receive them over-cordially, said,
'Alfred, I brought these people to see a lion, and
behold a bear!'

Again, you will hear it said that his son's 'Life' gives
too flattering and smooth a picture, that the 'seamy
side' is not shown. There was none to show, no side
that by any stretch deserves to be called 'seamy'.

> And was the day of my delight
> As pure and perfect as I say?
> The very source and fount of Day
> Is dash'd with wandering isles of night.

Foibles even the best have, of course. If the picture
is a bright one, after all that is as it should be. His
was an heroic and a glorious figure.

All I can say is that I found him consistently most
kind, and when I got over the first shyness, most genial
and cordial. His playfulness, his humour, were as
remarkable as his profundity and his sublimity. But
perhaps what struck me most was his transparent
candour. 'A terrible sagacity,' as poor Cowper says,
'informs the poet's heart.' It was so with Tennyson.
He saw through the shams, the conceit, the personal

D

motives of so many who came to him with some axe
or some penknife to grind, and he could not help
showing that he saw through them, and sometimes
telling them so.

Truth-teller was our England's Alfred named.

The general popularity which Tennyson attained in
England was indeed immense. He told Locker-
Lampson that as a boy he had desired it.   In later
life he viewed it more justly.   But it is certainly no
crime in one who never wrote down to gain it, and who
made special appeal to the learned even more than
the unlearned.   It will probably be conceded that he
was the ideal Poet Laureate, that he re-created, if he
did not create, the honour of that office. He was so,
because he was sincere in his loyalty to the powers
that be, to his Queen and his country, because his
laureation received the approval alike of the study and
the street, of the scholar at his desk, and of the man
of action in the forum or the field.   It may be doubted
if, whatever may be thought of him in esoteric circles,
even now that popularity has waned.   My friend
Dr. George Macmillan allows me to say that in the
twenty-five years during which they have been his
publishers, his House has printed nearly half a million
copies of the well-known complete one-volume edition,
and that, although the earlier poems, as fast as they
have come out of copyright, have been republished by
almost every publisher of note.   He is the one great
poet of the Victorian era whose effigy will be found
in that modern 'Temple of Fame' or of 'Notoriety,'
Madame Tussaud's Exhibition, along—the selection is
interesting—with Chaucer and Shakespeare, Burns and
Byron, Sir Walter Scott, Lord Macaulay, and Victor
Hugo. Every New Year's Day sees Calendars of
Shakespeare and Dickens and Tennyson. Of Tennyson
last year I noted at least three by different publishers.
I believe there has been no Academy Exhibition for

the last thirty years in which one or more of the
paintings have not been based on a passage in Tennyson.
This year certainly is no exception. I once began
making a list of the novels in England and America
whose titles are drawn from his works. It is, I can
assure you, a long list. But there are better tests than
these. Take any dictionary of quotations and note the
space allotted to Tennyson. As FitzGerald said long
since, 'Tennyson has stocked the English language
with lines, which once knowing one cannot forgo.'
In his own language,

> Jewels five-words-long,
> That on the stretched forefinger of all Time
> Sparkle for ever.

Take any Anthology of English poetry, I will not say
take the Second Series of the 'Golden Treasury', for
Mr. Palgrave, who owed so much to him in compiling
the First, may be thought to have been partial, but take
for instance the 'Tauchnitz Poetry Book of Modern
English Poets'. See the place he occupies. I will
instance one because it is among the most recent and
has a significance of its own. It is a little collection [1]
compiled the other day by three young girls, ranging
in age from six to sixteen, on the principle of putting in
the pieces which they and their friends have enjoyed.
Tennyson and Scott have there thirteen pieces each.
Only one other poet has as many as seven. I can only
compare his popularity with that of Virgil, who was at
once the hero and favourite of the city crowd and the
provincial empire of the Rome of his day, and yet
appealed at once and lastingly to the scholar, the statesman, and the philosopher. Will Tennyson's fame and
prominence endure like that of Virgil? Who shall say?
Like Virgil, in his own lifetime, he experienced many
veerings of the fickle breath of the *popularis aura*.
Like him he was criticized by poetasters and pedants,

[1] 'The Tripled Crown.' Henry Frowde, Oxford University
Press, London, 1908.

accused of plagiarism, affectation, and preciosity.   He
could not help feeling the criticisms, but he did not
greatly heed them.   What he thought may be best read,
in his own words in the little 'fable', as he calls it,
entitled 'The Flower', of which he may be said to have
given a comic version in an impromptu on 'Popularity',
preserved in the 'Life', or again set out at length in
the notable and inspiring allegory of 'Merlin and the
Gleam', written, as his son says, for those who cared to
know about his literary history, or briefly touched in
the delightful little piece already alluded to, 'Poets and
Critics,' in which he sings—

> What is true at last will tell:
> Few at first will place thee well;
> Some too low would have thee shine,
> Some too high—no fault of thine—
>   Hold thine own and work thy will!
> Year will graze the heel of year,
> But seldom comes the poet here,
>   And the critic's rarer still.

I ought to warn you that I myself am the most 'thick-
and-thin' admirer of Tennyson of my acquaintance.
My own feeling may best be expressed in what D. G.
Rossetti wrote near the end of his life to an artistic
friend: 'One can never open Tennyson at the wrong
page.'

I find it difficult to imagine that some of his lines and
pieces can ever be ignored or pass away, that the
world will ever forget the author of

> The old order changeth, yielding place to new,
> And God fulfils Himself in many ways
> Lest one good custom should corrupt this world.

or,

> But O for the touch of a vanish'd hand,
>   And the sound of a voice that is still!

or,

> 'Tis better to have loved and lost
> Than never to have loved at all.

or,

> Not once or twice in our rough island story
> The path of duty was the way to glory.

or, the 'Flower in the Crannied Wall', or 'Wages', or 'Crossing the Bar'.

What I would build on, if I attempt judicially to estimate his value as a poet, is his affinity with those poets who have lived and lasted down the ages.

> His likeness to the wise below,
> His kindred with the great of old.

To me he seems like Virgil and like Horace, like Chaucer and like Spenser, like Milton and like Gray. True and sympathetic to every fact and every *nuance* in the loveliness of nature, humorous in the observation of men, various as the whole gamut of human interest, deep in scholarly culture, in art rounded and finished, in expression exquisite—his place is surely with them. Yet after all what is literary immortality? He did not himself build on earthly immortality, or live for it. He felt, more perhaps than any other poet, the vastness of the universe as revealed to us by that modern science which he studied so incessantly and expressed so eloquently. His was 'a tiny spark of being' amid its 'deeps and heights', and yet, tiny spark that it was, it was a spark of an imperishable fire and had a value for himself and for its Creator. It is a theme he often hand ed, most aptly perhaps for us this evening in the noble piece 'Parnassus', published in his eightieth year, with which, should time permit, this Lecture will conclude.

Looking back over the hundred years, at the end of which we stand to-day, let us endorse the verdict pronounced by Oxford half a century ago : let us at any rate be thankful for his life and his life's work.

> Render thanks to the Giver,
> England, for thy son !

What he was to his own age remains as a great fact. He was the voice of the Victorian era, and those who wish to know what that voice was, even if it has, amid the new aspirations of another century, but a faint appeal to them, though to my mind, and I believe to that of many, his message is still potent and unexhausted, must go to him to learn it. Yes, let us be thankful for his life and for his example. For—as he himself has said so finely in the first piece I heard him read,—he was fond of reading it—

> For tho' the Giant Ages heave the hill
> And break the shore, and evermore
> Make and break, and work their will;
> Tho' world on world in myriad myriads roll
> Round us, each with different powers,
> And other forms of life than ours,
> What know we greater than the soul?
> On God and Godlike men we build our trust.

Belief in God, belief in the value and the immortality of his own existence, on these he built. He held by that old threefold cord, not easily broken, of Faith, Hope, and Love.

> We have but Faith: we cannot know;
> For Knowledge is of things we see;
> And yet we trust it comes from Thee,
> A beam in darkness: let it grow.

Faith at times might falter, but it returned again and yet again, and was stronger than ever at the last.

Hope might falter even more.

Love, that 'greatest of the three', was the strongest.

In his earliest days he formulated and proclaimed his creed.

> The poet in a golden clime was born
> With golden stars above;
> Dower'd with the hate of hate, the scorn of scorn,
> The love of love.

Throughout his life this was what he sought to give and longed to receive.

Let us repeat that tribute which in the hour of their bereavement comforted more than any other those who were near and dear to him, and offer yet again 'love and reverence to the memory of him who above all things loved Love!'

PARNASSUS

Exegi monumentum   .   .   .   .
Quod non .   .   .   .   .   .
Possit diruere .   .   .   .   .
.   .   .   .   .   innumerabilis
Annorum series, et fuga temporum.
HORACE.

I

WHAT be those crown'd forms high over the sacred
    fountain?
Bards, that the mighty Muses have raised to the height
    of the mountain,
And over the flight of the Ages! O Goddesses, help
    me up thither!
Lightning may shrivel the laurel of Caesar, but mine
    would not wither.
Steep is the mountain, but you, you will help me to
    overcome it,
And stand with my head in the zenith, and roll my
    voice from the summit,
Sounding for ever and ever thro' Earth and her listening
    nations,
And mixt with the great Sphere-music of stars and of
    constellations.

II

What be those two shapes high over the sacred fountain,
Taller than all the Muses, and higher than all the
    mountain?
On those two known peaks they stand ever spreading
    and heightening;
Poet, that evergreen laurel is blasted by more than
    lightning!

Look, in their deep double shadow the crown'd ones all
    disappearing!
Sing like a bird and be happy, nor hope for a deathless
    hearing!
Sounding for ever and ever? pass on! the sight
    confuses—
These are Astronomy and Geology, terrible Muses!

III

If the lips were touch'd with fire from off a pure Pierian
    altar,
Tho' their music here be mortal, need the singer
    greatly care?
Other songs for other worlds! The fire within him
    would not falter;
Let the golden Iliad vanish, Homer here is Homer
    there.

From 'Demeter and other Poems' (*published* 1889).

Oxford and Poetry in 1911

AN INAUGURAL LECTURE
DELIVERED IN THE SHELDONIAN THEATRE
ON JUNE 2, 1911

BY

T. Herbert Warren, M.A., Hon. D.C.L.
PRESIDENT OF MAGDALEN COLLEGE
PROFESSOR OF POETRY

1911

OXFORD AND POETRY IN 1911

Allora è buono ragionare lo bene quando ello è ascoltato.
DANTE, *Convivio*, iv. 27.

MR. VICE-CHANCELLOR,

To be given the right, and therefore the duty, to speak in this place, and from this Chair; to speak for Oxford and on the high theme of Poetry, is indeed to be accorded a position which might well overweight even the most competent and confident.

Only to aspire to be Professor of Poetry is, as an old friend said to me a short time ago, an honour.

Oxford has given me many honours. Some here may remember the 'smooth-tongued scholar' in Marlowe, who says

> my gentry
> I fetch from Oxford, not from heraldry.

Without adopting these words in their literal sense, I would say assuredly that Oxford has given me all the best honours I have, and those I would most care to have.

To strive to serve her is my privilege. May her own inspiration aid me and the traditions of this Chair! The traditions of this Chair. What are they? It has many, some old, some new.

There is one, a lost tradition, ·which I have been asked to revive, and to address you in Latin, to shroud, shall I say? my deficiencies in the 'decent obscurity of a learned language'.

And for certain reasons I might feel tempted to revive

it. There are some things which can be said so much
more neatly and easily, without fulsomeness or flattery,
in Latin than in English. But I doubt if to-day the
suggestion is a practical one. Whatever may have been
the feeling in Keble's own time, I think it has been
admitted since that the fact of his lectures being in
Latin has prevented their finding that vogue which they
deserved, or producing that effect which they might well
have produced.[1] Keble himself, in criticizing Copleston's lectures, condemned the practice and in strong
terms. 'A dead language,' he said, 'is almost a gag to
the tongue in delivering ideas at once so abstract and
so delicately distinguished.' He afterwards returned to
Latin himself on the ground that it would make him
more careful in pronouncing judgement. I do not think,
after reading his lectures, that he of all men needed
that added terror, and I hope I may not.

Another tradition of the Chair I know not if I have
broken. I should like in some small measure to have
done so, and you will sympathize when I tell you what
it is. I will give it you in the words of a poetess to
a poet, of Elizabeth Barrett to Robert Browning. In
one of those delightful early letters, she writes under
the date of January, 1848. 'You of the "Crown" and
of the "Lyre" to seek influence from the "Chair of Cas-
siopeia"! I hope she will forgive me for using her name
thus. I might as well have compared her (as a Chair
I suppose) to a Professorship of Poetry in the University
of Oxford according to the last election. You know the
qualification there is *not to be a poet.*'

But to come to traditions of the Chair more recent
and more living. I think naturally first, as you will be

[1] See p. 36.

thinking, of him who filled it last. I take to-day 'this
laurel',—the phrase is now so trite we hardly give due
credit to the admirable poet who coined it for us some
sixty years ago,—from the brow of one who uttered not
only 'nothing base', but nothing that had not, to my
mind at any rate, in his utterance of it, an indescribable
grace. *Ipsa mollities*, a certain 'Dorique delicacy', such
as the scholarly old diplomat and Provost of Eton who
has recently been made to live again for us so fully,
Sir Henry Wotton, found in the youthful Milton—these
phrases seem to me to describe more aptly than any
others the utterance of Professor Mackail. His criticism
of poetry was in itself a kind of poetry.

Nor can I forget, who could forget ? the recent tenure
of another, a friend from my undergraduate time, and
of the same Society, Professor Bradley, who in his five
years surely made an enduring mark, who reconciled
that ancient, ever recurrent, but ever reconcilable feud
of two great forces of the soul and departments of
the mind, and showed us how philosophy can handle
poetry.

I think, too, as my mind turns backward, of the author
of that delightful 'play of the youthful spirit', the 'Paradise of Birds', who in later years, amid the routine of
office conscientiously discharged, accomplished that vast
task which Pope projected, with which Gray dallied,
which Warton left half told, and has given us a definitive
History of English Poetry.

The Editor of that *Golden Treasury* which was so
much for my generation I knew and have heard, and
I have heard too the serious and gravely generous
author of the 'Bush aboon Traquair'.

The author, gallant and urbane, of the 'Private of the

Buffs' I never heard, but some here have doubtless done so.

And some few have even greater memories. When we think of this Chair and its tradition in the last century, two names stand out before all others, those of Matthew Arnold and of Keble. To the superficial observer they seem to stand out in sharp contrast.

They seem as far apart as the grave and the gay, the sacred and the secular, the saint and the Voltairian. In truth Arnold was no mere Voltairian. Keble again was no stiff or bigoted divine, no believer 'because it was impossible'.

It is not sufficiently remembered that Keble was the old college friend of Dr. Arnold and that he was Matthew Arnold's own godfather. It was not only Clough of whom it could be said—

The voice that from St. Mary's thrilled the hour,
He could not choose but let it in though loth.

Matthew Arnold, as an undergraduate, fell like Stanley, like Froude and Pattison and Jowett, like Coleridge and Temple,—who indeed of that time did not fall?—under the influence of the Tractarians. Many here will remember Arnold's moving description of Newman at St. Mary's, given in the Lecture on Emerson delivered in America, beginning, 'Forty years ago when I was an undergraduate at Oxford voices were in the air then which haunt my memory still. Happy the man who in that susceptible season of youth hears such voices! They are a possession to him for ever.'

And the debt was not only spiritual or moral, it was aesthetic also. They had as a common possession a deep love and reverence for Wordsworth, and it is worth while to compare Keble's studied yet happy dedication of his Lectures, with Arnold's Memorial Verses on

Wordsworth. Attention has often been called to the somewhat surprising title prefixed by Keble to these same Lectures, *De Poeticae Vi Medica*. Is it fanciful to suggest that Arnold's well-known expression about Wordsworth's '*healing* power' is borrowed from this heading?

But I have said enough and more than enough for the present moment on these two great names. They are not the only great names of the last century. Keble was preceded by a name not quite so memorable in the history of the Church or of sacred poetry, but still memorable in regard to these interests, and in relation to Church History and sacred scholarship certainly of first-rate eminence, that of Dean Milman.

And there is yet one more name belonging to the century which ought not to be forgotten, that with which it opens. Two of the three I have mentioned are Oriel names. So pre-eminently is this other name, that of Edward Copleston. There are few to which Oriel or Oxford owes more.

The Chair has been in existence for just two hundred years, and its history falls exactly within the bounds of two delimited centuries, the eighteenth and the nineteenth. I have mentioned, omitting living persons, four names of special note in the nineteenth century. Oddly enough the eighteenth presents exactly the same number, those of the first Professor, Joseph Trapp, of Joseph Spence, of Robert Lowth, and Thomas Warton.

Trapp was of Wadham. There is another debt to that most poetical College, which has, I think, never been properly recognized or put on record. The Chair owes its first tradition to one Wadham man, it owes its very existence to-day to another, a recent Head of that House, Mr. G. E. Thorley.

The third Professor was of New College, Joseph Spence. He is certainly memorable. His *Literary Anecdotes* are still agreeable and suggestive reading, and form also a valuable repertory of literary history.

His *Polymetis*, in the fine edition to be found in College Libraries, is a noble book. It had a deserved and far-reaching influence. One special debt we owe it. It was from an abbreviated school edition of Spence's *Polymetis* that Keats derived some of his early inspiration. We think too little, in these days of exact and exhaustive scholarship and archaeology, of those delightful, traditional, gossiping literary works, literary rather than scientific, of Lemprière, Tooke, and Spence. Without Spence we might never have had the 'Ode on a Grecian Urn'.

Of Lowth there is also much to be said. He was a man of mark and character both in letters and affairs. I may be pardoned for quoting at least one testimony. Every one knows the scathing criticism, couched in his inimitable style, which was passed by the great historian of my Society upon his University and his College. The two or three exceptions are not always noted.

In the well-known passage in which he advocates the value of public lectures, the historian himself concludes, 'I observe with pleasure that in the University of Oxford, Dr. Lowth with equal eloquence and erudition has executed this task in his incomparable Praelections on the Poetry of the Hebrews.'

Thomas Warton certainly calls for a lecture to himself, and it may perhaps peculiarly be due from one who is like him a resident. His burly features still look down on us in the Hall of Trinity and suggest his love of beer and bargees, mingled with his pioneer love of black-letter poets.

But it is not generally known that more than once, a greater than all these came within measurable distance of being Professor.

In 1867 Robert Browning was given the M.A. degree with the idea, in some quarters at any rate, that he might succeed Matthew Arnold as Professor. Arnold's own comment on the matter is to be found in his *Letters* (vol. i, p. 350).

'You will have been interested,' he writes, 'by the project of putting Browning up for the Chair of Poetry; but I think Convocation will object to granting the degree just before the election, for the express purpose of eluding the statute. If Browning is enabled to stand I shall certainly vote for him; but I think Doyle will get in.' The degree was carried, as we have seen, but whether for this reason or for any other the project of the Professorship was dropped, and Oxford and England lost a great opportunity.

It is on record, on the authority of Mr. Edmund Gosse, that Browning said, that had he been elected Professor, his first lecture would have been on Thomas Lovell Beddoes, 'a forgotten Oxford poet.' Beddoes had as it happened already been noticed from this Chair, though not, it is true, very favourably. Writing from Pembroke in 1825 to his friend Kelsall, he says, 'Mr. Milman, our Poetry Professor, has made me quite unfashionable here by denouncing me as one of a villainous School.' I, too, might be tempted to lecture on Beddoes, for he is a Bristol, as well as an Oxford poet. But his story, if not so sad as the better known story of Chatterton, is a sad one, and the study of it would savour somewhat of morbid pathology, however much Browning's animating vigour might have given it a new health, and would certainly have touched it sanely.

Ten years after Browning's possible candidature, another and quite a different possibility arose. In 1877 overtures were made from Oxford to William Morris to stand. His reply, which is given at length in Mr. Mackail's Biography, is illuminating to all who are interested in poetry. It is very like the well-known letter in which Gray gave his reasons for declining the office of Poet Laureate. Morris thought, he said, that the practice of any art rather narrowed the artist in regard to the theory of it. He doubted whether the Chair was more than an ornamental one, and whether the Professor of a wholly incommunicable art was not rather in a false position. 'Nevertheless,' he concludes, 'I would like to see a good man filling it, and if the critics will forgive me, somebody who is not only a critic.' The letter, like Gray's, was a little hard on persons less gifted than himself.

Is the Chair more than an ornamental one? Is the art wholly incommunicable? What is the relation of a University to poetry? Many Universities, all in a sense, but some in a special sense, would seem to have much about them that may be called poetical. It is a commonplace that Oxford is herself poetical.

So are other Universities, Cambridge, St. Andrews, Heidelberg. They are poetical in their history, their buildings, their amenities, their associations, their free and inspiring life.

And yet the *milieu* of a University is not, in the general sense, the *milieu* of poetry.

It is the business of Oxford to criticize, not to create; to prepare, not to practise. It is with few exceptions by going out from her, not by lingering within her walls,

that her sons achieve greatness in the field of letters as
well as in the field of affairs.

It is a hard saying for a resident, but I would say this
to any son of Oxford. If you want before all to be
a poet, if that is your first object, don't stay in Oxford.

Why not? you will reply.

> *Es bildet ein Talent sich in der Stille,*
> *Sich ein Charakter in dem Strom der Welt.*

Surely Oxford is *die Stille.* Yes, but in Poetry talent
is only half the battle, character is needed not less.

> Ah, two desires toss about
> The poet's restless blood,
> One drives him to the world without
> And one to solitude.

I hasten to add that there have been exceptions,
and that they are becoming every day more common
because the Universities are every day becoming so
much more open and various. I would say also that
this counsel is not for those whose natural home is
Oxford. For them it is like any other home, except that
it is unlike any other and better than most.

But the academic life does not suit very well with the
writing of poetry or indeed of original literature.

It is true that the author of the *Cloister and the Hearth*
and of *Peg Woffington* had been a Fellow at my College
when I first joined it for about forty years, and remained
so for some ten more. But he preferred the London
hearth to the Oxford cloister, and his life was more of
the town than the College.

Keble, again, wrote the poems which form the
Christian Year while he was a young resident Fellow
and Tutor, but at the time when his poetic powers were
quickest he liked Oxford least. 'I begin to be clear,' he

wrote when he was seven-and-twenty, 'that I am out of my element here,' and again a little later, 'I have made up my mind to leave Oxford, I get fonder and fonder of the country and of poetry and of such things every year of my life.' Shortly after, at the age of thirty, he left.

Dodgson and Pater, again, have been partial exceptions, and there are some living exceptions to-day whom I could name.

The great exception, the great example is Gray. What does Gray himself say about the academic life and the great world?

In a letter to Thomas Wharton, he writes as follows:—

'DEAR DOCTOR,—You may well wonder at my long taciturnity. I wonder too, and know not what cause to assign, for it is certain I think of you daily. I believe it is owing to the nothingness of my history, for except six weeks that I passed in town toward the end of spring and a little jaunt to Epsom and Box Hill, I have been here time out of mind in a place where no events grow, though we preserve those of former days by way of *Hortus Siccus* in our libraries. My slumbers were disturbed the other day by an unexpected visit from Mr. Walpole who dined with me, seemed mighty happy for the time he stayed and said he would like to live here: but hurried home in the evening to his new gallery which is all Gothicism and gold, and crimson and looking-glass. He has purchased at an auction in Suffolk ebony chairs and moveables enough to load a waggon.'

Yet Gray, from those College rooms which we may still see at Pembroke, indited the most popular poem in the language.

Gray, it has always seemed to me, would have been an ideal Professor of Poetry. For though, like all critics, he makes his mistakes, he is one of the best critics of Poetry, and equally strong in learning and in taste.

The functions of a University are just these, to preserve in its *Hortus Siccus* those events of former days,
and to grow in its Botanical Garden the typical plants of
the world : to compare their blossoming and their fruit-
age, to dissect their anatomy, to analyse them, to learn
their law, to know the best that has been thought and
written in all ages and places, to view things *sub specie
aeternitatis*, to provide a real standard.

It is this power that our study of the ancient classics
has given us in the past and that the modern classics
added to the ancient must still further give us, with a
larger induction, in the future.

This presentment of the classics fortunately coincides
with the special duties of the Professor. For what are
they ? When I was elected Professor I naturally read
the statute relating to the Chair. I found to my
pleasure that the Professorship was established for two
reasons, firstly because the reading of the 'old poets'
conduces to 'sharpening and making ready and nimble
the wits of the young', secondly because this same reading conduces 'to addition being made to more serious
literature, whether sacred or profane'.

My duties are then to lecture on the 'old poets' with
this twofold end in view. As to the sharpening of the
undergraduates' wits I am not sure that that is what
they most want. I remember how sharp they were in
my day. Still I gladly recognize that part of my duty is
to speak to the young. It is they after all who care
most about poetry, though they generally have their own
opinions pretty well made up—at any rate for the next
few months.

But here I find a difficulty which apparently my predecessors did not in the early days. Who are to-day
the old poets ? Down to Arnold's time my predecessors

seem to have confined themselves, though with increasing liberty of allusion and digression, to the Greek and Latin Classics. Keble, however, allowed himself considerable latitude, and Arnold of course set an example of absolute freedom, not only as regards period but as regards subject. He tells us ingenuously in one of his letters that he threw in the famous lectures on translating Homer because he was supposed, and indeed I think we may say with some reason, not to have lectured enough on poetry.

It was natural that the early Professors should be thus limited. They were so by the custom of the University. They were so by natural causes. Two hundred years ago when Professor Trapp began to lecture, who were the old poets in England and in France? We can best answer that by asking who were the new poets? In 1711, the year in which Trapp began, Louis XIV was still reigning in France and Queen Anne in England.

The recent poets in France were Corneille and Molière, Lafontaine, Racine, and Boileau. In England, Milton and Dryden were hardly old, Pope and Addison were still living and at work.

As for modern German poetry it simply did not exist.

A hundred years later these had become really old writers. Who in turn were the recent and the new? Voltaire and Rousseau had been dead just a generation, but they were still recent. Madame de Stael and Chateaubriand were in middle age. Béranger was thirty-one. Lamartine had just come of age. Hugo was a boy of nine. Schiller had died at the age of forty-two in 1805, but Goethe was still active. Burns was still recent, Scott as a lad had seen him, Scott who was now just between his poems and his novels. The *Lyrical Ballads* had been published some fifteen years, and followed up by the *Poems* with their famous Prefaces. Byron had come of age, had published *English Bards and Scotch Reviewers*, and then dashed off on *Childe Harold's Pilgrimage*. Keats was a surgeon's apprentice among his gallipots, but reading Spenser and translating the *Aeneid*. Shelley had just come up to University College and was just going to get himself sent down again, after two terms' residence. Landor had been sent down from Trinity for an explosion of a different kind a few years before. Tennyson and Mrs. Browning were babes in arms, and Robert Browning was not yet born.

Now these in their turn, are 'souls of poets dead and gone'.

To-day another hundred years have passed by. The Victorian Age itself is now classic, or is rapidly becoming so. It will soon be as classic as the age of Queen Anne. Two years ago, in two successive months, its last representatives vanished from this scene, Swinburne in April, Meredith in May, of 1909. They seemed to pass at once, as the poet says, *sideris in numerum*, and to be added to the great glittering constellation of the Victorian Era. We are beginning then to be in a position to deal with the Victorian Age as a whole, and I think we may do so with some advantage. We stand now sufficiently far off to treat it to some extent historically, yet near enough to be aided by living tradition, and to be saved by this tradition from many of those mistakes to which the hypotheses of a later age, after the facts have been forgotten, must always be liable.

But the situation has changed for the Professor of Poetry in Oxford in two hundred years in another and not less important way.

Two hundred years ago, even one hundred years ago, there was very little public lecturing in Oxford on the poets. Gibbon in his later life made it a complaint that the Professors did not lecture either at Oxford or at Cambridge. 'The silence,' he says, 'of the Oxford Professors, which deprives the youth of public instruction, is imperfectly supplied by the Tutors as they are styled, of the several Colleges.'

But, for the most part, there were very few Professors to lecture, even if they had all discharged their duty in this regard.

To-day the field of English, both in literature and in language, is covered by a brilliant band of Professors, Readers, and Lecturers. The *Times*, in a leading article on the day of the election to this Chair, said, and justly, that my friend Professor Raleigh has written books which are just such as any Professor of Poetry might have written—if he could.

But, Mr. Vice-Chancellor, it is not only the Professor of English Literature who divides the field with and raises the standard against the unfortunate Professor of Poetry of to-day. The Professor of Greek does just the same. So again does the Professor of Latin and the Professor of German, and the Lecturers in French and Italian and Spanish. All these gentlemen are so many Professors of Poetry. They are so partly by their own gifts, and partly also by the nature of their office. It may happen, it does happen, that some of them are also in no small degree, but in a very marked degree, poets. The same is true of the keen-witted scholar whom the sister University has just annexed to herself, the author of the *Shropshire Lad* who is the Cambridge Professor of Latin. Need I say how largely it is true too of Dr. Verrall? But in point of fact the same has been true for a long time both here and at Cambridge, and true not only of the Professors but of the College

Lecturers. It was true of Sir Richard Jebb. It was eminently true of that vivid younger scholar, critic, and poet, Walter Headlam.

You may see the same phenomenon in Scotland, and no less strikingly in poetic Ireland. You may see it in London University, and in the provincial Universities and Colleges.

Meanwhile, it is all the more important to ask what room there is left for the Professor of Poetry as such. What ought he to be, and to do? It has been said, 'You should obtain for your Professor a practising poet.' Is that in order that he might speak from experience about the technique of his art, shall I say the tricks of his trade? I imagine not. You will find it, I think, difficult to persuade him to do so, and few would be either competent or prepared to follow many lectures of such a kind. But it is very true that the best criticism of the poets has been written by the poets, whether in prose or in verse. The popular saying which finds expression in so many forms, that a critic is a poet, or a creative artist, who has failed, contains at best only half the truth. The good poets have seldom failed as critics. On the contrary, so far as they have touched it, they have signally succeeded. I am inclined to think that the truth is rather that the critics have failed as poets than that the poets have failed as critics. I had already written this when I found that it had been anticipated by the poet Shenstone, who says, 'Every good poet includes a critic: the reverse will not hold.' Some of the greatest critics are indeed not known as poets, but it will, I think, generally be found that they have at one time or another written poetry, from the days of Plato and Aristotle to those of Sainte Beuve, who always declared that when the 'integrating molecule in himself was reached, it would

c

be found to have a poetical character'. Matthew Arnold, the most original and memorable critic among my predecessors, was also undoubtedly the best and most memorable poet. It was when he tried to pass directly from the critic to the poet that he failed. He wrote *Merope*, his least known and his least successful long poem, just after he became Professor. He said himself, 'She is calculated rather to inaugurate my Professorship with dignity than to move deeply the present race of *humans*.' His best work in poetry was all done before he filled this Chair. The same was true, though less strikingly, of his predecessor, Keble. The reason in both cases, no doubt, is partly natural. The best poetry of both was written by both in their younger and less critical days. Where the poet and the critic coexist, the critic tends, as years go on, to gain upon the poet, partly from the influence of the world outside, partly from internal causes. But these examples, and many others, go to prove that the practice of poetry is the best preparation for the practice of criticism. Of the great critics in our own language, some have been poets hardly less great, like Dryden, Pope, and Coleridge. Others, while not so excellent in verse, like Addison and Johnson, must still rank among the poets.

The same has continued true in our own time. There are no more suggestive and illuminating lights of criticism, even if they are only rare intermittent flashes, than the *obiter dicta* of excellent poets, whether those of Sophocles or Goethe, of Ben Jonson or Gray, of Tennyson or Meredith. One of the best of critics notwithstanding his occasional caprice, his prejudice against persons as dissimilar as Euripides and Byron, 'George Eliot' and Walt Whitman, was Swinburne. You require, it is true, to know how to read, and if necessary to transpose, his notation. He reminds me of an examiner with whom I once acted, long since dead, whose marking was admirable, if you only understood his scale, and could translate it into normal usage. Swinburne estimated in superlatives or the opposite. His marks were all $a+$ or $\delta-$. Meanwhile the difficulty of filling the Chair in the way suggested is the familiar one. 'First catch your poet.' We have seen how Morris declined; others nearer in time and space have done the same.

How then does poetry stand at the present moment, more particularly in England? Where are we in its evolution? Have we any data either of dead reckoning, or of sounding, or of observation, by which we can determine our bearings? Let us look at the poetic history of the past century. In 1825 Hazlitt, that brilliant and sincere, if too pungent and polemic writer, gave to the world a series of portraits which he collected under the title of *The Spirit of the Age*. About a score of years later the author of *Orion*, Richard Hengist Horne, thought the time had come to issue a *New Spirit of the Age*.[1]

The criticisms are still interesting; yet more interesting is it to see who are the personages criticized. Who were Hazlitt's figures? He begins with Jeremy Bentham and William Godwin, he ends with Lamb and Washington Irving. Between these come Coleridge, Edward Irving, Scott, Byron, Southey, Wordsworth, Sir James Mackintosh, Malthus, Canning, Gifford, Jeffrey, Lord Brougham, Sir Francis Burdett, Lord Eldon, Wilberforce, Cobbett, Campbell, Crabbe, Tom Moore, and Leigh Hunt. It will be remarked that neither Shelley nor Keats finds a place. In the account of Byron it is noted that the news of his death arrived even while the paper on him was being composed. Of

[1] See p. 36.

the figures selected by Hazlitt as typical of the Age of 1825, only two survive in Horne's book as typical of the Age of 1844. These are Wordsworth and Leigh Hunt, 'two laurelled veterans,' 'links between the past and the present' as he describes them. Who are Horne's other figures? It is interesting to recall the names of the men and women who in 1844 appeared to the critic to embody the spirit of the era. The list is a very long one. I will not give it you in full. It may suffice to say that it begins with Charles Dickens (Thackeray significantly does not appear), the Earl of Shaftesbury, 'Thomas Ingoldsby,' and Landor: that it contains Dr. Pusey and Captain Marryatt, Tennyson, Macaulay and his victim Robert Montgomery, Macready, Harriet Martineau, Elizabeth Barrett, Robert Browning, and Carlyle, and ends with Sir Henry Taylor and the author of *Festus*. There is this difference between the two. Hazlitt in 1825 is pessimist and looks backward. His essay on Coleridge opens with this striking statement: 'The present is an age of talkers and not of doers, and the reason is that the world is growing old. We are so far advanced in the Arts and Sciences, that we live in retrospect and doat on past achievements.'

Was this how the age really appeared to a perspicacious mind in 1825? 'Far advanced in the Arts and Sciences! "Figure it to yourselves," as the French say. Five years before the opening of the first railway, five years off from 1830.'

Horne, on the other hand, is optimist and looks forward. What has intervened? A gigantic stirring and awakening alike spiritual and material. They were, indeed, in 1825, in the small hours, in the dead, weary night before the dawn. When Byron died, Tennyson

and his friends, as you remember, thought the world
was at an end.   Our world was only just beginning.

The era ran its well-known course.   We have another
picture of it.   A little more than twenty years later
again, Matthew Arnold, in a volume styled *New Poems*,
included a remarkable and characteristic piece entitled
'Bacchanalia, or The New Age'.   May I be allowed
to make rather a long quotation from the middle of this
poem?

'The epoch ends,' he writes :—

> The epoch ends, the world is still.
> The age has talk'd and work'd its fill—
> The famous orators have shone,
> The famous poets sung and gone,
> The famous men of war have fought,
> The famous speculators thought,
> The famous players, sculptors, wrought,
> The famous painters fill'd their wall,
> The famous critics judged it all.
> The combatants are parted now—
> Uphung the spear, unbent the bow.
> The puissant crown'd, the weak laid low.
>
> .   .   .   .
>
> And o'er the plain, where the dead age
> Did its now silent warfare wage—
> O'er that wide plain, now wrapt in gloom,
> Where many a splendour finds its tomb,
> Many spent fames and fallen mights—
> The one or two immortal lights
> Rise slowly up into the sky
> To shine there everlastingly,
> Like stars over the bounding hill.
> The epoch ends, the world is still.
>
> Thundering and bursting
> In torrents and waves—
> Carolling and shouting
> Over tombs, amid graves—
> See on the cumber'd plain
> Clearing a stage,
> Scattering the past about
> Comes the new age.

Bards make new poems,
Thinkers new schools,
Statesmen new systems,
Critics new rules.
All things begin again;
Life is their prize;
Earth with their deeds they fill,
Fill with their cries.

The passage is applicable, that is part of its merit, to any marked and sundering change from an old to a new era. But it seems indubitable that Arnold was thinking of his own era, of the end and break-up of the old political régime, culminating in 1848, of the death of Wordsworth in 1850 (preceded by Coleridge and Southey), in other words of the 'new age' heralded by Horne in 1845. This becomes yet more clear if we read the Memorial verses, headed 'April, 1850', and first published in *Fraser's Magazine* at the time of Wordsworth's death, which took place on April 23 of that year. It is not perhaps easy to say exactly what Arnold held to be the true limits of Wordsworth's 'period', for, like every other critic, he regarded him as having outlived his day. He ranks him, however, with Byron and Goethe as a poet of 'the iron age', 'the iron time', 'Europe's dying hour'.

That had been the time of Wordsworth's real impact. His influence gradually grew with the age which he formed. Horne's prose says again the same as Arnold's poetry: 'After twenty years of public abuse and laughter William Wordsworth is now regarded by the public of the same country as the prophet of his age.'

Arnold's poetic treatment of the New Age, it will be noticed at once, is far more general and wide in its scope than that of Horne's prose volumes. But this is accidental.

In the Preface to his first edition Horne writes,
'Should the design of the projectors be fully carried
out the work will comprise the Political Spirit of the
Age, in which of course the leading men of all parties
will be included, the Scientific Spirit of the Age, the
Artistical Spirit of the Age, and the Historical, Biographical, and Critical Spirit of the Age.'

Horne then fully intended to be as all-embracing in
his diagnosis and analysis as Arnold is in his suggestion.
In point of fact the new age was perhaps most marked
in the realm of painting, the most central, notorious, new
departure being that of the since famous Pre-Raphaelite
Brotherhood which started in the autumn of the year 1848.
The name for it was found by Dante Gabriel Rossetti in the
summer of that year, after he had read Lord Houghton's
Life and Letters of Keats.   It was the result of the friendship of three young art students, Rossetti, Millais, and
Holman Hunt, who had joined forces in this year.
Holman Hunt described it to me himself when he was
here painting 'May Day on Magdalen Tower'.   After
a *reconnaissance* in 1849 they made their real venture
in 1850 and 1851, when the battle began.   They were
at once violently attacked by the critics of the old school.
Ruskin, himself a new writer, rallied to their side.   They
may be said to have received their first Oxford influence
through this channel.   Then began *The Germ*.   Its oddly-
sounding title had not then the scientific associations
which now attach to the word.   Six years later first
Burne-Jones and then William Morris were introduced
in London to the 'P. R. B.', and the next year the
'P. R. B.' itself came to Oxford.   Rossetti was brought
by Ruskin to aid in the designs of the new Museum,
and seeing the new Debating Room of the Union,
formed the idea of the decoration of the roof.   In 1858

'George Eliot' published *Scenes of Clerical Life*, Fitz-
Gerald *The Rubaiyat of Omar Khayyam*, and William
Morris *The Defence of Guinevere*. The next year came
Darwin's *Origin of Species*, Meredith's *Ordeal of Richard
Feverel*, and Mill's volume on *Liberty*. It may well be
said that the new era had now established itself. It
culminated in 1870, when Morris finished the *Earthly
Paradise*, and Rossetti published his Poems. In the
meantime other names of note had added themselves,
in particular Swinburne and Christina Rossetti.

This age then again, ran its course in some twenty to
five-and-twenty years, and this, the period of a generation, we may take it, is the period of an age of poetry.
Many writers live through two, as we saw that Wordsworth did, while Keats and Shelley and Byron lived
only through one. Tennyson, and Browning though
less in evidence, lived through and wrote in three, for
not only were they both in full activity during this
period which we have just indicated, from 1850 to 1870,
but they continued to write, Browning for twenty, and
Tennyson for more than twenty years longer. Tennyson
was indeed like Nestor.

> Τῷ δ' ἤδη δύο μὲν γενεαὶ μερόπων ἀνθρώπων
> ἐφθίαθ', οἵ οἱ πρόσθεν ἅμα τράφεν ἠδ' ἐγένοντο
> ἐν Πύλῳ ἠγαθέῃ, μετὰ δὲ τριτάτοισιν ἄνασσεν.

But at last Nestor too went to join Antilochus, and yet
a new generation appeared.

We are now nearly twenty years again from Tennyson's death. We may again look out for yet a newer
spirit, for the 'newest spirit' of the 'newest age',
Were we to set ourselves once more the task of Horne,
who are the men and what are the forces we should
have to describe ?

They are not wanting, I think, and many of them are

not far to seek. The statesmen, the soldiers, and the
jurists, all the men of action ; the divines and the men
of science, the novelists, the actors, are all round us.
And the poets? It is usual indeed to say that we have
no poets, at any rate no great poets, among us. It is
true that in all the arts and activities of the soul and
mind we have lost in the last twenty or five-and-twenty
years great names and great figures, not in poetry alone,
but in painting and sculpture, in creative prose literature,
in history, in science and philosophy. Only here and
there a solitary figure like that of Sir Joseph Hooker
or Dr. Alfred Wallace links us to the intellectual past.
But neither science nor literature nor even poetry is
dead. Despite the absence of conspicuous and household names of poets pure and simple, I would confidently assert that we have still poets among us who
have written pieces which have as good a chance of living
in the Anthologies of the future as many of the pieces
which appear in the Anthologies of the present. There
has always been this complaint of the dearth of good
new poets. Somewhere about 1880 it must have been
that I met Browning for the first time, and I remember
the talk turned on this very topic. Browning said,
' Well, anyhow we are not worse off than they were at
the beginning of the century,' and he quoted the doggerel
Latin lines which I had never heard before, which are
attributed to Porson :

> Poetis laetamur tribus
> Pye, Petro Pindar, parvo Pybus,
> Si ulterius ire pergis,
> Adde his Sir James Bland-Burges.

The hundred years which have elapsed since the
beginning of the Romantic movement have enormously
enlarged the resources of poetry. Its modes have been

many times multiplied both in France and in England. We too have had our Romanticists, our Parnassians, and our Symbolists. Whatever may be thought of Tennyson, Morris, Swinburne, Bridges, or Kipling, as poets, they have, whether in the revival or modification of the old, or in the addition of the new, added signally to the range of English metrification, and to our conception of the possibilities of music and harmony in English verse.

Now for the first time we are beginning systematically to teach our students their own language and literature. France has long done it. Greece always did it. Who shall say what the effect will be on the English literature of the future? Who can say again what may not be the effect of such a vast Thesaurus as will be, when it is completed, the *New English Dictionary*?

Certainly the young English poet of to-day ought to be better equipped than the young poet of the past in technique. And I believe he is. It is, I think, the abundance of models and the diffusion of education which account for the diffusion of technical skill of a very creditable excellence.

But it is asked, Why are there no new great poets? For my part I do not doubt that they too will by and by again arrive. Great men are always scarce, and to be a really great poet you must be a great man. It may indeed be that the present age is not one whose first or second preoccupation is with poetry. Politics, science, business, affairs, activities, the preparation for war, the contests with the elements, exploration, commerce, all these may predominate. But all this only points to the fact that the world is moving and living, if it is not at the moment meditating or singing in an equal degree. That a new age is arriving we all feel, some with

optimism, some with pessimism, some with mingled
hope and apprehension. There have been, no doubt, in
the past, tracts and periods of literary sterility. The
present condition of the United States of America
certainly does not seem to favour literary production.
But both there and in Germany, where it cannot be
doubted that great changes, intellectual as well as
material, in the condition of a vast and powerful nation
have been, and are, in process, a revolution in this
regard may rapidly occur. You young people, who
have the whole of the next new age before you, you,
I hope, are optimistic, resolute, and prudent, but
optimistic; critical I am sure you are, for you would
not be young if you were not, but criticism of others'
enthusiasms or of past ideals may go with a great deal
of enthusiasm and new ideals of one's own. The
world surely was never more interesting for young or
old, perhaps never more achingly interesting, with an
intensity half pleasurable, half painful, than at present.
We are reminded of the lines which the young poet
wrote in the dawn of the Victorian Era :

> Ev'n now we hear with inward strife
>   A motion toiling in the gloom—
>   The Spirit of the years to come
> Yearning to mix himself with Life.
>
> A slow develop'd strength awaits
>   Completion in a painful school ;
>   Phantoms of other forms of rule,
> New Majesties of mighty states.
>
> The warders of the growing hour,
>   But vague in vapour, hard to mark ;
>   And round them sea and air are dark
> With great contrivances of Power.

Are we not to-day nearing a new 1830, pregnant with
change? We see new nations in either hemisphere

and in every portion of the globe; Canada a nation, Australia, New Zealand, South Africa nations, United Italy, United Germany, solid established historical facts, the Germanic and the Slavonic combinations growing and coming together, Turkey and Egypt feeling after modern efficiency, Japan broad awake, and China awakening, the United States an active and expansive world-power, South America with its immense physical riches one of the great potencies of the commercial world; the constant attrition of privilege, the growth of democracy, confronting this strengthening of nationality; freedom and order everywhere competing, science with its illimitable vistas alike of theory and of application, always at work upon both the moral and material life; these are some of the main factors of the new momentous age. Religion in many forms is certainly not less alive to-day than formerly; indeed, I trust it is more alive than ever. The theatre is vigorous, full of leaders and ideas. The novel, which was thought to be nearing exhaustion of subject thirty years ago, shows at least no sign of extinction.

How poetry will deal with these new themes, how it is beginning even now to deal with them, I may perhaps attempt to discuss in future discourses.

Meanwhile where are the English poets of the next age? Perhaps in Oxford. Perhaps here to-day. And yet, it may also be, not here, even though they belong to Oxford. That they may belong to Oxford I think not unlikely. Oxford, it is true, has not always had her share of the poets of the country. It is certainly strange that while even Cambridge men like Dryden and Wordsworth and FitzGerald have admitted that Oxford is herself full of poetry, and at least not less so than her sister, she has in the past produced far fewer of the great poets than Cambridge. What the reason of this may be it is not easy to pronounce. Partly it is a matter of accident. I remember well in younger days, when I had more of the spirit of schoolboy rivalry, my amusement and pleasure too when I came on the passage in a letter to Murray in which Byron describes his experiences and feelings when he began his undergraduate career. 'I was wretched', he says, 'at leaving Harrow, to which I had become attached during the last years of my stay there, wretched at going to Cambridge instead of Oxford because there were no rooms vacant at Christ Church.'

The whole letter, which contains the famous passage in which the 'Tutor' advised Byron's friend, to whom his rooms were lent in his absence, not to damage any of the furniture, 'for Lord Byron, Sir, is a man of tumultuous passions,' is exceedingly entertaining. It was then an accident that Byron did not come here, and similar accidents may have determined the choice of others of the long list. But it must be admitted that it is too long to be all due to accident. It is more interesting to inquire whether it is in any way connected with our studies. Mr. Gladstone, in the very interesting personal recollections of Arthur Hallam which appeared in the *Daily Telegraph* some thirteen years ago, and which, I think, have still never been republished, enters with characteristic thoroughness into the speculation of what would have been the effect on the intellect of Arthur Hallam if he had been sent, as Mr. Gladstone, like a good Oxonian, clearly indicates he thinks he ought to have been, by his father, to Oxford instead of to Cambridge, and in place of devoting himself or rather failing to devote himself to the studies of Cambridge, had read for the Final 'Greats' School.

Whatever the reason the fact remains that at that time, and for a few years longer, Cambridge was certainly predominantly the University of English Poetry, as Oxford was predominantly the University of English Prose.

In the last fifty years the balance has perhaps considerably shifted. Certainly the University of Matthew Arnold himself, of William Morris and others well known, need not hide its head, and to-day we have not to look very far from Oxford, or to search very deeply amongst living Oxford men, to see that we have still less reason to complain. Who the next generation of Oxford poets will be I will not attempt to pronounce. They will not perhaps be discovered by the Professor of Poetry. The wind of the spirit bloweth whither it listeth and the new princes of Poetry come not usually 'with observation'. They will more probably be discovered by the young for themselves, by their own contemporaries, in some youthful coterie or *camaraderie.*

Such little circles appear from time to time in Oxford. Silently, stealthily they come together, like fairy rings in the night, sometimes only leaving a mysterious mark upon the morning grass, and afterward melting away even as they came; sometimes growing into more lasting strength of flower and fruit. Such was the little coterie of Birmingham schoolboys, who, coming to Oxford in the 'fifties', gathered new friends and forces to themselves, and by and by, as we have seen, merged in the still more famous 'brotherhood' of London which turned the world of art and taste upside down. A more recent example was that later friendship to which my immediate predecessor belonged, which, when the 'seventies' were passing into the 'eighties', sent flying to and fro those 'Waifs and

Strays' of poesy, fresh and fragrant, if immature, like
the green, fluttering leaves and seedlets which blow
about the quadrangles and strew the College lawns in
May-time, or coined those merry epigrams which by
and by found their way into the great world. Such,
in another spring, a dozen years later, were the four
friends who put forth a shy little volume so happily
entitled *Primavera.* Twenty years have again gone
by and yet another *Primavera* may be due. But I do
not count on finding its authors here. They do not
invariably attend lectures even on poetry.

> Ite hinc inanes, ite rhetorum ampullae,
> Inflata rore non Achaico turba!

> Away, haunt not thou me,
> Thou vain Philosophy!
> Little hast thou bestead,
> Save to perplex the head,
> And leave the spirit dead.

Such has very often been the language of the poetic
undergraduate. But even if they are not here I may
perhaps offer to them, in their absence, a few words
of practical advice. Do not think, any of you, because
you have a turn for versification, even a very pretty
turn, that you are necessarily poets. The gift for
versification is very widely diffused.

It is perhaps hardly less widely diffused than the gift
for drawing or music. Few clever men, with a literary
turn at any rate, are quite without it. Statesmen, divines,
judges, architects, artists, have always had it. Half the
great men in letters and affairs of the last generation
possessed it. They were not quite poets, though some
of them came very near it. The same has always been
the case and is doubtless the case to-day. But if you
have the gift, cultivate it, at any rate in youth. It is

at least a delightful and also an educative exercise. I think that the art of versification, and even of poetry, might be more taught than it is, as part of a literary and mental training. You will soon find out, life will teach you, whether poetry is your vocation. It is that only for one in a hundred thousand.

Some people seem to think I ought to be prepared to give lessons in poetry. They write and solicit my advice. They ask to be recommended some manual of poetry. They invite me to correct their verses. I am not saying that this instruction could not be given at all. One of the greatest of poets gave it, or something very like it; Dante, who was, as it pleases me to think, a Professor of Poetry at the University of Bologna. A lesser poet of more recent times, de Banville, offered, I believe, to teach poetry in so many lessons. I do not propose to follow his example.

Poetry is not to be regarded as a profession amongst professions. Parents and guardians have always said the same thing about it, and they are right—what Tennyson's grandfather said to Tennyson and Pope's father to Pope, and Cowper to poetry itself, what Ovid's father long before said to Ovid.

Maeonides nullas ipse reliquit opes.

' Even Homer left no fortune,' or as I suppose we ought to put it, to be up to date, the syndicate for promoting the rise of the Greek Epic did not pay its shareholders.

If you merely want fame and fortune for their own sakes, seek them in other lines, but if indeed poetry is your vocation, then walk worthy of it. If the magic gleam does glance on your path, ' follow the gleam! '

Art thou poor yet hast thou golden slumbers,
         Oh, sweet content!

Meanwhile is the Oxford of to-day a favourable ground for the production of poetry or poets? The Oxford of sixty years ago, says a living poet, speaking of the time of Burne-Jones and Morris, was singularly unsympathetic. And as regards direct teaching this would seem to have been so.

Oxford herself was perhaps at that time more beautiful than to-day. The whisper of the last enchantments of the 'Middle Age' was less mingled and confused with the whirr of modern science and modern commerce. But on the other hand the ideas of modern science were also wanting. The opportunities of studying both science and art were meagre and scant. Ruskin had not enriched the Galleries with his gifts or with his Drawing School. Morris and Burne-Jones went toward the end of their undergraduate time as a favour to see the Combe Collection of Pre-Raphaelite art at the private house of the owner at the University Press. Now any undergraduate can go and study it for himself, excellently displayed as it is to-day, in the Ashmolean Buildings.

There was then no exhibition of plastic art of any educative kind in Oxford. We remember how much Keats owed to the Elgin Marbles, savagely denounced as their transference to London had been by Byron. The student at Oxford had no equivalent opportunity. To-day he has the whole range of Professor Gardner's Department and of the Ashmolean Collections.

Music, it is true, had never quite died out. Like architecture and with architecture it had maintained its living continuity in Oxford under varying changes of fortune and taste.

But Music in England, especially in the last fifty

years, has made great advance, and is to-day an influence far more present and energetic than it then was.

I am inclined to believe more in these indirect influences than in any direct education of the poet. And yet I am doubtful whether influences more indirect still may not be yet more potent.

The chance-blown seed lighting on the happy corner may produce blooms which 'outredden', and 'outperfume' too, 'all voluptuous garden roses'.

The free intercourse of quick, youthful minds in College and University life, the stimulus of original and enthusiastic teachers—these all, history tells us, have been powerful if not to produce, at least to foster original and creative minds.

I said the world was never more interesting than to-day. Nor I think was there ever a greater call for the intuition of the poet to interpret the new age to itself, and Oxford should surely contribute her share toward this end. What is her inspiration? How did Matthew Arnold fifty years ago, from this place, define her spirit? 'Sweetness and light.'—The harmonizing of poetry and of truth; the search for truth, guided by the splendour of beauty.—If I had to rewrite after fifty years this formulation of the Oxford spirit and say how it lives and appears among us to-day, for that it does live and appear I believe and hope, I would say that the best spirit of Oxford is shown in the combination, in every field, of research with reverence. Oxford has a unique opportunity in her history and her material incarnation, in her old studies supplemented as they are to-day by her new. To her Humanities she has at last added Science, to her Metaphysics the Physics she so much needed, and for which for so long she cared too little. But let her be careful now in adding the new to keep the old. Let her recognize that in the things of the spirit the human element enters in. You cannot treat men and their actions, either those of to-day or those of yesterday, as if they were only automata responding to a mechanical stimulus. You cannot so interpret history or language, or so work upon human nature. We see the Oxford spirit perhaps best in some of our leading workers in that region where it is needed most, but it is needed in every field of learning, and I think—I would fain think— we see it, and not seldom, in each in turn.

Oxford has been in time past a far-famed home of Theology; she has been a far-famed home of Philosophy; she has been a famed school of the historian, the economist, and the statesman; she is beginning to be a school of Natural Science; let her become more than of yore—I think she is beginning to become that also—a nursery, a training ground, a home, of poets.

For it is just here that that special power can help us, that first and finest of the Fine Arts, that Muse which is, as we know, more philosophical than History, more potent with mankind in general than Philosophy, more penetrating in its eloquence, and in its influence more permanent, than Rhetoric—the Muse, the 'divine' Muse, of Poetry.

NOTES

¹ p. 4. I am glad to think that this drawback is about to be removed. The Oxford Press will before long produce, with the aid of the Warden of Keble, a translation of these Lectures by Mr. E. K. Francis.

² p. 19. Hazlitt's *Spirit of the Age* has been republished in Bohn's Standard Library. Horne's *New Spirit of the Age* is included in the World's Classics (Henry Frowde. Oxford University Press. Price 1s.).

Robert Bridges
Poet Laureate

Readings from his Poems

A PUBLIC LECTURE
DELIVERED IN THE EXAMINATION SCHOOLS
ON NOVEMBER 8, 1913

BY

T. Herbert Warren, M.A., Hon. D.C.L.

PRESIDENT OF MAGDALEN COLLEGE
PROFESSOR OF POETRY

1913

PREFATORY NOTE

THIS lecture as here published differs slightly in form from what it was as delivered. On the one hand the text is a little longer, as want of time made it necessary to omit then some passages given in these pages. On the other hand some of the pieces read as illustrations, when the lecture was delivered, are not reproduced, but are given by reference to the pages of the Oxford Book, *The Poetical Works of Robert Bridges,* excluding the Eight Dramas: Humphrey Milford, Oxford University Press, 1913. The different forms and prices of this edition will be found at the end.

Lines sent with a copy of the 'Shorter Poems'

Take, friend of all that's good and fair,
    This book of daintiest verse,
And let each coy, retirèd air
    Its music rare rehearse.

The silver Thames by summer kiss't,
    The rustling brakes of spring,
Or autumn woods when gales are whist,
    Such songs as these they sing.

Such song in England's flowering day
    Made merry England brave,
From honied Chaucer shrewdly gay
    To Wither blithely grave.

                      T. H. W.

READINGS FROM THE POET LAUREATE

WITH AN INTRODUCTION

UNDOUBTEDLY the event of the vacation for us in Oxford, the event of the year in the English literary world, was the appointment of our neighbour, the friend of many of us, Mr. Robert Bridges, to be Poet Laureate. ' The friend of many of us.' I ought to tell you at the outstart that I am an old friend, and I speak with the partiality of an old friend. You may discount my opinion, if you will, proportionately. But it is my belief that it is an event and an appointment of no small or brief importance.

I would begin with one word, or rather really two words, of congratulation. I would congratulate Mr. Bridges in your name and in the name of his university, of which he has shown himself not only such a worthy, but such a loyal and affectionate son. And I would congratulate that other son of Oxford, the Prime Minister, and thank him for not having listened to those in Parliament and elsewhere, who would fain have persuaded him to abolish this historic and picturesque office.

The history of the Laureateship is not very well known. To recount it would require a special lecture. I will only say that it is partly the fault of the poets themselves if it is less continuously creditable than it might have been. Some years ago I had the opportunity of hearing Mr. Gladstone's opinion about the office. He said to me that ' the history of the office was curious and seemed

to show that an appointment, to be prosperous, required
to combine a number of conditions '. It has had, of
course, its ups and downs. Oddly enough, it was vacant
just a hundred years ago this summer by the death of
the then holder, whose name was Pye, a member of my
own college.

Mr. Bridges has, in the Collection of Sonnets entitled
' The Growth of Love ', a delightful sonnet in which he
notes how by a happy chance so many of the names
of the great poets are themselves beautiful and musical,
and might seem to have been chosen for their beauty
and euphony.

' Thus may I think ', he writes,

> the adopting Muses chose
> Their sons by name, knowing none would be heard
> Or writ so oft in all the world as those,—
> Dan Chaucer, mighty Shakespeare, then for third
> The classic Milton, and to us arose
> Shelley with liquid music in the word.

Mr. Pye's name was not poetical, however spelt, and
was often made game of. The Laureateship at that time
was very down. But why was it down ? The fault lay not
with the Kings or the Prime Ministers. They had offered
it in the previous century to one of the very best poets of
the century, to Gray. Gray refused it, in a clever and
characteristic letter. But in this very letter he said he
hoped some one might be found to restore its credit, and
having refused, he shortly after wrote the Installation
Ode, a pre-eminently occasional, laudatory, laureate piece
containing some splendid and some most beautiful verses,
but the concluding lines of which are absolutely in the
vein which he and others disparaged.

> The star of Brunswick smiles serene
> And gilds the horrors of the deep.

In the year 1813 the laurel was offered—again to one of the best poets of the day—to Sir Walter Scott. One of the reasons why Scott declined it was that Gray had done so. It was then given to Southey, then to Wordsworth, and then to Tennyson. Tennyson received it as we all know,

> Greener from the brows
> Of him who uttered nothing base.

He left it not only greener, but more glorious still, fragrant and fertile with the flower and fruit of some forty years. The poet's laurel, be it remembered, is the ' odorous bay '.[1]

When the Exhibition of 1862 was opened and Tennyson's Ode was sung, one of the newspapers reported that the poet-laureate was present ' clothed in his green *baize* '.

Tennyson died just one-and-twenty years ago. A child born on the day of his death would, this autumn, exactly have reached his majority. Born four or five years earlier, so that he could just remember Tennyson, he would be to-day five- or six-and-twenty. It is the period of a generation. During all that time the laurel has certainly been, to put it gently, somewhat in the shade. But if it is not cut down it is an evergreen tree, and once more it is shining in the sun.

Habemus poetam laureatum! We have a laureate, in the true English line of English poetry, of Chaucer and Spenser, of Milton and Gray, of Wordsworth and Tennyson.

But I am not going to praise, or to appraise, my old friend. I am not going to attempt any critical study of his work or his works. I have done so before now, and I may perhaps be allowed to mention to you the name of a little volume in which some three-and-twenty years ago I ventured to introduce and commend him to

readers of poetry.   It was a volume in Mr. A. H. Miles's
series of the ' Poets and the Poetry of the Century ',
and it was entitled *Robert Bridges and Contemporary
Poets.*[2]

I was asked to do this by Mr. Miles, and Mr. Bridges
himself aided me in the task by giving me a few autobiographical notes, which I still possess, and of which
I made use.

Among the ' contemporary poets ' whom it contained
were Frederic W. H. Myers, Edward Dowden, Ernest
Myers, Gerard Hopkins (with an introduction from
Mr. Bridges' own pen), Arthur O'Shaughnessy, Andrew
Lang, Edmund Gosse, W. E. Henley, H. D. Rawnsley,
R. L. Stevenson, Alice Meynell, A. Mary F. Robinson,
William Watson, and Rudyard Kipling.

In 1906, fifteen years later, it was revised and re-
issued under the title *Bridges to Kipling.*   The ladies
were removed to another volume and some new poets
were added, among them Henry Newbolt and Laurence
Binyon.

What, with your kind concurrence, I should desire to
do to-day is, to ask you to judge, and to help you to
judge, for yourselves, of this fine poet, for such he is,
and his production, giving such amount of introduction
and explanation as may enable you to understand his
poems better.

For it is the truth that his poems have not been, and
still are not, as well known as they ought to be.   I find,
for instance, that comparatively few know that he has
already written a beautiful piece in what might be considered a peculiarly laureate vein.   It was not written to
command and is of course all the better for that.   It
was written, however, for Queen Victoria's ' Diamond
Jubilee'.   It is headed '*Regina Cara*, Jubilee-Song, for

Music, 1897'. It has a characteristic Latin 'Envoy'.
It will be found on p. 364 of the Oxford edition.

It is a commonplace to say that Mr. Bridges is not
a 'popular' poet. In a sense that is true. He has
never sought to be popular. He does not live in
the street. His poetry is not known to the 'man in the
street', whether on the pavement or on the top of the
tram. May I say that the cult of him is not one which
falls under the formula—

> *Quod semper, quod ubique, quod ab ' omnibus' ?*

He left the street long ago, for the very reason that he
did not wish for this sort of worship.

> And country life I praise,
> And lead, because I find
> The philosophic mind
> Can take no middle ways ;
> She will not leave her love
> To mix with men, her art
> Is all to strive above
> The crowd, or stand apart.

So he wrote in the 'Invitation to the Country' (Oxford
edition, p. 253).

But his critics sometimes go further than this and say
that he has deliberately shunned popularity, that he has
only brought out his poems in the rare editions of a
private press or in separate and isolated pamphlets,
which, like the Sibyl's leaves, he has allowed the winds of
chance to scatter, and has never gathered together again.
I do not think that is quite fair.

We have all heard of the timid gentlewoman who had
seen better days and was reduced to selling muffins, and
who cried her wares in ever so soft a voice, saying,
'Muffins ! Muffins ! I hope nobody will hear me !' Well, I don't
think Mr. Bridges was ever quite like that, but he has

sometimes reminded me of his own ' flame-throated
robin ' of whom he writes :

> Thus sang he ; then from his spray
> He saw me listening and flew away.

But of this and of his poems I want you to judge for
yourselves. If we could understand them I think we
should find that of him, as of other poets, his poems
themselves were the best biography. But that you may
understand them, I will attempt a brief outline of his
career, giving it when I can in his own words.

He was born, then, at Walmer, in 1844. Some of you
may remember the lines which stood in the earliest
versions of Tennyson's Ode on the Death of the Duke
of Wellington :

> Where shall we lay the man whom we deplore ?
> He died on Walmer's lonely shore.

Tennyson was nearly six when Waterloo was fought.
He was forty-three when the great Duke died, in 1852.
Mr. Bridges, in his turn, was then a boy of eight.

There is a charming autobiographical poem of his
styled ' The Summer House on the Mound ', which
describes how he used to watch, through a telescope from
his father's garden, the ships in the Channel, and how, in
particular in 1854, he saw the English Fleet under
Napier making its way to the Baltic, and among the
vessels ' the Admiral ship The Duke of Wellington '.

Tennyson, you may remember, heard the booming of
the guns at Portsmouth as he wrote ' Maud ', in the
January of 1854, and he watched the ' ships of battle '
' slowly creeping ' under the cliffs at Freshwater. I remember Mr. Bridges telling me that the ' Letter to F. D.
Maurice ' was a poem he much liked.

Let me now read you Mr. Bridges' own description.
(Oxford edition, pp. 334-5.)

> One noon in March upon that anchoring ground
> Came Napier's fleet unto the Baltic bound :
> Cloudless the sky and calm and blue the sea,
> As round Saint Margaret's cliff mysteriously,
> Those murderous queens walking in Sabbath sleep
> Glided in line upon the windless deep :
> For in those days was first seen low and black
> Beside the full-rigg'd mast the strange smoke-stack,
> And neath their stern revolv'd the twisted fan.
> Many I knew as soon as I might scan,
> The heavy *Royal George*, the *Acre* bright,
> The *Hogue* and *Ajax*, and could name aright
> Others that I remember now no more ;
> But chief, her blue flag flying at the fore,
> With fighting guns a hundred thirty and one,
> The Admiral ship *The Duke of Wellington*,
> Whereon sail'd George, who in her gig had flown
> The silken ensign by our sisters sewn.
> The iron Duke himself,—whose soldier fame
> To England's proudest ship had given her name,
> And whose white hairs in this my earliest scene
> Had scarce more honour'd than accustom'd been,—
> Was two years since to his last haven past :
> I had seen his castle-flag to fall half-mast
> One morn as I sat looking on the sea,
> When thus all England's grief came first to me,
> Who hold my childhood favour'd that I knew
> So well the face that won at Waterloo.

A little later Mr. Bridges went to Eton. This was
it may certainly be said, fortunate for Eton and fortunate
for him—fortunate for him because Eton, whatever may
be its failings, is certainly a good school for a poet, not
only from its associations, its splendours, its delightful
amenities, but still more from its free and varied life. It
leaves them more alone, gives them more scope to be
themselves, than many schools which are better for more
average, ordinary boys. This may be seen in the Eton

poets, in Gray and Shelley, in Swinburne, and above all in Mr. Bridges.

It was fortunate for Eton, since none of her sons have written so happily about Eton and for Eton as he : none above all with such ideal truth to her real nature, to what she was meant to be.

Gray loved her, and in the formal eighteenth century he discerned and declared her historic tradition, her dedication to learning.

> Ye distant spires, ye antique towers
>   That crown the watery glade,
> Where grateful Science still adores
>   Her Henry's holy shade.

Swinburne loved her and has written of her beauty and her associations :

Still the reaches of the river, still the light on field and hill,
Still the memories held aloft as lamps for hope's young fire to fill,
Shine, and while the light of England lives, shall shine for England still.

But Mr. Bridges has seen more deeply. Eton is too often thought of, as Oxford is also sometimes thought of, as a place of elegant education for elegant youth, for the *jeunesse dorée*, a smart and fashionable school where a good deal of cricket and rowing and other athletic enjoyment accompany the acquisition of a tincture of the classics, a knowledge of the manners and ways of society and ' all things fitting gentleman's attire '.

Mr. Bridges appreciated and enjoyed all this to the full, but he and his best friends found something more in the College of St. Mary the Virgin of Eton, the fair foundation of the royal and murdered saint.

I wonder whether any here know the Charter of the Foundation of Eton. It is headed by a beautiful illumination representing King Henry VI dedicating his college to her Patron.

An intimate friend of Mr. Bridges, Mr. Lionel Muirhead, when they had just left school and were at Oxford together, painted a picture representing more fully the same dedication, and containing symbolical portraits of the friends, Mr. Dolben, Mr. Stuckey Coles, and Mr. Bridges himself.

Mr. Bridges has most happily combined this inspiration and this view of Eton with her other aspects in the charming ' Eton Ode ' written for the ' Ninth Jubilee of the College '. (Oxford edition, p. 313.)

Mr. Bridges has written again, more than once, about Eton, about his own life there, in the ' Eclogue for the Fourth of June ', Oxford edition, p. 330, about her sorrow for her sons, in the ' Ode in memory of the Old-Etonians whose lives were lost in the South African War ' (Oxford edition, p. 393).

The same spirit pervades them all. It was a spirit common to himself and his friends, as may be seen, not only from this painting of one of them, but from the faithful, vivid, and humorous picture which he has drawn of their little coterie in the memoir which he wrote for the edition of his friend Mr. Mackworth Dolben's poems.

At Eton Mr. Bridges was, as might be gathered from his poems, a scholar and an athlete in happy combination. It was the same when he came to Oxford.

He chose Corpus, of which college a kinsman of his, Dr. Thomas Edward Bridges, had been President for twenty-one years, dying the year before the Poet Laureate was born. He pursued the usual classical course, reading for ' Greats ', and taking his degree with Honours in 1867.

He had originally intended to seek Holy Orders, and had come to Oxford with introductions to Dr. Pusey and Canon Liddon, who remained his friends during his undergraduate time. He gave up this idea, however, and after his degree travelled with his friend Mr. Muirhead in the East. Later he travelled with this same companion on the Continent.

Mr. Muirhead has kindly given me in a letter some account of their travels. He writes :

' In January 1868 R. B. and I went by sea to Alexandria, and thence to Cairo, where after spending some time we went leisurely up the Nile, seeing everything we could, as far as Assouan, and did not return to Cairo till the beginning of May. R. B. wrote poems even in those days, and I find in my sketch-book a small pencil drawing of him smoking his pipe with the legend beneath : " R. B. as he appeared when he composed his ode." The ode is no longer in existence unless the Pyramids and the Nile with their " eternal recollections " (*vide* " Now in wintry delights ") keep it in mind. I have also got a sketch of him writing in one of the temples at Phylae : the Nile has now drowned the temple, though Osiris has fortunately preserved the poet.

In May we went by Jaffa to Jerusalem where we spent several weeks seeing the surrounding country, the Dead Sea, and going south to Hebron. R. was then suddenly summoned to England and I continued my journeyings alone.

In March 1874 we went to Italy, seeing Pisa, Florence, Perugia, Siena, Orvieto, Rome, Naples, Pompeii, Paestum, Sorrento.

In November 1881 we went to Amiens, Turin, Genoa, Nervi, Rapallo, Spezzia, and to Florence and Rome in

1882. Thence R. went on to Sicily, leaving me in Rome. Some of the sonnets in the Growth of Love were written at Florence in 1882—"Life-trifling Lions", for instance, I *think* may be so dated—though a great number of the sonnets were written much earlier (the first edition of some of them was in 1876) and some of those dealing with Florence date from 1874 ; without much more research than I can give I should be afraid of venturing on dogmatic statement about dates.'

This travel widened his views and gave him in his own language :

> Mirrors bright for the magic cave,

of memory. They gave him in particular a living idea of Greece and Egypt which no book learning alone can supply.

I note not a few reminiscences of them in his poem. One of the best instances may be found in a poem of which I am specially fond, 'Achilles in Scyros'. Let me quote one passage from this poem. It is about Achilles and Homer.

> But lo, I am come to give thee joy, to call
> Thee daughter, and prepare thee for the sight
> Of such a lover, as no lady yet
> Hath sat to await in chamber or in bower
> On any wallèd hill or isle of Greece ;
> Nor yet in Asian cities, whose dark queens
> Look from the latticed casements over seas
> Of hanging gardens ; nor doth all the world
> Hold a memorial not where Ægypt mirrors
> The great smile of her kings and sunsmit fanes
> In timeless silence : none hath been like him ;
> And all the giant stones, which men have piled
> Upon the illustrious dead, shall crumble and join
> The desert dust, ere his high dirging Muse
> Be dispossessèd of the throne of song.

Among his contemporaries and friends at Oxford were Dr. Sanday, Mr. Andrew Lang, and Mr. Gerard Hopkins, a very interesting, poetic, pathetic figure, of whom he has written a brief memoir, to be found, as I have already mentioned, in the little volume, *Bridges to Kipling*.

As an oarsman Mr. Bridges achieved some remarkable successes, stroking the Corpus Eight and carrying it to the head of the river, while at Paris as stroke of the Oxford Etonians he, I believe, performed greater feats still, and I often find, when I ask his contemporaries what he was like, that it was in this capacity that he made the strongest impression on them.

I remember well that when I was getting up a list of supporters to nominate him for the Professorship of Poetry I found that Bishop Chavasse had been with him at Corpus, and with some hesitation I asked the Bishop if he would let me add his name. 'Most assuredly I will', he said. ' I steered the Eight for him at Corpus and I have the greatest respect and regard for him.'

The river may be said to stream like a shining thread through his poems, and the oarsman is a very frequent figure in them. In this he is a true son of Oxford.

ELEGY

Clear and gentle stream !
Known and loved so long,
That hast heard the song
And the idle dream
Of my boyish day ;
While I once again
Down thy margin stray,
In the selfsame strain
Still my voice is spent,
With my old lament
And my idle dream,
Clear and gentle stream !

Where my old seat was
Here again I sit,
Where the long boughs knit
Over stream and grass
A translucent eaves :
Where back eddies play
Shipwreck with the leaves,
And the proud swans stray,
Sailing one by one
Out of stream and sun,
And the fish lie cool
In their chosen pool.

Many an afternoon
Of the summer day
Dreaming here I lay ;
And I know how soon,
Idly at its hour,
First the deep bell hums
From the minster tower,
And then evening comes,
Creeping up the glade,
With her lengthening shade,
And the tardy boon
Of her brightening moon.

Clear and gentle stream !
Ere again I go
Where thou dost not flow,
Well does it beseem
Thee to hear again
Once my youthful song,
That familiar strain
Silent now so long :
Be as I content
With my old lament
And my idle dream,
Clear and gentle stream.

This delightful little ' Elegy ', as he calls it, which opens
the book of the ' Shorter Poems ', was one of the first
of his writings, and appears in the earliest book of poems.

' There is a hill beside the silver Thames ' (Oxford edition, p. 248) is again one of the most characteristic and beautiful of his pieces. Another poem a little later, characteristically headed ' Indolence ' (Oxford edition, p. 270), describes a voyage by boat from Oxford to Abingdon.

When he came back from travel he determined to study medicine. He joined St. Bartholomew's Hospital and made himself thoroughly proficient.

He took the M.B. degree at Oxford, and in course of time held several hospital appointments. In particular he was on the staff at St. Bartholomew's and at the Children's Hospital in Great Ormonde Street. He also practised generally. He much preferred treating young children to treating adults, as he very wittily said, for two reasons, firstly that they could not tell him untruths about their symptoms, secondly because they were obliged to take the remedies which he prescribed for them.

He was moreover very fond of children. One of the most touching and beautiful poems in the whole of his collected works, arising, I believe, out of his hospital time, is the poem ' On a Dead Child ' (Oxford edition, p. 267). I wonder how many here know it. I will venture, though it is not an easy poem to read, to read it.

ON A DEAD CHILD

Perfect little body, without fault or stain on thee,
  With promise of strength and manhood full and fair !
    Though cold and stark and bare,
The bloom and the charm of life doth awhile remain on thee.

Thy mother's treasure wert thou ;—alas ! no longer
  To visit her heart with wondrous joy ; to be
    Thy father's pride ;—ah, he
Must gather his faith together, and his strength make
    stronger.

To me, as I move thee now in the last duty,
   Dost thou with a turn or gesture anon respond ;
      Startling my fancy fond
With a chance attitude of the head, a freak of beauty.

Thy hand clasps, as 'twas wont, my finger, and holds it :
   But the grasp is the clasp of Death, heartbreaking and
      stiff ;
      Yet feels to my hand as if
'Twas still thy will, thy pleasure and trust that enfolds it.

So I lay thee there, thy sunken eyelids closing,—
   Go lie thou there in thy coffin, thy last little bed !—
      Propping thy wise, sad head,
Thy firm, pale hands across thy chest disposing.

So quiet ! doth the change content thee ?—Death,
      whither hath he taken thee ?
   To a world, do I think, that rights the disaster of this ?
      The vision of which I miss,
Who weep for the body, and wish but to warm thee and
      awaken thee ?

Ah ! little at best can all our hopes avail us
   To lift this sorrow, or cheer us, when in the dark,
      Unwilling, alone we embark,
And the things we have seen and have known and have
      heard of, fail us.

As a set-off to this sad poem let me read you another,
a glad poem on a child. It is entitled ' The Garland of
Rachel '.

The heroine was the little newly-born daughter of
Mr. Henry Daniel, at that time Bursar, now Provost, of
Worcester College. She was born on September 17, 1880.
It was Mr. Humphry Ward who suggested the ' Garland ',
after the model of the famous Guirlande de Julie of the
Hôtel Rambouillet, and it was printed the next year.

There were eighteen contributors: (1) her father himself;
(2) Mr. Albert Watson, afterwards Principal of B.N.C.
(in Latin) ; (3) Mr. Austin Dobson ; (4) Andrew Lang ;

(5) John Addington Symonds ; (6) Mr. Robert Bridges ;
(7) ' Lewis Carroll ' ; (8) Sir Richard Harington (Latin) ;
(9) A. Mary F. Robinson, afterwards Madame Darmesteter;
(10) Mr. Edmund Gosse ; (11) Mr. Francis W. Bourdillon ;
(12) W. E. Henley (in French) ; (13) Mr. W. J. Courthope ;
(14) Frederick Locker ; (15) Mr. Humphry Ward ; (16)
Mr. Ernest Myers ; (17) Margaret L. Woods ; (18)
Mr. C. J. Cruttwell.

Mr. Daniel printed the slender volume. Mrs. Daniel
added the floral lettering or ' miniation ' in red ink.
Mr. Alfred Parsons, R.A., then a young Somerset friend,
contributed three designs, for head and tail pieces and for
the tops of the pages.

Here is Mr. Bridges' poem :

' RACHEL'S GARLAND '

Press thy hands and crow,
Thou that know'st not joy :
Rouse thy voice and weep,
Thou that know'st not care :
Thou that toil'st not, sleep :
Wake and wail nor spare,
Spare not us, that know
Grief and life's annoy.

Thine unweeting cries
Passion's alphabet,
Labour, love, and strife
Spell, or e'er thou read :
But the book of life
Hard to learn indeed,
Babe, before thee lies
For thy reading yet.

Thou when thou hast known
Joy, will laugh not then :
When grief bids thee weep,
Thou wilt check thy tears :

> When toil brings not sleep,
> Thou, for others' fears
> Fearful, shalt thine own
> Lose and find again.

To-day the child for whom the garland was then twined, has a nursling of her own, and her poet wears the nation's laurel.

Another poem belonging to this period and phase I will not read. It is exceedingly clever and amusing, but it is in Latin, and I am not lecturing in Latin. It is entitled *Carmen Elegiacum Roberti Bridges de Nosocomio Sti. Bartholomaei Londinensi,* and is an account written in the ' longs and shorts ' so dear to Eton, of that hospital and its staff. It is addressed to Dr. Patrick Black, and has a very neat and fluent Introduction dated from 52 Bedford Square, on the Ides of December, and a merry motto :

> *Si qua videbuntur casu non dicta latinè*
> *In qua scribebam barbara terra fuit.*

Indeed, the whole piece is full of a delightful playfulness. ' Dear to Eton,' I said, and Mr. Bridges himself writes :

> *Audeo quae quondam propter Thamesina fluenta*
> *Progeniem docuit mater Etona suam.*

It was published in 1877. It was exhibited at the Royal College of Physicians on St. Luke's Day last, when Dr. Bridges was entertained by the President and Fellows as the guest of the evening. Another production of his, one of the wisest and wittiest things of the kind I know, is not a poem at all, but that very prosy thing a Report ; an account in prose of the treatment, the gratuitous and necessarily rather perfunctory treatment, of the ' casualty ' patients at a London Hospital.

Mr. Bridges became then a Fellow of the Royal College of Physicians. But as regards his poetry the most

important effect of this period of his career is the influence
of his medical and scientific study upon his thought. He
possesses and exhibits a grasp of Natural Science, so
potent a factor in our time, such as will be found in no
English poet before Tennyson, and in no other poet
since Tennyson.   Good specimens of it may be seen in
the Hexameter Epistle to ' L. M. ' (his friend Mr. Lionel
Muirhead), the first of the ' Poems in Classical Prosody '.
(O.B. p. 411).

Fond as he was, however, of Science, and strong as
was his belief in its importance, he loved poetry better,
and became convinced that it was his vocation. This is
shown in the ' Spring Ode ' (Oxford edition, p. 254) :

> Thrice happy he, the rare
> Prometheus, who can play
> With hidden things, and lay
> New realms of nature bare ;
> Whose venturous step has trod
> Hell underfoot, and won
> A crown from man and God
> For all that he has done.—
>
> That highest gift of all,
> Since crabbèd fate did flood
> My heart with sluggish blood,
> I look not mine to call ;
> But, like a truant freed,
> Fly to the woods, and claim
> A pleasure for the deed
> Of my inglorious name :
>
> And am content, denied
> The best, in choosing right ;
> For Nature can delight
> Fancies unoccupied
> With ecstasies so sweet
> As none can even guess,
> Who walk not with the feet
> Of joy in idleness.

And still more forcibly in Sonnet 62 in the ' Growth of
Love ' (Oxford edition, p. 213) :

> I will be what God made me, nor protest
> Against the bent of genius in my time,
> That science of my friends robs all the best,
> While I love beauty, and was born to rhyme.
> Be they our mighty men, and let me dwell
> In shadow among the mighty shades of old,
> With love's forsaken palace for my cell ;
> Whence I look forth and all the world behold,
>
> And say, These better days, in best things worse,
> This bastardy of time's magnificence,
> Will mend in fashion and throw off the curse,
> To crown new love with higher excellence.
> Curs'd tho' I be to live my life alone,
> My toil is for man's joy, his joy my own.

A very interesting autobiographic piece which describes
this period of his life and his conflict of inclinations is the
' Recollections of Solitude ' (Oxford edition, p. 367).

In the end it may be said of him that, ' he was not
disobedient to the heavenly vision ', for indeed, it was
a ' call '. He chose poetry not from ambition but from
love, for better, for worse, for richer, for poorer. This is
how that shy mistress ought to be wooed, and how she
is to be won and wedded.

He has a beautiful little poem upon this theme
(Oxford edition, pp. 286-7) :

> O Love, my muse, how was 't for me
>   Among the best to dare,
> In thy high courts that bowed the knee
>   With sacrifice and prayer ?
>
> Their mighty offerings at thy shrine
>   Shamed me, who nothing bore :
> Their suits were mockeries of mine,
>   I sued for so much more.

> Full many I met that crowned with bay
>   In triumph home returned,
> And many a master on the way
>   Proud of the prize I scorned.
>
> I wished no garland on my head
>   Nor treasure in my hand ;
> My gift the longing that me led,
>   My prayer thy high command,
>
> My love, my muse ; and when I spake
>   Thou mad'st me thine that day,
> And more than hundred hearts could take
>   Gav'st me to bear away.

In 1882 then, at the age of 38, he gave up London and Medicine and retired to the country, and to Berkshire, in which county he has lived ever since. For a number of years he had his home at Yattendon, on the downs above Pangbourne. Now, to our advantage, he is settled near Boar's Hill.

His first volume of poems was published in 1873 when he was nine-and-twenty. It is now exceedingly rare, and so are the thin, paper-covered pamphlets which succeeded it during the next few years. Some of the poems contained in these he has never reprinted. There is one in particular, a very fine Lucretian piece on 'Nature', which I have often wished he would reprint.

In 1876 he published what must be regarded as one of the most characteristic of his works, the sequence of Sonnets entitled ' The Growth of Love '. As then given to the world it consisted of twenty-four numbers. In 1879, and again in 1880, he published volumes, entitled simply, ' Poems by the author of the Growth of Love '. Then in 1883, the year after he had left London, came a notable event in his literary career, the printing for the first time of one of his plays by his now intimate friend

Mr. Henry Daniel, the present Provost of Worcester College.

The history of the 'Daniel Press' is a chapter apart, a chapter of real moment, as is beginning to be more and more evident in the history of printing and poetry in our time. But it deserves, and would require, a separate lecture to do it justice.

The first long poem printed by Mr. Daniel for Mr. Bridges was the noble and beautiful play which opens the Oxford Book, *Prometheus the Fire-Giver*, ' A Mask in the Greek Manner ', as he calls it. Both the Greek manner and the manner of Milton, especially of *Comus*, are distinctly traceable in it, as the first few lines alone would suffice to show. And yet it is thoroughly original. It reveals all Mr. Bridges' qualities. It revealed them, as I well remember, to me, for it was the first of his poems I read. It was reprinted in 1884 by Mr. Bell, and it was in this form that I came upon it. Just after it appeared I had asked my friend and predecessor in this Chair, Mr. J. W. Mackail, if there was any new poet who could write really good blank verse. He said, ' Yes, there is one ', and advised me to get *Prometheus*. I got it and read it, and from that day I have never had any doubt that Mr. Bridges was a true and a *new* poet, a poet that is with a new and quite independent style of his own. This last point I think struck me as much as anything. His blank verse is not like that of Tennyson except when Tennyson also resembles Milton, nor like that of Swinburne or Shelley or Keats. In *Prometheus* it is obviously reminiscent of Milton, but it has a *differentia* of its own.

I set myself to procure everything of this new and delectable poet, and, very soon after, I had the good luck to make his personal acquaintance. For the next half-dozen years he went on in his quiet, sequestered way, printing and publishing his poems and plays, now with his friend Mr. Daniel, now with Messrs. Bell, now with Mr. Edward Bumpus, the plays chiefly with the latter.[3]

He was not well known, but he had his poetic friends, and other good judges spoke up for him from time to time. Notably Mr. Andrew Lang, in his *Letters on Literature*, 1889, quoted and praised, with equally happy discrimination and warmth, several of his pieces, above all the ' Elegy on the Lady killed by grief for the death of her betrothed ' (Oxford edition, p. 238).

It is interesting to read Lang's criticism again to-day, written in 1889, nearly a quarter of a century ago, before Browning had published his last volume, or Tennyson his last but one.

' The name of Mr. Robert Bridges ', he says, ' is probably strange to many lovers of poetry who would like nothing better than to make acquaintance with his verse. But his verse is not so easily found. This poet never writes in magazines ; his books have not appealed to the public by any sort of advertisement, only two or three of them have come forth in the regular way. The first was " Poems, by Robert Bridges, Batchelor of Arts in the University of Oxford. *Parva seges satis est.* London : Pickering, 1873 ".

This volume was presently, I fancy, withdrawn, and the author has distributed some portions of it in succeeding pamphlets, or in books printed at Mr. Daniel's private press in Oxford. In these, as in all Mr. Bridges' poems, there is a certain austere and indifferent beauty of diction, and a memory of the old English poets, Milton and the earlier lyrists. I remember being greatly pleased with the " Elegy on a Lady whom Grief for the Death of Her Betrothed Killed ".

Let the priests go before, arrayed in white,
And let the dark-stoled minstrels follow slow,
Next they that bear her, honoured on this night,
And then the maidens in a double row,
    Each singing soft and low,
    And each on high a torch upstaying :
Unto her lover lead her forth with light,
With music, and with singing, and with praying.

This is a stately stanza.

In his first volume Mr. Bridges offered a few rondeaux
and triolets, turning his back on all these things as soon
as they became popular. In spite of their popularity,
I have the audacity to like them still, in their humble
twittering way. Much more in his true vein were the
lines, " Clear and Gentle Stream ", and all the other verses
in which, like a true Etonian, he celebrates the beautiful
Thames (Oxford edition, p. 248) :

There is a hill beside the silver Thames,
Shady with birch and beech and odorous pine :
And brilliant underfoot with thousand gems
Steeply the thickets to his floods decline.
    Straight trees in every place
    Their thick tops interlace,
And pendant branches trail their foliage fine
    Upon his watery face.
        .   .   .   .   .   .
A rushy island guards the sacred bower,
And hides it from the meadow, where in peace
The lazy cows wrench many a scented flower,
Robbing the golden market of the bees :
    And laden barges float
    By banks of myosote ;
And scented flag and golden flower-de-lys
    Delay the loitering boat.

I cannot say how often I have read that poem, and how
delightfully it carries the breath of our river through
the London smoke. Nor less welcome are the two poems

on spring, the " Invitation to the Country ", and the
" Reply " (Oxford edition, pp. 252–7).'

Professor Dowden also in the *Fortnightly*, and
Mr. Humphry Ward and Mr. Thursfield in the *Times*
spoke up for him.

It was about 1890 that he began to take his real rank.
In 1889 Mr. Daniel reprinted for him the ' Growth of
Love ', now increased to seventy-four sonnets, while he
published four plays, *Palicio*, *The Return of Ulysses*,
The Christian Captives, and *Achilles in Scyros*, with
Bumpus and with Messrs. Bell, the first edition of the
collection called the ' Shorter Poems '. It was this little
volume that made him more widely known. A reprint
was called for the same year, and two more in 1891 and
1894. Its further history will be found on page 224 of
the Oxford edition.

In the year 1891 it was that Mr. Alfred Miles,
had the courage and prescience to entitle his new volume
' Robert Bridges and Contemporary Poets '.

In 1898 Canon R. W. Dixon, his old friend, wrote a
most discerning and emphatic commendation of him for
a series of portraits by Will Rothenstein, of which more
anon.

In 1899 Messrs. Bell issued a shilling edition of the
' Shorter Poems ', to which a fifth book had been added
in 1894, and this was again reprinted the same year.

This same year, 1899, saw the publication by a new firm,
Messrs. Smith, Elder & Co., of a collected edition of all
his works in six volumes.⁴ This is a very attractive
edition. It contains the so-called ' New Poems ' and the
plays, and has a number of notes on the history of the
poems.

In 1903 he made another new departure, publishing
with Mr. Daniel the first of the ' Poems in Classical

Prosody ' which grew out of the theories and experiments of his friend, the Radley Master, Mr. William Johnson Stone. ' Will Stone's versification ', as he calls it in the first of the poems so written and published, the first, that is, of the Epistles.

In 1912, last year, Oxford gave him the degree of Doctor of Letters ; and in the autumn the University Press, to its lasting credit, ranked him living with the dead immortals,—οἴῳ πεπνῦσθαι, τοὶ δὲ σκιαὶ ἀΐσσουσιν—and put him into the series of Oxford Poets, in the volume which I hold in my hand, and am using to-day. It was a bold step, but it has been abundantly justified.

This edition adds to the poems collected before a series of so-called ' Later Poems ' which, as will be seen, have appeared in a variety of periodicals and papers, ranging from the *Sheaf* and the Corpus College *Pelican* to the *Monthly* and *English* Reviews.

Last July he was appointed Poet Laureate, and when at the end of the month I asked for a copy of the cheap edition, I was told it was all sold out.

There are then seven years which are landmarks in the Poet Laureate's poetical career, namely, 1873, 1883, 1890, 1899, 1903, 1912, and 1913.

Besides his verse, he has also written a good deal of criticism in prose, some avowed and some anonymous. Specially noteworthy are the criticisms of Keats which he wrote as an Introduction to Mr. Bullen's edition, his prose tractate on *Milton's Prosody* (published with the Clarendon Press in 1893), and his recent deliverance on *English Pronunciation* issued from the same source. These should be remembered by any one who wishes to study his poetry with thoroughness, and to understand his art and its development completely.

But I want now to let these poems speak for themselves,

and to give, through them, and in his own language, some indication of the character of his genius and his work.

Has it any dominant note ? I think it has. ' 'Tis Love, Love, Love,' says the old French *refrain*, ' that makes the world go round.' C'est l'Amour qui fait le monde à la ronde. That is the secret of all life. And this is certainly Mr. Bridges' creed. But love implies an object, it is of many kinds, love of husband, wife, child, and friend, of man in general, of beauty in man's work, in all the various arts, of the fair face of nature, and containing and crowning all these, the love of God.

Mr. Bridges has put his creed into one of the shorter of the ' Shorter Poems ', No. 9 of Book IV, a little poem that has all his art yet all his naturalness, his sincerity and artistic simplicity (Oxford edition, p. 286) :

> My eyes for beauty pine,
> My soul for Goddës grace :
> No other care nor hope is mine ;
> To heaven I turn my face.
>
> One splendour thence is shed
> From all the stars above :
> 'Tis namèd when God's name is said,
> 'Tis Love, 'tis heavenly Love.
>
> And every gentle heart,
> That burns with true desire,
> Is lit from eyes that mirror part
> Of that celestial fire.

' Every gentle heart.' *Amore e cor gentil son una cosa* as the great Italian lover-poet sang. ' Love and the gentle heart are one same thing.' Mr. Bridges has had above all, and always, the ' chivalrous heart '.

The next two poems ' run division ', as the old phrase was, on the same theme. Number 10 shows us how by following truly his true love of beauty he won the unique reward of the sincere, who are faithful to their love and themselves. His ambition was to succeed in Science, his vocation was to succeed in poetry. He followed his vocation.

> I wished no garland on my head
> Nor treasure in my hand.

The garland is on his head now and I hope some treasure in the hand, but just because he did not seek them they were added to him.

Love is the theme of his two longer poems—'The Growth of Love' and 'Eros and Psyche', which takes the old fairy tale of True Love and the Soul, from Apuleius' tinsel setting, and gives of it a new, a healthy and heavenly reading.

> The poet in a golden clime was born,
>   With golden stars above.
> Dowered with the hate of hate, the scorn of scorn,
>   The love of love.

So wrote another Poet Laureate in his youth some eighty years ago.

How does the Poet Laureate of to-day put it? (Oxford edition, p. 303):

> Since to be loved endures,
>   To love is wise :
> Earth hath no good but yours,
>   Brave, joyful eyes.
>
> Earth hath no sin but thine,
>   Dull eye of scorn :
> O'er thee the sun doth pine
>   And angels mourn.

The counterpart of joy is sorrow, and the measure of love is grief. This too is worthily expressed in Mr. Bridges' poems. One of the most touching of them

all is the poem on the death of his wife's brother, Maurice
Waterhouse (Oxford edition, p. 309) :

I never shall love the snow again
    Since Maurice died :
With corniced drift it blocked the lane,
And sheeted in a desolate plain
    The country side.

The trees with silvery rime bedight
    Their branches bare.
By day no sun appeared ; by night
The hidden moon shed thievish light
    In the misty air.

We fed the birds that flew around
    In flocks to be fed :
No shelter in holly or brake they found.
The speckled thrush on the frozen ground
    Lay frozen and dead.

We skated on stream and pond ; we cut
    The crinching snow
To Doric temple or Arctic hut ;
We laughed and sang at nightfall, shut
    By the fireside glow.

Yet grudged we our keen delights before
    Maurice should come
We said, In-door or out-of-door
We shall love life for a month or more,
    When he is home.

They brought him home ; 'twas two days late
    For Christmas day :
Wrapped in white, in solemn state,
A flower in his hand, all still and straight
    Our Maurice lay.

And two days ere the year outgave
    We laid him low.
The best of us truly were not brave,
When we laid Maurice down in his grave
    Under the snow.

Perfect mastery of his instrument, delicate dainty harmony and rhythm, these will be found everywhere. Like a consummate skater or dancer, there is nothing he cannot do, no figure he cannot cut, no step he cannot execute, and with grace. ' But', they say, ' he is wanting in passion and in feeling for the common joys and sorrows of life.' The little poem ' A Villager ' is surely enough to refute that charge (Oxford edition, p. 319):

> There was no lad handsomer than Willie was
> The day that he came to father's house :
> There was none had an eye as soft an' blue
> As Willie's was, when he came to woo.
>
> To a labouring life though bound thee be,
> An' I on my father's ground live free,
> I'll take thee, I said, for thy manly grace,
> Thy gentle voice an' thy loving face.
>
> 'Tis forty years now since we were wed :
> We are ailing an' grey needs not to be said :
> But Willie's eye is as blue an' soft
> As the day when he wooed me in father's croft.
>
> Yet changed am I in body an' mind,
> For Willie to me has ne'er been kind :
> Merrily drinking an' singing with the men
> He 'ud come home late six nights o' the se'n.
>
> An' since the children be grown an' gone
> He 'as shunned the house an' left me lone :
> An' less an' less he brings me in
> Of the little he now has strength to win.
>
> The roof lets through the wind an' the wet,
> An' master won't mend it with us in 's debt :
> An' all looks every day more worn,
> An' the best of my gowns be shabby an' torn.

E

No wonder if words hav' a-grown to blows ;
That matters not while nobody knows :
For love him I shall to the end of life,
An' be, as I swore, his own true wife.

An' when I am gone, he'll turn, an' see
His folly an' wrong, an' be sorry for me :
An' come to me there in the land o' bliss
To give me the love I looked for in this.

Love of his country will be found in the ' Fair Brass '
(Oxford edition, p. 349), a delightful quietly original and
very characteristic lyric, on a subject so apt that it seems
strange it has never been handled before, and in the
Peace Ode (Oxford edition, p. 439).

It remains to speak of two points which go together, of
Mr. Bridges' knowledge and skill in music, and of his command of that rare and difficult art, the art of writing
hymns.

My own knowledge of music is slight. I only know
enough to believe that I can see for myself, what others
tell me, that Mr. Bridges' knowledge is deep and true.
His love of it certainly breaks out again and again in
his poems. He has written an Ode to Music for the
Bicentenary Commemoration of Henry Purcell (Oxford
edition, p. 394). He dedicated ' Eros and Psyche ' to the
celestial spirit ' of the same rare English composer. In the
' Christian Captives ' he introduces the music of *Anerio*
and *Allegri*, and he writes charmingly about music in the
sonnet to Joseph Joachim, and critically about it, in
the first Epistle in Classical Prosody (Oxford edition,
p. 411).

Of his hymns it is hardly possible to give a fair idea in
a short time, or by one or two specimens. He excels both
in translation and in original work. I first came across
a hymn of his, a translation from the Latin, in that very

pleasant book *Translations from Prudentius*, edited by
his friend the Rev. Francis St. John Thackeray, the
' Morning Hymn '. I was at once attracted by it and
I have always, when I have returned to it, thought it
very beautiful. It is, however, somewhat long, and I will
only quote the first two stanzas :

> Nox et tenebrae, et nubila
>   Confusa mundi, et turbida,
>   Lux intrat, albescit polus,
>   Christus venit, discedite !
>
> Caligo terrae scinditur
>   Percussa solis spiculo
>   Rebusque jam color redit
>   Vultu nitentis sideris.
>
> Night and gloom and cloud
>   The world's confusion and shroud !
>   Light enters, the sky grows bright,
>   Christ comes, take ye your flight.
>
> The darkness of earth is torn
>   By the level spears of the morn,
>   The colours return and play
>   In the smile of the star of day.

In 1899 he published a Hymn Book of his own, *The
Yattendon Hymnal*, a most original volume based on his
own personal experiment and experience with his rustic
choir in his parish church on the Berkshire Downs. It
is described as ' Hymns in Four Parts with English Words
for singing in Church, edited by Robert Bridges '. In
the preface he makes acknowledgement to his friend
Mr. Henry Ellis Wooldridge, some time the Slade Professor
of Fine Art, for the music. It was published in various
forms. The *Edition de Luxe*, at a guinea a part, is a
magnificent volume, so is the next largest form, but
there are also quite cheap editions procurable at a very

small price, from Messrs. Blackwell. I will quote one Hymn from this book, No. 82 :

> My heart is fill'd with longing
> And thick the thoughts come thronging
>   Of my eternal home ;
> That all desire fulfilleth
> And woe and terror stilleth :
> Ah, thither fain, thither fain would I come.
>
> Creation knows no staying,
> And with the world decaying
>   May love itself decay :
> Yea, as the earth grows older
> Her grace and beauty moulder,
> Her joy of life passeth, passeth away.
>
> But Thou, O Love supremest,
> Who man from woe redeemest,
>   My Maker, Thee I pray,
> My soul with night surrounded;
> Above the abyss unsounded,
> Lead forth to light, lead to Thy heavenly day.

I said at the beginning of this Lecture that I would not myself praise or appraise my friend, but I do not feel precluded from quoting the appreciation of another. Let me conclude by reviving an appreciation written some sixteen years ago. It is that of Mr. Richard Watson Dixon. It will be found in the letter-press of a volume entitled *English Portraits*, by Will Rothenstein, published in 1898, opposite a portrait of Mr. Bridges himself.

' Among "them that know"', the writer there says, ' there is continual wonder that wider recognition is not given to the genius of Robert Bridges. His generation hesitates to place him where in heart it feels that he ought to be placed : but the reason for not doing a thing should scarcely be that it ought to be done. The living generation ought to give the signal to posterity. One or two fair opportunities have been lamentably lost. . . .

. . . .

One of his dramas contains the most ludicrous situation ever invented, another the most pathetic. His sc ets are a collection that will stand among the first three or four, unless his generation befool posterity by its reticence. His Shorter Poems are as new an application to nature as photography. To poetry as an art he has rendered a special service. The influence of his " new prosody " is apparent everywhere. We know of Milton and of Keats what we should not have known without him. It is perhaps a pity that the masters so seldom write on one another. If Milton had written on Shakespeare we should have known things that we shall never know.' . . .

The whole is to my mind an excellent piece of English and an admirable piece of criticism. The author was the lifelong friend of William Morris and of Burne-Jones. He was an excellent and approved writer himself. ' Among them that know ', to use his own phrase, he is accounted, I believe, one of the best of our Church historians, and he was also himself a poet. If you would know more of him let me commend to you the two little volumes, *Selected Poems by R. W. Dixon, with a Memoir by Robert Bridges*, Smith, Elder, and the *Last Poems of Richard Watson Dixon, selected and edited by Robert Bridges*, Henry Frowde, 1905.

Dixon was a warm friend of Mr. Bridges. Make allowance for that friendship if you will, as I have asked you to do for mine. He put his opinions strongly. I told him at the time, I remember, how much the strength and courage of his words pleased me. He said that he

had not written when he had the chance without deliberation.

Yet friendship is not all a disadvantage to the critic.
Is not the deepest truth about a poet that spoken by a
poet ?

> And you must love him ere to you
> He will seem worthy of your love.

If only he could have been spared to know that Bridges'
generation has not ' befooled posterity by its reticence ',
that ' the living have given the signal '.   If Dixon could
have lived to see this day !

---

¹ This fact is stated in an interesting letter of Gray to Walpole.
He is criticizing, and I fear correcting, the book of an Oxford
professor of poetry, Spence's *Polymetis*, and he says :

' There are several little neglects, that one might have told
him of, which I noted in reading it hastily : on page 311 a discourse about orange trees occasioned by Virgil's *Inter odoratum
lauri nemus*, where he fancies the Roman *Laurus* to be our Laurel,
though undoubtedly the bay tree, which is *odoratum*, and (I believe)
still called *Lauro*, or *Allovo*, at Rome.'

² Another critique of mine appeared in the *Literary Year Book*
for 1900.

³ He published *Eros and Psyche*, Bell, 1885.   *Nero*, Bumpus,
1885.   *The Feast of Bacchus*, Daniel, 1889.   *Elements of Milton's
Blank Verse*, in Mr. Beeching's edition, 1887.   *Prosody of Paradise
Regained and Samson Agonistes*, Blackwell, Oxford, 1889.

⁴ A seventh volume is understood to be now in preparation
which will complete this edition up to date.

' ROBERT BRIDGES '

(Reprinted from *The Oxford Magazine.*)

LOVING the joy of earth, and well belovéd,
    Home at the last he is come :
Home to the light of applause he has not sought for,
Now, with the wreath of a fame he never wrought for,
    England rewards her son.

The meadow-sweet, and streamlets of the Isis,
    Have had their poet long,
And the greater themes of high Hellenic story
He has touched again with a tender, mellowing glory,
    Master of Attic song.

O eagle-eyed, knowing the lofty music
    That Milton also knew,
To-day the heart of the land with thee rejoices,
Hearing, far from the murmur of city voices
    Thy magic known to few.

                                    H. F. B. B.-S.

HENRY BIRKHEAD

AND THE FOUNDATION OF THE OXFORD CHAIR OF POETRY

A PUBLIC LECTURE DELIVERED
IN THE EXAMINATION SCHOOLS
ON OCTOBER 19, 1908

BY

J. W. MACKAIL

M.A., LL.D., FORMERLY FELLOW OF BALLIOL COLLEGE
PROFESSOR OF POETRY IN THE UNIVERSITY OF OXFORD

1908

HENRY BIRKHEAD

AND THE FOUNDATION OF THE OXFORD CHAIR OF POETRY

Two hundred years ago to-day, on Tuesday, the 19th of October, 1708, the first Professor of Poetry in the University of Oxford delivered his inaugural lecture. We are much overdone nowadays with commemorative celebrations in various multiples of centuries; but the occasion is fitting to say something, among ourselves here and not as part of any public ceremonial, about the founder of the Professorship and the circumstances in which it was founded. The name of Henry Birkhead is almost forgotten; nor, but for this foundation of his, would it have any particular claim on our regard or remembrance. But some duty of piety is owed, by the wholesome tradition of this University, to the memory of its founders and benefactors; and while there is little to say about Birkhead himself, he is in a way the type or average representative of his period; and his period is one of no little importance in the history of English poetry; for it was that of Milton.

In the first place, then, I propose to say what little there is to be said about the founder himself; next to give an account of the foundation of the Professorship of Poetry, and in connexion with that to consider the circumstances in which it was founded as illustrating (which they do in a very interesting way) the attitude of the academic mind towards poetry at the end of the seventeenth

century, and the point in its secular progress which
poetry had then reached.

With regard to the life of Henry Birkhead I find little
to add to the facts which have been collected by the
industry and research of Mr. A. H. Bullen in the *Dictionary
of National Biography*. The Birkheads, Bircheds, or
Birketts, were a Northumbrian family, of whom there
are many records in the registers of Durham Cathedral
and of different parishes in that county during the sixteenth and seventeenth centuries. Of our founder's
father nothing seems to be known except that he was,
or became, a Londoner, and, according to Aubrey, ' kept
the Paul's Head' near St. Paul's Cathedral. Henry
Birkhead was born there, in 1617, according to the most
probable statement. His father must have been a thriving
man, for he gave him the best education which London
then provided. This was at Farnaby's famous school in
Cripplegate—the school which for a whole generation
educated hundreds of eminent Englishmen. It was then
at the height of its fame, the first classical school in
England, and known throughout Europe. Its size was
almost double that of the neighbouring foundation of
St. Paul's; three hundred boys attended it, of whom
a large proportion were of high birth and many became
distinguished in after life. Farnaby himself was reckoned
one of the foremost scholars of his age.

From school, Birkhead proceeded to Trinity College,
Oxford, where he was admitted a commoner in 1633—
at an age of sixteen according to Aubrey's chronology,
of twenty, if Anthony Wood is right in dating his birth
in 1613—and was elected a scholar in 1635. The next
that we hear of him is interesting; it gives evidence
that he was a scholar of fine parts, and perhaps also
that the accusation made against him in one of the few

notices that there are of him after his death, of weakness and conceitedness, may have had some foundation. Under Jesuit influence, then working strongly if secretly in Oxford, he joined the Church of Rome, and left Oxford to enter as a student at the great English Jesuit College at St. Omer. As often happened in that age of fluctuating religious opinions, his conversion to Catholicism was brief. Within a year or two he rejoined the Church of England ; and on the recommendation of Archbishop Laud, the Visitor of the College, was elected in 1638 a Fellow of All Souls. He was an Anglican and Royalist, but accepted things as they came, and submitted quietly to the Cromwellian Commissioners. While at All Souls he sustained his reputation as a scholar and man of letters, and also studied law and medicine. He associated on friendly terms with other Oxford scholars of both parties ; for one of his friends, and joint author with him of a volume of Latin poems which ran into a second edition during the Commonwealth, was Henry Stubbe, a violent opponent of authority in Church and State, who was expelled from Christ Church and from his keepership of the Bodleian Library for scandalous attacks on the clergy, but had the reputation of being 'the best Latinist and Grecian in Oxford'. Birkhead himself remained at All Souls for nineteen years. In 1657 he resigned his fellowship and went to live in London, where he had chambers in the Temple. At the Restoration he became Registrar of the Diocese of Norwich, a post which he continued to fill for the next twenty years. Of his later life we know nothing : he lived, says Wood, in a retired and scholastical condition. Two volumes of Latin poems, and a few contributions to miscellanies of English and Latin verse, all included within the period of his residence at All Souls, are the sum total of his published works. A MS. play, written by him, and entitled *The Female Rebellion*, is among the collections in the Bodleian. Mr. Bullen, who is probably the only person alive who has read it, reports that it has little or no merit : I have not had an opportunity of verifying this judgement, but it may no doubt be accepted as right.

He died at his house in Westminster at a very advanced age in 1696, and was buried in St. Margaret's Church, as I find from the parish records, on the 30th September of that year. It was a year of capital importance in English history, the year of the renovation of the currency and the restoration of public credit which opened for England, after a century of distress and confusion, that long era of commercial prosperity under which the Empire was created.

The will under which this Chair was founded had been made by him three years before his death. It is a document of much human interest ; and as it is brief, and has never been published, I make no apology for quoting it in full, omitting only the parts of it which are common form.

' I give and bequeath unto Mrs Margaret Jones my niece because I think she is well provided for five shillings Item I give and bequeath to her brother John Donaldson if he be alive one shilling   Item I give and bequeath to Stephen Donaldson the younger brother of the said John Donaldson if he be alive one shilling   Item I give and bequeath to Jane Stevenson whom I have formerly called and written to as my wife to save her credit in the world though I was never married to her nor betrothed to her or did she ever so much as desire me to marry her or be betrothed to her   She is of Monkwearmouth in the County of Durham I write this in the presence of God who knowes she has been extream false and many wayes

exceeding injurious to me And therefore I bequeath
to her but one shilling Item I give and bequeath to
Mrs Mary Knight ats Geery my sister five shillings

'Item I give and bequeath to Henry Guy of Westminster Esq (The sum is left blank in the original
document.)

'I doe hereby nullify and revoke all wills formerly by
me in any wise made particularly one last Will and
Testament made by me to my best remembrance in the
yeare of our Lord 1688 and in the moneth of December
I constitute and appoint hereby the forenamed Mary
Knight and forenamed Henry Guy executrix and executor
of this my last will and testament, to whom I bequeath
and give all my lands tenements and hereditaments
whatsoever with their appurtanences scituate in the
parish of Sutton or thereabouts near Abbington in Bark-
shire and my lease of lands scituate in the parish of
Monkwearmouth in the county of Durham with its
appurtanences held by me of the Reverend Dean and
Chapter of Durham with all the rest of my goods and
chattells of what kind soever In trust to maintain as
far as it can for ever a Publick Professor of Poetry in
the University of Oxford '

There is something pitiable, and almost tragic, in the
hot spurt of anger that breaks here from the lonely old
man of eighty. From the specific allusion to the previous
will of five years before, the natural inference is that the
miserable story dated back only to then, and was the
case of an old scholar and recluse fallen into senility and
become the prey of a woman who looked forward to
inheriting his property, but played her game badly.

The Henry Guy named as co-executor with his sister,
and described in the letters of administration as *armiger*,
was no doubt the politician of that name, a member of

Christ Church and of the Inner Temple, and Member
of Parliament for Hedon in Yorkshire. He was Secretary
to the Treasury when the will was made, and probably
a neighbour of Birkhead's in Westminster. It is not
surprising, in view of the terms of the will, that both he
and Mrs. Knight declined to undertake the executorship.
Mrs. Knight very probably regarded the legacy of five
shillings as little short of a direct insult. Guy, a short
time before Birkhead's death, had been removed from
his post at the Treasury and committed to Newgate for
accepting bribes ; he was presumably in no state of mind
to undertake an onerous and unremunerative duty, and
is not known to have felt the least interest in poetry.
Letters of administration were consequently granted in
the ensuing December to the Syndic General of the
University of Oxford.

The delays of legal procedure were in any case then
great ; Jane Stevenson had very possibly made some such
havoc in the property as Becky Sharp did later with that
of Joseph Sedley, and there appears in particular to
have been some long negotiation with the Dean and
Chapter in regard to the Durham property. In the
inaugural lecture of the first professor they are spoken
of as themselves benefactors to the University in the
matter, and almost as co-founders. How this exactly
was I have not been able to discover. The present
Dean, who takes an interest in the matter as it affects
both Durham and Oxford, has very kindly had search
made for me in the Chapter Records. From the Receiver's
books it appears that the rent of certain property which
had been paid by Birkhead for 1696–7 was paid by the
University for 1697–8, and that in 1698 the University
was mulcted in the customary fine on renewal of the
lease. But from that point the records become defective :

' Our Chapter clerk in Queen Anne's day,' the Dean writes to me, ' was a neglectful rascal.' It would seem that at some time within the ten years 1698–1708, the Dean and Chapter gave up the rent and made a present to the University of the estate. In any case, the University acquired the estate in some way, for they afterwards sold it. Had this not been done, it is possible either that the endowment of the Chair would be much larger than it is, or, and this is perhaps more likely, that it would have been before now dealt with by statute, whether by the University itself or by a Commission, and its application varied. For, as we shall see presently, Professorships of Poetry do not seem to be in consonance with modern ideas about the organization and staffing of universities.

At all events, it was not until eleven years later that the statute establishing the Chair was framed. It passed Convocation on the 13th July, 1708. The preamble of the statute is in the following terms : I quote from an old translation of the original Latin :

' Seeing that the reading of the old poets contributes not only to give keenness and polish to the natural endowment of young men, but also to the advancement of severer learning whether sacred or human ; and also forasmuch as the said Henry Birkhead hath, for the purpose of leaving with posterity a record of the devotion of his mind to literature, founded a poetical lecture in the University of Oxford, to be given for all future times ; and hath by his last will bequeathed a yearly income for its support ; we decree, &c.'

The provisions of the statute itself, which are in main substance still those in force, are as follows :

1. The Reader is to be either M.A. or B.C.L., or holder of some higher degree in the University.

2. He is to be elected in full Convocation, and at the

end of five years may be elected afresh or some other
person appointed, provided that no Reader is to be continued in office beyond ten years, and that no other
person of the same House is to succeed him without
interval.

3. He is to lecture in the Natural Philosophy School on
every first Tuesday in full term (with arrangements for
postponement if that Tuesday should be a Saint's Day)
at 3 p.m., and also in the Theatre at the Encaenia, ' before
the philological exercises commence.'

4. The income of the foundation is to be received and
accounted for by the Vice-Chancellor, and a fine of £5
to be deducted from the Reader's salary on each occasion
when he neglects to lecture, and applied to the uses of
the University.

When the terms of the statute were being debated,
a proposal was made, by no less a person than Dean
Aldrich, that there should be Encaenia terminally, for
the recitation of compositions in prose and verse by
young gentlemen, and that on each of these occasions
the Professor of Poetry should make a speech.   The
proposal was negatived ; and I am very glad of it.

This statute remained unaltered till 1784, when the
hour of lecturing was altered from 3 to 2 p.m., and the
regulation as to the additional lecture at Commemoration
omitted.   In 1839 the precise regulation as to the day
and hour of the terminal lectures was dropped, and it
was enacted in more general terms that the professor was
to read one solemn lecture every term.   The more recent
changes by which reappointment for a second term of
five years was forbidden, and the inconvenient regulation
which did not allow two successive professors to belong
to the same college was repealed, are modern and familiar.
A ten years' occupancy of the Chair had up till then been

the rule ; of the twenty-one professors who successively held the Chair until the power of reappointment was abolished a few years ago, all but four were re-elected for a second term. The new rule, whatever may be thought of it by the occupant of the Chair for the time being, is probably in the interest both of poetry and of the University. That the foundation should have, but for this single change, remained practically the same in its terms for two centuries may be taken, if we like, partly as an indication of the sagacity of its founders when they drew the original statute, partly as an instance of the innate conservatism of Oxford, and of her far from deplorable tendency rather to make the best of existing institutions than to cast them into the melting-pot.

Of the particular aims which Birkhead had in view in his foundation we have no evidence. Thomas Smith, of Magdalen, writing at the time of the foundation of the Chair, says that he knew Birkhead, and that the current story after his death was that he had left considerable sums to the Society of Poets : ' of which,' he adds, ' I know no such formal establishment.' His general ideas, however, may probably be taken as substantially represented by the preamble of the statute of 1708. Poetry was then, from the academic point of view, one of the liberal arts. The inaugural lecture of the first Oxford professor laid it down as a sort of axiom that instruction in the art was both possible and desirable : ' artem poeticam institutionem et admittere et mereri.' There were similar Chairs or lectureships in other European Universities. I do not know whether this was at all generally the case, and have come on but few actual instances. In 1705, there is a record of a visit to Oxford, and admission while there ' to the privileges of the Publick Library ', of one ' Mr. Bergerus, Professor of

Poetry in the University of Wittemberg'. This must
have been J. W. von Berger, one of three brothers who
were all professors, each in a different faculty, at that
University. The title of his Chair is, however, given in
the *Biographie Universelle* not as Poetry, but as Eloquence.

The title is fancifully suggestive. One can hardly help
wondering whether the lectures of some predecessor of
his were attended by Hamlet, and whether their influence reappears in that able and wayward scholar's
tendency to drop into poetry and his keen interest in
dramatic criticism. But the University of Wittenberg
itself, Chair of Poetry and all, has long since disappeared.
Still the most flourishing of the Universities of Protestant
Germany till well on in the eighteenth century, it fell
into decay during the Napoleonic wars, and was merged
in 1816 in that of Halle. The Vereinigte Friedrichs-
Universität Halle-Wittenberg has no Chair of Poetry.
Indeed, in the possession of such a Chair Oxford stands,
as far as I can ascertain, alone. There is no Chair of
Poetry, other than ours, in the British Empire. There
is none at Athens or Rome, at Bologna or Berlin. There
is none in the many Universities, with their multi-
farious professorships, which have been founded in the
United States of America. At the Sorbonne there are
Chairs of Latin Poetry and of French Poetry; but
that is a different thing. The nearest and the sole
approach to a Chair of Poetry like ours ·is in the
University of Budapesth, where there is half a one;
at least there is, among the ordinary professorships, one
of *Aesthetik und Poetik*. With these exceptions, if they
be exceptions, the Oxford Professor of Poetry has no
colleague in the two hundred and twenty Universities now
catalogued, and spread over the whole civilized or
partially civilized world.

Two hundred years ago the foundation of a Readership in Poetry was a sort of symbol of the generally accepted view that the laws of the art had become fixed, and its principles had become a matter, as one might say, of international agreement in the republic of letters. The *Poetics* of J. C. Scaliger had, ever since their publication in 1561, after Scaliger's death, been received throughout Europe as a sort of textbook of the art. The seventeenth century had gone on building on these foundations; and what was expected of a Professor of Poetry, here or elsewhere, was the same sort of work, in comment and consolidation, that was being done in France by the joint labours of the two Daciers. But in England poetry had taken a course of its own; and the immense and splendid production of a century had been followed by a body of poetical criticism which included work of great excellence and value. Sidney's *Apology* and the treatise attributed to Puttenham belong to the Elizabethan age proper. Through the whole century of the transition there was a constant stream of discussion on the principles and practice of the art; Dryden, who died in the last year of the seventeenth century, was the first critic of his age. Soon after this Chair was founded, Addison began in the *Spectator* the series of literary papers, which remained for more than half a century, until the appearance of Johnson's *Lives of the Poets*, the last word in English poetical criticism. Within the limits which it had then assigned itself, poetry settled down, during that half century and longer, into an art of fixed rule. The new Renaissance of poetry first foreshadowed in the writings of Gray, Percy, and Warton, did not rise in its full splendour until the last years of the eighteenth century. Coleridge, its inaugurator, also opened up the new Renaissance of poetical criticism. But Oxford was then and for years afterwards still firmly rooted—or, shall we say, fast stuck ?—in the old tradition.

In Oxford itself poetry, and poetical criticism as we should now understand that term, were two hundred years ago at a low ebb. There was no nest of singing-birds here then such as there had been earlier, and was to be again more than once later. Among the Oxford versifiers of Queen Anne's reign no one attained immortality ; the thin but delicate piping of Tickell, a poet best remembered now as Addison's devoted pupil and panegyrist, is the only note that remains audible now. He was deputy-professor of Poetry during the third year of the existence of the Chair, when Trapp, according to the easy-going fashion of those days, had gone off to Ireland as chaplain to the Irish Lord Chancellor. Henry Felton of Edmund Hall might perhaps be still remembered as a poet if he had written many things like these two melodious stanzas, ' occasion'd by a Ladies making a copy of Verses : '

> In Antient Greece when Sappho sung
> And touch'd with matchless Art the Lyre,
> Apollo's Hand her Musick strung
> And all Parnassus form'd the Quire.

> But sweeter Notes and softer Layes
> From your diviner Numbers spring,
> Such as himself Apollo plays,
> Such as the Heavenly Sisters sing.

The lines have something of the purity and sweetness of an early Blake. But Felton, unlike Crabbe, appears to have said farewell to the Muses when he became domestic chaplain to the Duke of Rutland. Other Oxford poets of the period can hardly be mentioned but in a spirit of levity. A single typical instance may suffice ; the

entry in Hearne's diary in May, 1710, where he notes
that ' Mr. Stubbe of Exeter, an ingenious Gentleman, has
publish'd a Poem called *The Laurell and the Olive*, in-
scrib'd to his dear Friend and Acquaintance Mr. Bubb,
who is likewise an ingenious Gentleman, and has a Copy
of Verses before this Poem in two pages to Mr. Stubbe '.
Such were then, and such with allowance for difference
of fashion still are, the frail blossoms of the flying terms.
But it had not then become the fashion that a young man
should stop writing poetry when he put on his Bachelor's
gown. Poetry was at least regarded as an art to be practised by grown men, not as an exercise or amusement to
be outgrown with boyhood. In such a change of fashion
there may be both loss and gain.

Among the English poets of the preceding generation,
Cowley still retained his curious pre-eminence, though now
he shared it with Dryden. Milton, as a republican and
regicide, was an abomination to all orthodox Anglicans ;
and in Oxford any praise bestowed on him was faint and
grudging, while eager credence was given to an absurd
legend that he had died a Papist. Pope only became
known after the appearance of his *Pastorals* in 1709.
The older poets were, however, becoming the subject of
critical study. One of the first acts of Atterbury when
he became Dean of Christ Church in 1712 was to give
his countenance and assistance to Urry in preparing the
edition of Chaucer which, with all its faults and imper-
fections, was the first attempt made at forming a satisfactory text of the poems, and was only superseded by
that of Tyrwhitt more than half a century later. Perhaps
a fair judgement may be formed of the way in which
poetry was generally read and studied in the University
by looking at the names mentioned in the published lectures of the first professor. His inaugural lecture makes

no mention of any but Greek and Roman poets ; in the other lectures the English poets named are, except for Spenser and Shakespeare, all those of his own age or that immediately preceding it, of the period, that is, when poetry in this country had been attacking and achieving the task of becoming fully civilized, of throwing off its insular and national character, and joining— one might almost say, merging in—the general international current of European letters. The knowledge of our older poetry, with but few exceptions, did not extend beyond students and antiquarians.

It was the age of poetical translations ; and these were not only translations into English of foreign masterpieces, but translations into Latin of English originals. Fanshawe, half a century earlier, had started the fashion by his translation of Fletcher's *Faithful Shepherdess* into Latin verse. Sir Francis Kynaston, about the same time, had made a Latin translation of Chaucer's *Troilus and Cressida* : it was dedicated, like the second edition of the volume of Milton's Latin poems, to Rouse, the principal librarian of the Bodleian. Henry Bold, of New College, translated the *Paradise Lost* into Latin verse within a few years after its publication. All this work was on the same lines and directed towards the same object, the testing of English poetry by a universally recognized classical standard, and the vindication for it of a certain classical quality and international value.

It would be a mistake to suppose that the Professorship of Poetry was generally thought of at the time as an institution of high importance, or one which might exercise a powerful influence over thought and taste : still less was there any idea that the interpretation of poetry should be in the hands of its chosen exponent nothing short of the interpretation of life. The statutory lectures of the professor either were rhetorical exercises, or dealt with the laws of poetry regarded as a formal code, and with the art of poetry in a narrowly technical meaning. The extraneous duties which he was expected to undertake were of a trivial kind : to write a prologue to be spoken before the theatrical performance in Oxford of some play by Betterton or Vanbrugh, or a set of complimentary verses on some public occasion. A little while before he was elected to the Chair of Poetry, Trapp had been desired by the Vice-Chancellor to write encomiastical verses upon the new English edition of Spanheim's treatise *De Nummis*, a copy of which had just been presented by the author to the Bodleian. Pegasus had been got well into harness ; and it was the Professor of Poetry's function to keep him there, and see to it that the harness fitted. It is clear enough from all the indirect evidence, of which there is abundance, that this was what was meant. It is clear enough too that this was what actually happened, so far as the earlier Professors of Poetry refrained from following the notorious Oxford fashion of totally neglecting their duties. Of one Oxford professor of that time a contemporary notes that ' having got the place by a Corrupt Interest among the Electors ' he turned out ' so dull a Reader that after a few Lectures he could get no Hearers, and so makes the Place in a manner a *sine-cure*, as most other Publick Readers do '. The last words are venomous, but seem not to be wholly untrue. But as regards the estimation in which the Chair of Poetry was held at its foundation we have direct and tangible evidence. The first professor was elected without competition ; and this was not, we are told, because of any striking or supereminent fitness on his part, but because others ' did not stir for it on account of the smallness of the salary'. The salary was £25, which

would represent, I am told, something like £75, or rather
more, perhaps nearly £100, at the present day. Poetry
and poetical criticism cannot of course be weighed in
terms of money ; but in a salaried appointment, the
importance of the office generally bears some kind of
relation to the amount of the stipend. It is a further
fact, which may induce various reflections according as
one looks at it, that the first Professor of Poetry received,
for the copyright of a volume of the lectures given by
him during the first two years of his tenure of the Chair,
just twice the sum that Milton received for the copyright
of *Paradise Lost*. But poets, with a few remarkable
exceptions, have not been good men of business.

Ample materials exist from which, without going deeply
into records, one can form a picture in one's mind of the
Oxford of two hundred years ago, alike in its material, its
social, and its intellectual aspect. The general impression
that one receives is of an Oxford not so very unlike the
Oxford of the present day. Like the present time, it
was an age of building here, in a new manner and on
an imposing scale : we owe to it many of the buildings
which are now among the most striking and characteristic
of those which adorn the city. ' Lord Arundell's Stones,'
as they were called, were still lying in the Theatre yard,
but the building in which they were housed until a few
years ago was in preparation. Peckwater quadrangle
was rising in Christ Church ; the stately Church of All
Saints on the site of an old and ruinous Gothic predecessor in High Street ; and, further down, the massive
and dignified façade of Queen's, even then the subject of
great controversy, and called a ' great staring pile ' by
those who held by the smaller and richer Jacobean architecture which was then, as it still remains, predominant
in Oxford. It was while that last building was in progress

that, one November evening, the Provost—known familiarly in the University as Old Smoothboots—fell into one of the open cellars ' and was like to have broke his Neck '. He was popularly supposed to have been drunk at the time : for hard drinking was then common even among Heads of Houses and other high officials. When one Fletcher, a scholar of University, was expelled for abusing and striking the Proctor, Harris of Wadham, in the open street, ' there are not wanting credible witnesses,' we are told, ' who say that Harris was more in drink himself than Fletcher.' But University was a difficult college to keep in hand. As an illustration of undergraduate life in Queen Anne's time, and its remarkable likeness to that of our own day, the following account of an incident which took place there in 1706 is worth recording. A newly-appointed Bursar of University had entered on his duties full of zeal for reform. ' Amongst these laudable undertakings,' says the chronicler, ' is chiefly to be mention'd the College Garden which having been almost ruinated and quite out of Repair, he order'd to be cover'd with Green Turff, planted with Trees and Flowers, and the Walks to be gravell'd, to the great Beauty of the Place and Satisfaction of the rest of the Fellows : and there was no one of the College appear'd at present displeas'd with it but the Master : which perhaps being known to one Robinson (a commoner of that House, and Nephew to Mr. Smith, lately Senior Fellow and now in London, who it seems was always averse to this Reform) a day or two after it was finish'd with two or three more of the College, got into the Garden in the Night time, pull'd up some of the Ews spoil'd others, and did other Mischief, to the no small Grief of the Doctor and the rest of the Fellows ; it being such a piece of Malice as one would think could not enter into the thoughts of any person of common Breeding, and indeed seldom or never heard of in the University, but in this College, where they have had some other Instances of the same Nature, and have had some lads noted for this Diabolical Wickedness ; and without doubt 'twas from them Mr. Robinson was instructed, he being reckon'd at first a civil modest Youth, and to be very good natur'd. One reason which instigated him I hear is because the Doctor and the rest of the Society had taken care that all the undergraduates and Bachelors should dine and sup in the Hall, or to undergo a penalty for it, which it seems had been neglected before, to the disgrace somewhat of the College, this being a proviso in all College and Hall Statutes, and if kept up redounds much to the Honour of the University.'

Only a little before this, the Master of University, Dr. Charlett, together with the President of Magdalen and the Provost of Queen's, had been dining with the Warden of New College, ' where they staid till 9 of the clock,' says the letter-writer who tells the story, ' but 'tis highly scandalous to say they drunk to excess, the Warden of New College being not in a very good State of health, and neither of the other noted for being hard Drinkers.' When the dinner-party broke up, Dr. Charlett's boy lighted him home with one of the New College silver tankards instead of a lantern ; ' which was not perceived till they came home, because '—here our authority seems to be blowing hot and cold—' because the President of Magdalen and Provost of Queen's accompany'd him.' However this may have been, the incident ' made a great Noise in Town '. The boy was turned off, and disappears from history. ' But I am heartily sorry,' the narrator goes on to say, ' any one should hence take occasion to blacken the Doctor's character, who (notwithstanding some Failings, to which all are subject) is a man of several excellent Qualifications, and if he had Abilities would be one of the Greatest Encouragers of Learning that have appeared of late.'

But it would be an entire mistake to suppose, from incidents like these, that Oxford was a place entirely given over to idleness and good living. It was full of scholars of wide erudition and vast industry. It was eminent in the study of law and medicine, and of the physical sciences as they were then understood, as well as in its own peculiar field of classical scholarship and theology. Research into the history and antiquities of England was pursued zealously and actively. Rent asunder and half crippled as it was by the furious political and theological controversies of the time, it found even in these a stimulus to the study of ecclesiastical and constitutional history. The University Press was continually bringing out treatises and editions which at least showed no lack of labour and of learning. And it was a subject of regret then, as it has so often been in later times, that many of the finest scholars in Oxford contented themselves with amassing knowledge without communicating it, and carried it all to the grave with them when they died.

Yet, when all is said, it is true that Oxford had then entered on the long period of quiescence, almost of stagnation, which lasted until the early years of the nineteenth century, and the reputation of which still clings to it after almost another century of progress, reform, and revolution. But all through that period it bred fine scholars and accomplished critics; it remained a seat of learning which, if often narrow, pedantic, and insular, was solid and unostentatious. It kept within itself the springs of intellectual life, and the potentiality of reform and advance, the power of adapting itself, though slowly and cumbrously, to new conditions imposed on it by an altered world. It slept, but was not dead ; and thus it is that it is still alive now.

What may be said of the University of Oxford generally may also be said of the Chair of Poetry during the eighteenth century. It slept, or at least dozed : its occupants are names now forgotten, with the exception of Warton, and, to some degree, of Spence and Lowth. It clung hard to its academic and conservative traditions. The great renaissance of poetry at the end of the century was long in reaching it, and reached it at last in the dimmed and distorted form that it took when passed through the absorbent and refractive medium of Anglo-Catholicism. Until Arnold, fifty years ago now, gave the Chair a higher importance and spoke from it to a wider audience, it is to other sources that we must go to trace the progress of poetical criticism, whether such criticism be regarded as the technical exposition of an art or as the appreciation of poetry as a living thing and a power over life. The reading of the old poets, named in the original statute as the object towards the promotion of which the Chair was founded, had sunk into a matter of routine, into a branch of scholarship in the narrower meaning of that ambiguous word. But the greater part of all life is routine ; and the reading of the old poets, in whatever spirit it be pursued, at all events ensures that they shall be read. They themselves, not what is said about them, must do the rest. Yet what can be said about them is endless, and endlessly interesting. Poetry itself, like all organic functions of life, may be incapable of exact definition. The works of the great poets cannot receive any final and conclusive appreciation ; each age, one might almost say each individual mind among their readers, must appreciate them for itself, and find in them what it brings the power and the will to find. But in the art of poetry, as in other arts, it is possible to distinguish, to disengage, to illuminate, to pass on to others something of the meaning and beauty that otherwise might not reach them. There are a thousand ways of doing this; for art like nature is inexhaustible; and the foundation of this Chair 'for all future times' requires no justification, since for all future times the need of this elucidative and constructive appreciation will remain, and the instinct towards it be part of human nature. The progress of poetical criticism means the progress of the study of poetry; and that follows endlessly the endless progress of poetry itself. So long as there is a University of Oxford, so long is it permissible to look forward to a succession of occupants of this Chair of Poetry, who one after another will set themselves to realize, in the terms of their own time and in the communication of their own experience, the object which, after his manner and in consonance with the ideas of his age, was in the mihd of the Founder : who one after another will be commissioned by the University herself to speak in her name of poetry, as a function, interpretation, and pattern of life.

SAMUEL JOHNSON

THE LESLIE STEPHEN LECTURE

DELIVERED IN THE SENATE HOUSE

CAMBRIDGE 22 FEBRUARY 1907

BY

WALTER RALEIGH

KING'S COLLEGE CAMBRIDGE

PROFESSOR OF ENGLISH LITERATURE IN THE UNIVERSITY OF OXFORD

SAMUEL JOHNSON

THE honour that the University of Cambridge has done me by asking me to deliver the first Leslie Stephen lecture is the best kind of honour, for it appeals even more to affection than to pride. Like most men whose trade is lecturing, I have known many Universities; but none of them can be so dear to memory as the first, the place of my early friendships, and dreams, and idleness.

A quarter of a century ago I heard Leslie Stephen lecture in the Divinity Schools of this place. I saw him once again, on the uplands of Cornwall, but I never again heard his voice. You will not expect from me, therefore, any reminiscences, or intimate appreciation of his character. But I can say something of what I believe was very imperfectly known to him, the regard and reverence that was felt for him by a younger generation. A busy man of letters, always occupied with fresh tasks, has little time to study the opinions of his juniors. He makes his progress from book to book, without looking back, and knows more of the pains of doing than of the pleasures of the thing done. Far on in his career, while he is still struggling with his difficult material, he discovers, to his surprise, that the younger world regards him as a triumphant dictator and law-giver. Something of this kind I think happened to Leslie Stephen. He woke up, late in life, to find himself an established institution. He was pleased, and half-incredulous, and he turned to his weary task again. But indeed he had been famous and influential far longer than he knew. The work in literary criticism that was done by him, and by Sir James Fitzjames Stephen, was unlike most of the criticism of the last age. Amid a crowd of treatises which directed attention chiefly to the manner of an author, it was a solid comfort to come across a critic who made it his business to grasp the matter, and who paid even a poet the compliment of supposing that he had something to say. There is no finer literary model than bare matter of fact; and Leslie Stephen's style, 'the lean, terse style' as it has been called, constantly aimed at this perfection. The *Dictionary of National Biography*, under his control, became a gymnasium for authors, a gymnasium where no one was permitted to exercise his muscle until he had stripped himself of those garments which ordinary literary society expects authors to wear. It was Leslie Stephen's aim to prove that this avoidance of superfluity is not the negation of criticism. He was nothing if not critical, but he endeavoured to identify his criticism with the facts, to make it the wall of the building, not a flying buttress. When he relaxed something of his rigour and severity, as he did in his latest studies, his ease was like Dryden's, the ease of an athlete; and the native qualities of his mind, his sincerity and kindliness and depth of feeling, are nowhere more visible than in his latest and best prose. He still keeps close to his subject, but he permits himself an indulgence which he had formerly refused, and sometimes, for a few delightful sentences, speaks of himself.

There is no need for haste in estimating his work and his services to good letters. These will not soon be forgotten. I like to think that he would have approved my choice of a subject for the first of the lectures associated with his name. His enjoyment of books, he said at the close of his life, had begun and ended with Boswell's *Life of Johnson*. Literature, as it is understood for the purposes of these lectures, is to include, so I am informed, biography, criticism, and ethics. If I had been commanded to choose from the world's annals a name which, better than any other, should serve to illustrate the vital relations of those three subjects to literature, I could find no better name than Samuel Johnson. He was himself biographer, critic, and moralist. His life is inseparable from his works; his morality was the motive power of all that he wrote, and the inspiration of much that he did. Of all great men, dead or alive, he is the best known to us; yet perhaps he was greater than we know.

The accident which gave Boswell to Johnson and Johnson to Boswell is one of the most extraordinary pieces of good fortune in literary history. Boswell was a man of genius; the idle paradox which presents him in the likeness of a lucky dunce was never tenable by serious criticism, and has long since been rejected by all who bring thought to bear on the problems of literature. If I had to find a paradox in Boswell I should find it in this, that he was a Scot. His character was destitute of all the vices, and all the virtues, which are popularly, and in the main rightly, attributed to the Scottish people. The young Scot is commonly shy, reserved, and self-conscious; independent in temper, sensitive to affront, slow to make friends, and wary in society. Boswell was the opposite of all these things. He made himself at home in all societies, and charmed others into a like ease and confidence. Under the spell of his effervescent good-humour the melancholy Highlanders were willing to tell stories of the supernatural. 'Mr. Boswell's frankness and gayety,' says Johnson, 'made everybody communicative.' It was no small part of Boswell's secret that he talked with engaging freedom, and often, as it seemed, with childish vanity, of himself. He had the art of interesting others without incurring their respect. He had no ulterior motives. He desired no power, only information, so that his companions recognized his harmlessness, and despised him, and talked to him without a shadow of restraint. He felt a sincere and unbounded admiration for greatness or originality of intellect. 'I have the happiness,' he wrote to Lord Chatham, 'of being capable to contemplate with supreme delight those distinguished spirits by which God is sometimes pleased to honour humanity.' But indeed he did not confine his interest to the great. He was an amateur of human life; his zest in its smallest incidents and his endless curiosity were infectious and irresistible. No scientific investigator has ever been prompted by a livelier zeal for knowledge; and his veracity was scrupulous and absolute. 'A Scotchman must be a very sturdy moralist,' said Johnson, 'who does not love Scotland better than truth.' Boswell was very far indeed from being a sturdy moralist, but he loved truth better than Scotland, better even than himself. Most of the stories told against him, and almost all the witticisms reported at his expense, were first narrated by himself. He had simplicity, candour, fervour, a warmly affectionate nature, a quick intelligence, and a passion for telling all that he knew. These are qualities which make for good literature. They enabled Boswell to portray Johnson with an intimacy and truth that has no parallel in any language.

We owe such an enormous debt of gratitude to Boswell that it seems ungrateful to suggest what is nevertheless obviously true, that the Johnson we know best is Boswell's Johnson. The *Life* would be a lesser work than it is if it had not the unity that was imposed upon it by the mind of its writer. The portrait is so broad and masterly, so nobly conceived and so faithful in detail, that the world has been content to look at Johnson from this point of view and no other. Yet it cannot be denied, and Boswell himself would have been the first to admit it, that there are aspects and periods of Johnson's career which are not and could not be fully treated in the *Life*. When Johnson first saw Boswell in Tom Davies's back shop, he was fifty-four years old and Boswell was twenty-two. The year before the meeting Johnson had been rescued, by the grant of an honourable pension, from the prolonged struggle with poverty which makes up so great a part of the story of his life. He had conquered his world; his circumstances were now comparatively easy and his primacy was universally acknowledged. All these facts have left their mark on Boswell's book. We have some trivial and slight memorials of Shakespeare by men who treated him on equal terms of friendship or rivalry. But Johnson, in our conception of him, is always on a pedestal. He is Dr. Johnson; although he was sixty-six years of age when his own University gave him its honorary degree. The fact is that we cannot escape from Boswell, any more than his hero could; and we do not wish to escape, and we do not try. There are many admirers and friends of Johnson who are familiar with every notable utterance recorded by Boswell, who yet would be hard put to it if they were asked to quote a single sentence from *The Rambler*. That splendid repository of wisdom and truth has ceased to attract readers: it has failed and been forgotten in the unequal contest with Boswell. ‘ It is not sufficiently considered,’ said Johnson, in an early number of *The Rambler*, 'that men more frequently require to be reminded than informed.' I desire to remind you of the work of Johnson, the writer of prose; and I am happy in my subject, for the unique popularity of Boswell has given to the study of Johnson's own works a certain flavour of novelty and research.

It will be wise to face at once the charge so often brought against these writings, that they are dull. M. Taine, who somehow got hold of the mistaken idea that Johnson's periodical essays are the favourite reading of the English people, has lent his support to this charge. Wishing to know what ideas had made Johnson popular, he turned over the pages of his *Dictionary*, his eight volumes of essays, his biographies, his numberless articles, his conversation so carefully collected, and he yawned. 'His truths,' says this critic, 'are too true, we already know his precepts by heart. We learn from him that life is short, and we ought to improve the few moments granted us; that a mother ought not to bring up her son as a fop; that a man ought to repent of his faults and yet avoid superstition; that in everything we ought to be active and not hurried. We thank him for these sage counsels, but we mutter to ourselves that we would have done very well without them.' I will not continue the quotation. It is clear that M. Taine's study of Johnson was limited to a table of contents. What he says amounts to this—that Johnson's writings are a treasury of commonplaces; and in this opinion he certainly has the concurrence of a good many of Johnson's fellow countrymen, who have either refused to read the works or have failed after a gallant attempt.

A commonplace, I take it, is an oft-repeated truth

which means nothing to the hearer of it. But for the most perfect kind of commonplace we must enlarge this definition by adding that it means nothing also to the speaker of it. Now it cannot be denied that Johnson's essays are full of commonplace in the first and narrower sense. When he came before the public as a periodical writer, he presented the world with the odd spectacle of a journalist who cared passionately for truth and nothing at all for novelty. The circulation of *The Rambler* was about five hundred copies, and the only number of it which had a great sale was a paper by Richardson, teaching unmarried ladies the advantages of a domestic reputation and a devout bearing at church as effective lures for husbands. Johnson's papers often handle well-worn moral themes in general and dogmatic language, without any effort to commend them to the reader by particular experiences. He did not conceal from himself the difficulty of making any impression on the wider public—'a multitude fluctuating in pleasures or immersed in business, without time for intellectual amusements.' In many passages of his works he shows a keen appreciation of the obstacles to be surmounted before an author can capture the attention and wield the sympathies of his readers. The chief of these obstacles is the deep and sincere interest which every author feels in his own work and which he imagines will be communicated automatically to the reader. 'We are seldom tiresome to ourselves.' Every book that can be called a book has had one interested and excited reader. It is surely a strange testimony to the imperfection of human sympathy and the isolation of the single mind that some books have had only one.

An author's favourite method of attack in the attempt to cross the barrier that separates him from his reader is the method of surprise. The writer who can startle his public by an immediate appeal to the livelier passions and sentiments is sure of a hearing, and can thereafter gain attention even for the commonplace. This method was never practised by Johnson. He despised it, for he knew that what he had to say was no commonplace, so far as he himself was concerned. Among all his discourses on human life he utters hardly a single precept which had not been brought home to him by living experience. The pages of *The Rambler*, if we can read them, are aglow with the earnestness of dear-bought conviction, and rich in conclusions gathered not from books but from life and suffering. It is here that the biography of the writer helps us. If he will not come to meet us, we can go to meet him. Any reader who acquaints himself intimately with the records of Johnson's life, and then reads *The Rambler*, must be very insensible if he does not find it one of the most moving of books. It was so to Boswell, who says that he could never read the following sentence without feeling his frame thrill: ' I think there is some reason for questioning whether the body and mind are not so proportioned that the one can bear all which can be inflicted on the other; whether virtue cannot stand its ground as long as life, and whether a soul well principled will not be separated sooner than subdued.'

Almost every number of *The Rambler* contains reflections and thoughts which cease to be commonplace when the experiences that suggested them are remembered. For more than thirty years of his mature life Johnson was poor, often miserably poor. There are three degrees of poverty, he said—want of riches, want of competence, and want of necessaries. He had known them all. He spoke little of this in his later years;

there is no pleasure, he said, in narrating the annals of beggary. But his knowledge of poverty has expressed itself more than once in the quiet commonplaces of *The Rambler*. Again, he was tortured by what he called indolence, but what was more probably natural fatigue consequent upon the excessive nervous expenditure of his bouts of hard work. And this too finds expression in *The Rambler*. 'Indolence,' he says, 'is one of the vices from which those whom it infects are seldom reformed. Every other species of luxury operates upon some appetite that is quickly satiated, and requires some concurrence of art or accident which every place will not supply; but the desire of ease acts equally at all hours, and the longer it is indulged is the more increased. To do nothing is in every man's power; we can never want an opportunity of omitting duties.' The topics of *The Rambler* are many, but the great majority of them are drawn from the graver aspects of life, and it is when he treats of fundamental duties and inevitable sorrows, bereavement, and disease, and death, that Johnson rises to his full stature. When he ventures to emulate the tea-table morality of the *Spectator* he has not a light or happy touch. Yet his knowledge of the human mind is not only much more profound than Addison's, it is also more curious and subtle. In an essay on bashfulness he first investigates its causes, and finds the chief of them in too high an opinion of our own importance. Then he applies the remedy:

'The most useful medicines are often unpleasing to the taste. Those who are oppressed by their own reputation will, perhaps, not be comforted by hearing that their cares are unnecessary. But the truth is that no man is much regarded by the rest of the world. He that considers how little he dwells upon the condition of others, will learn how little the attention of others is attracted by himself. While we see multitudes passing before us, of whom, perhaps, not one appears to deserve our notice, or excite our sympathy, we should remember that we likewise are lost in the same throng; that the eye which happens to glance upon us is turned in a moment on him that follows us, and that the utmost which we can reasonably hope or fear is, to fill a vacant hour with prattle, and be forgotten.'

This is prose that will not suffer much by comparison with the best in the language. It is strange to remember, as we read some of the noblest of Johnson's sentences, that they were written in a periodical paper for the entertainment of chance readers. His essay on Revenge concludes with an appeal not often to be found in the pages of a society journal: 'Of him that hopes to be forgiven, it is indispensably required that he forgive. It is therefore superfluous to urge any other motive. On this great duty eternity is suspended; and to him that refuses to practise it, the throne of mercy is inaccessible, and the Saviour of the world has been born in vain.'

The passages that I have quoted from *The Rambler* are perhaps enough to illustrate what Johnson means when he speaks, in the last number, of his services to the English language. 'Something, perhaps, I have added to the elegance of its construction, and something to the harmony of its cadence.' Later criticism has been inclined to say rather that he subdued the syntax of his native tongue to a dull mechanism, and taught it a drowsy tune. But this is unjust. It is true that he loved balance and order, and that the elaborate rhetorical structure of his sentences is very ill-adapted to describe the trivial matters to which he sometimes applies it, such as the arrival of a lady at a country house. 'When a tiresome and vexatious journey of four days had brought me to the house, where invitation, regularly sent for seven years together, had at last induced me to pass the summer, I was surprised, after the civilities of my first reception, to find, instead of the leisure and tranquillity which a rural life always promises, and, if well conducted, might always afford, a confused wildness of care, and a tumultuous hurry of diligence, by which every face was clouded and every motion agitated.' In a sentence like this, the ear, which has been trained to love completeness and symmetry, shows itself exorbitant in its demands, and compels even the accidents of domestic life to happen in contrasted pairs. The idle antithetical members of the sentence have been compared to those false knobs and handles which are used, for the sake of symmetry, in a debased style of furniture. But this occasional fault of the formal Johnsonian syntax is of a piece with its merits. The sentence is very complex, and when no member of it is idle, when every antithesis makes room for some new consideration, it can be packed full of meaning, so that it exhibits a subject in all its bearings, and in a few lines does the work of a chapter. When Johnson is verbose and languid, it is often because his subject is slight, and does not yield him matter enough to fill his capacious style. The syntax is still a stately organ, fitted to discourse great music, but the bellows are poor and weak. When his mind gets to work on a subject that calls forth all his powers, his vigour and versatility, displayed within a narrow compass, are amazing. There is nothing new to add to his brief conclusion in the question of the second sight, which he investigated with some care during his Highland journey. 'To collect sufficient testimonies,' he says, 'for the satisfaction of the public, or of ourselves, would have required more time than we could bestow. There is, against it, the seeming analogy of things confusedly seen and little understood; and, for it, the indistinct cry of national persuasion, which may be perhaps resolved at last into prejudice and tradition. I never could advance my curiosity to conviction; but came away at last only willing to believe.'

In *The Lives of the Poets* his style reaches its maturity of vigour and ease. The author of these *Lives* is Boswell's Johnson, the brilliant talker, the king of literary society,

> Who ruled, as he thought fit,
> The universal monarchy of wit.

Yet for the light that they throw on Johnson's own character I doubt whether any of the *Lives* can compare with *The Life of Richard Savage*, which was published almost twenty years before the meeting with Boswell. The character of Savage was marked, as Boswell truly observes, by profligacy, insolence, and ingratitude. But Johnson had wandered the streets with him for whole nights together, when they could not pay for a lodging, and had taken delight in his rich and curious stores of information concerning high and low society. The *Life of Savage* is a tribute of extraordinary delicacy and beauty, paid by Johnson to his friend. Only a man of the broadest and sanest sympathies could have performed this task, which Johnson does not seem to find difficult. Towards Savage he is all tenderness and generosity, yet he does not for an instant relax his allegiance to the virtues which formed no part of his friend's character. He tells the whole truth; yet his affection for Savage remains what he felt it to be, the most important truth of all. His morality is so

SAMUEL JOHNSON 15

entirely free from pedantry, his sense of the difficulty of
virtue and the tragic force of circumstance is so keen,
and his love of singularity of character is so great, that
even while he points the moral of a wasted life he never
comes near to the vanity of condemnation. It is abundantly clear from the facts, which he records with all
the impartiality of a naturalist, that Savage, besides
being hopelessly self-indulgent and dissolute, was violently egotistic, overbearing, and treacherous to his
friends. Johnson's verdict on these faults is given
in the closing sentences of the *Life*: ' The insolence
and resentment of which he is accused were not easily
to be avoided by a great mind, irritated by perpetual
hardships, and constrained hourly to return the spurns
of contempt and repress the insolence of prosperity;
and vanity surely may be readily pardoned in him,
to whom life afforded no other comforts than barren
praises and the consciousness of deserving them. Those
are no proper judges of his conduct, who have slumbered
away their time on the down of plenty; nor will any
wise man easily presume to say, " Had I been in Savage's
condition, I should have lived or written better than
Savage." '

If we try to picture Johnson in his most characteristic
attitude we usually see him sitting on that throne of
human felicity, a chair in a tavern, and roaring down
opposition. It was thus that Boswell knew him best,
and though the same record exhibits him in many other
aspects, yet the predominant impression persists. So
Johnson has come to be regarded as a kind of Chairman
to humanity, whose business it is to cry ' Order, Order,'
an embodiment of corporate tradition and the settled
wisdom of the ages.

Yet we may think of him, if we like, in a less public

fashion, as a man full of impulse and whim, quaint in humour, passionate in feeling, warm in imagination, and, above all, original. You can never predict what Johnson will say when his opinion is challenged. Doubtless he loved paradox and argument, but he was no dialectician, and behind the play of talk his fancies and tastes were intensely individual. He disliked all talk that dealt with historical facts, especially the facts of Roman history. He never, while he lived, desired to hear of the Punic War. Others besides Johnson have been distressed and fatigued by talk that is merely an exercise of memory. But his method of escape was all his own. When Mrs. Thrale asked his opinion of the conversational powers of Charles James Fox, 'He talked to me at club one day,' said Johnson, 'concerning Catiline's conspiracy—so I withdrew my attention, and thought about Tom Thumb.'

Johnson is famous for his good sense and sound judgement, but his good sense abounds in surprises. There is a delightful touch of surprise in his comparison of a ship to a jail. 'No man will be a sailor who has contrivance enough to get himself into a jail; for being in a ship is being in a jail, with the chance of being drowned.' And again, 'A man in jail has more room, better food, and commonly better company.' The same dislike of the sea expresses itself in a paper of *The Rambler* which discusses the possibility of varying the monotony of pastoral poetry by introducing marine subjects. But unfortunately the sea has less variety than the land. 'To all the inland inhabitants of every region, the sea is only known as an immense diffusion of waters, over which men pass from one country to another, and in which life is frequently lost.'

Wherever you open the pages of Johnson's works

you will find general truths sincerely and vigorously expressed, but behind the brave array of dogma you will find everywhere the strongest marks of an individual mind, and the charm and colour of personal predilections. The Romantic writers must not be allowed the credit of inventing the personal note in literature. What they invented was not themselves, but a certain sentimental way of regarding themselves. Johnson despised all such sentiment. 'When a butcher tells you,' he said, 'that his heart bleeds for his country, he has in fact no uneasy feeling.' Rousseau is not more individual in his cultivation of sentiment than Johnson in his dislike of it. He carried this dislike to strange extremes, so that all gesticulation and expression of the emotions became suspect to him. Of the preaching of Dr. Isaac Watts he says, 'He did not endeavour to assist his eloquence by any gesticulations; for, as no corporeal actions have any correspondence with theological truth, he did not see how they could enforce it.' Perhaps the best example of this fixed distaste for demonstrative emotion may be found in his contempt for the actor's profession. It is dangerous to quarrel with Boswell, but it seems to me impossible to accept his suggestion that Johnson's opinions concerning stage-players had their origin in jealousy of the success of Garrick. Such jealousy is utterly unlike all that we know of Johnson. On the other hand, a hatred of show and a fierce resentment at the response of his own feelings to cunningly simulated passion are exactly what we should expect in him. The passages in which he has expressed himself on this matter are too many and too various to be attributed to a gust of personal ill-feeling. One of the most delightful of them occurs in his notes on the character of Bottom in *A Midsummer*

c

Night's Dream. 'Bottom,' he says, 'seems to have been bred in a tiring-room. He is for engrossing every part, and would exclude his inferiors from all possibility of distinction.' Again, 'Bottom discovers a true genius for the stage by his solicitude for propriety of dress, and his deliberation which beard to choose among many beards, all unnatural.'

The sonorous and ponderous rotundity of Johnson's style, and the unfailing respect that he pays to law and decorum, have partly concealed from view the wilfulness of his native temper. Obedience to law can never be the soul of a man or of a writer. It is the converted rebels who give power to the arm of government. If there has ever been a writer of a sober, slow, and conforming temper, who has left memorable work behind him, it will be found, I think, that for the greater part of his life he acted as a poor mechanical drudge in the service of his own youthful enthusiasm, and painfully filled out the schemes which were conceived in a happier time. All enduring literary work is the offspring of intense excitement. Johnson did most of his reading piecemeal, in a fever of agitation. If any man praised a book in his presence, he was sure to ask, 'Did you read it through?' If the answer was in the affirmative, he did not seem willing to believe it. He very seldom read a book from beginning to end; his writing, moreover, was done at high speed, and often at a great heat of imagination. Some writers use general statements as a mask to conceal ignorance and emptiness; Johnson prefers them because they lend smoothness and decency to passion. He states only his conclusions; but the premises, although they are not given, are vividly present to his mind. When it becomes necessary, as a guarantee of sincerity and knowledge, to exhibit in full all that is implied in a general statement, he reverses his favourite method, and permits his imagination to expatiate on his material with all the visionary activity of poetry. His review of Soame Jenyns's *Free Enquiry into the Nature and Origin of Evil* furnishes a splendid instance of this imaginative power, which expands an abstract proposition into all its detailed consequences. Soame Jenyns was a gentleman with a taste for metaphysic, who had offered some conjectures, in the glib optimistic vein of Pope, towards the explanation of failure and suffering. In the course of his essay he touches, with a light hand, on the possible compensations and advantages of pain and poverty. In order to demonstrate that all partial evil is universal good he constructs an airy hierarchy, or graduated scale of imaginary beings, each rank of whom he supposes to derive benefit from the pains of those who inhabit another grade. Johnson's piety and humility, his profound sense of the reality of human suffering and the weakness of human faculty, were outraged by this fantastic philosophy. 'To these speculations,' he says, 'humanity is unequal.' In a passage of relentless satire Soame Jenyns is introduced, for the first time, to the meaning of his own hypothesis. 'He imagines,' says Johnson, 'that as we have not only animals for food, but choose some for our own diversion, the same privilege may be allowed to some beings above us, *who may deceive, torment, or destroy us for the ends only of their own pleasure and utility*. This he again finds impossible to be conceived, *but that impossibility lessens not the probability of the conjecture, which by analogy is so strongly confirmed.*

'I cannot resist the temptation of contemplating this analogy, which, I think, he might have carried further, very much to the advantage of his argument. He might have shown that *these hunters, whose game is man,* have many sports analogous to our own. As we drown whelps and kittens, they amuse themselves now and then with sinking a ship, and stand round the fields of Blenheim or the walls of Prague, as we encircle a cock-pit. As we shoot a bird flying, they take a man in the midst of his business or pleasure, and knock him down with an apoplexy. Some of them, perhaps, are virtuosi, and delight in the operations of an asthma, as a human philosopher in the effects of an air-pump. To swell a man with a tympany is as good sport as to blow a frog. Many a merry bout have these frolic beings at the vicissitudes of an ague, and good sport it is to see a man tumble with epilepsy, and revive and tumble again, and all this he knows not why. As they are wiser and more powerful than we, they have more exquisite diversions, for we have no way of procuring any sport so brisk and so lasting as the paroxysms of the gout and the stone, which undoubtedly must make high mirth, especially if the play be a little diversified with the blunders and puzzles of the blind and deaf. We know not how far their sphere of observation may extend. Perhaps now and then a merry being may place himself in such a situation as to enjoy at once all the varieties of an epidemical disease, or amuse his leisure with the tossings and contortions of every possible pain exhibited together.

'One sport the merry malice of these beings has found means of enjoying to which we have nothing equal or similar. They now and then catch a mortal proud of his parts, and flattered either by the submission of those who court his kindness or the notice of those who suffer him to court theirs. A head thus prepared for

the reception of false opinions and the projection of
vain designs they easily fill with idle notions, till in
time they make their plaything an author: their first
diversion commonly begins with an ode or an epistle,
then rises perhaps to a political irony, and is at last
brought to its height by a treatise of philosophy. Then
begins the poor animal to entangle himself in sophisms
and flounder in absurdity, to talk confidently of the
scale of being, and to give solutions which himself
confesses impossible to be understood. Sometimes,
however, it happens that their pleasure is without much
mischief. The author feels no pain, but while they
are wondering at the extravagance of his opinion, and
pointing him out to one another as a new example of
human folly, he is enjoying his own applause and that
of his companions, and perhaps is elevated with the
hope of standing at the head of a new sect.

'Many of the books which now crowd the world may
be justly suspected to be written for the sake of some
invisible order of beings—for surely they are of no use
to any of the corporeal inhabitants of the world. . . .
The only reason why we should contemplate Evil is,
that we may bear it better; and I am afraid nothing
is much more placidly endured for the sake of making
others sport.'

Johnson, it may be remarked, does not answer
Soame Jenyns's argument; he concentrates on it the
vivifying heat of his imagination, and it shrivels under
the glow. He felt no respect for a structure of theory,
however ingenious and elaborate, which is built up
from facts imperfectly realized. 'Life,' he says, 'must
be seen before it can be known.' Because he had seen
much of life, his last and greatest work, *The Lives of the
Most Eminent English Poets*, is more than a collection

of facts : it is a book of wisdom and experience, a treatise on the conduct of life, a commentary on human destiny.

Those *Lives* will never lose their authoritative value as a record. The biographer must often consult them for their facts. The student of Johnson will consult them quite as often for the light that they throw on their author, who moves among the English poets easily and freely, enjoying the society of his peers, praising them without timidity, judging them without superstition, yet ready at all times with those human allowances which are more likely to be kept in mind by a man's intimates than by an indifferent posterity. When Johnson undertook the *Lives* he was almost seventy years of age ; he had long been familiar with his subject, and he wrote from a full mind, rapidly and confidently. He spent little time on research. When Boswell tried to introduce him to Lord Marchmont, who had a store of anecdotes concerning Pope, he at first refused the trouble of hearing them. ' I suppose, Sir,' said Mrs. Thrale, with something of the severity of a governess, ' Mr. Boswell thought, that as you are to write *Pope's Life*, you would wish to know about him.' Johnson accepted the reproof, though he might very well have replied that he knew more than was necessary for his purpose. An even better instance of his in-difference may be found in his criticism of Congreve. Congreve's dramatic works are not bulky, and were doubtless to be found in any well-appointed drawing-room. But Johnson would not rise from his desk. ' Of Congreve's plays,' he says, ' I cannot speak dis-tinctly ; for since I inspected them many years have passed ; but what remains upon my memory is, that his characters are commonly fictitious and artificial, with very little of nature and not much of life.' Then follows an admirable critical summary of Congreve's peculiar merits in comedy.

This magnanimous carelessness with regard to detail helped rather than hindered the breadth and justice of Johnson's scheme. There are many modern biographies and histories, full of carefully authenticated fact, which afflict the reader with a weight of indigestion. The author has no right to his facts, no ownership in them. They have flitted through his mind on a calm five minutes' passage from the notebook to the immortality of the printed page. But no man can hope to make much impression on a reader with facts which he has not thought it worth his own while to remember. Every considerable book, in literature or science, is an engine whereby mind operates on mind. It is an ignorant worship of Science which treats it as residing in books, and reduces the mind to a mechanism of transfer. The measure of an author's power would be best found in the book which he should sit down to write the day after his library was burnt to the ground.

The *Lives of the Poets* has not a few of the qualities of such a book. It is broadly conceived and written, it has a firm grasp of essentials, the portraits are lifelike, and the judgements, on the whole, wonderfully fair. There has been much extravagant talk among Romantic critics of Johnson's prejudices, and even of his incapacity as a judge of poetry. Time will avenge him on these critics ; and Time has begun to do its work. The minor poets of our own day may well be glad that Johnson is not alive among them.

His occasional errors cannot be concealed ; they are known to every schoolboy. Sometimes he allows his own matured and carefully considered views on certain general literary questions to interfere with the impartial examination of a particular poem. He disliked irregular metres and fortuitous schemes of rhyme. He held the pastoral convention in poetry to be artificial, frigid, and over-worn. These opinions and tastes led him into his notorious verdict on *Lycidas*. And yet, when the noise of the shouting shall have died away, it may be questioned whether most of the points attacked by Johnson would ever be chosen by admirers of the poem for special commendation. Is there nothing artificial and far-fetched about the satyrs and the fauns with cloven heel? Is the ceremonial procession of Triton, Camus, and St. Peter an example of Milton's imagination at its best? In short, does the beauty and wonder of the poem derive from the allegorical scheme to which Johnson objected? But I am almost frightened at my own temerity, and must be content to leave the question unanswered.

There were certain of the English poets whom Johnson, it is plain, disliked, even while he admired their work. His account of them is inevitably tinged by this dislike; yet his native generosity and justice never shine out more brightly than in the praises that he gives them. He disliked Milton; and no one has ever written a more whole-hearted eulogy of *Paradise Lost*. Unless I am deceived, he disliked many things in the character of Addison, yet any one who would praise Addison nobly and truly will find himself compelled to echo Johnson's praises. A more profound difference of feeling separated him from Swift. He excuses himself from writing a full account of Swift's life, on the ground that the task had already been performed by Dr. Hawkesworth. But Hawkesworth's *Life* is a mere piece of book-making, and it seems likely that Johnson was glad to be saved from a duty that had no attractions for him. The con-

trast between himself and Swift may be best expressed
in their own words: 'I heartily hate and detest that
animal called man,' said Swift, 'although I heartily love
John, Peter, Thomas, and so forth.' Johnson's attitude
was the reverse of this. He used to say that the world
was well constructed, but that the particular people
disgraced the elegance and beauty of the general fabric.
Yet it was he, not the hearty lover of 'John, Peter,
Thomas, and so forth', who had the deeper sense of the
tie that binds man to man. That men should dare to
hate each other in a world where they suffer the like
trials and await the same doom was hardly conceivable
to Johnson. That a man should dare to stand aloof from
his kind and condemn them was a higher pitch of arrogance, destined to end in that tempest of madness and
hate which is the Fourth Book of *Gulliver's Travels*.

Lastly, it cannot be denied that Johnson did scant
justice to Gray; although here, again, his praise of the
Elegy could hardly be bettered. The causes of this
imperfect sympathy are easy to understand. Gray was
a recluse poet, shy, sensitive, dainty, who brooded on
his own feelings and guarded his own genius from contact with the rough world. 'He had a notion,' says
Johnson, 'not very peculiar, that he could not write
but at certain times, or at happy moments; a fantastic
foppery, to which my kindness for a man of learning and
virtue wishes him to have been superior.' Surely this
impatience will seem only natural to those who remember
the story of Johnson's life. He had lived for thirty
years, and had supported others, solely by the labours
of his pen. The pay he received was often wretchedly
small. Fifteen guineas was the price of the copyright
of the *Life of Savage*. He was driven from task to task,
compelled to supply the booksellers with what they

demanded, prefaces, translations, or sermons at a guinea a piece. In spite of sickness and lassitude and intense disinclination, the day's work had to be done, and when work did not come to hand, it had to be sought and solicited. It is not easy for us to imagine the conditions of literature in London when Johnson first came there, and for many years after,—the crowds of miserable authors, poor, servile, jealous, and venal. Immersed in this society he laboured for years. The laws that he imposed on his drudgery were never broken. He made no personal attacks on others, and answered none on himself. He never complied with temporary curiosity, nor enabled his readers to discuss the topic of the day. He never degraded virtue by the meanness of dedication. There was nothing in his writings to disclaim and nothing to regret, for he always thought it the duty of an anonymous author to write as if he expected to be hereafter known. When at last he was known, there was still no escape from hack-work and the necessities of the day. The books which he has added to the English Classics were written for bread—the *Dictionary*, the periodical papers, *Rasselas*, the Preface and Notes to Shakespeare (which will some day be recognized for what they are, the best and most luminous of eighteenth-century commentaries on Shakespeare's drama), and the *Lives of the Poets*.

This is the greatness of Johnson, that he is greater than his works. He thought of himself as a man, not as an author; and of literature as a means, not as an end in itself. Duties and friendships and charities were more to him than fame and honour. The breadth and humanity of temper which sometimes caused him to depreciate the importance of literature, have left their mark on his books. There are some authors who exhaust themselves in the effort to endow posterity, and distil all their virtue in a book. Yet their masterpieces have something inhuman about them, like those jewelled idols, the work of men's hands, which are worshipped by the sacrifice of man's flesh and blood. There is more of comfort and dignity in the view of literature to which Johnson has given large utterance: 'Books without the knowledge of life are useless; for what should books teach but the art of living?'

PROSE RHYTHM IN ENGLISH

BY

ALBERT C. CLARK

FELLOW OF QUEEN'S COLLEGE

A LECTURE DELIVERED ON JUNE 6, 1913

1913

PROSE RHYTHM IN ENGLISH

THE suggestions which I venture to put forward in this lecture occurred to me recently while I was reading Saintsbury's *History of English Prose Rhythm*. I realize that I am guilty of temerity in writing upon a subject which lies outside the range of my usual work, and can only excuse myself by saying that I have studied similar phenomena in ancient and mediaeval prose. Some three years ago I published a paper upon the mediaeval *cursus*, which contained a brief introduction to the study of numerous prose.[1] Since, however, I cannot hope that more than a few of my listeners may have seen this, I must begin by repeating a few points.

For the origin of prose rhythm we must go to Cicero. Nature, he tells us, has placed in the ears a register which tells us if a rhythm is good or bad, just as by the same means we are enabled to distinguish notes in music. Men first observed that particular sounds gave pleasure to the ear, then they repeated them for this end. Thus, practice came first and was succeeded by theory. The rhythm of prose is based on the same principle as that of verse. This in ancient prose was the distribution of long and short syllables; in our own tongue it is the arrangement of stressed and unstressed syllables. The difference between the rhythms of prose and verse is said to be one of degree. In verse the metre is constant and unbroken, in prose the measures are loose and irregular. In this respect prose is said to resemble lyric poetry, a very suggestive remark.

The theory of ancient writers is, that the whole sentence is pervaded or ' winged ' by rhythm, or ' number ', but that this number is most noticeable in the cadence, or *clausula*. The sentence is termed period, and its parts are called *commata* and *cola*. There is a cadence at the end of the colon, and to a less extent at the end of the comma, similar to that at the end of the period. At the end of each there is a beat or κρότος, similar to that used in music or poetry. Whenever the speaker paused to draw fresh breath, he punctuated by a *numerus*, or cadence. Thus, as I have said elsewhere, ' the *numeri* coincide with the beats and reveal the secret of

---

[1] *The Cursus in Mediaeval and Vulgar Latin*, Oxford, 1910.

ancient punctuation.'[1]   So also in the twelfth century A. D. Pope
Gregory VIII speaks of the pause in the middle of a sentence *post
punctum vel post metrum*.[2]   In this connexion it is interesting to notice
that the person who is said to have invented *numeri*, i. e. the use
of rhythmical cadences in prose, Thrasymachus of Chalcedon, is
also said to have first pointed out the nature of the κῶλον and the period.
We still use the terms comma and colon, but in a new sense, i. e. to
mark the grammatical construction.   For this the ancients did not
care, their punctuation was founded on delivery.   Their ears were far
sharper than ours, and their speech was more musical.   Thus, we
hear of an occasion when a Roman orator brought down the house by
a sentence ending with a double trochee, while a Greek audience
would beat time with a monotonous speaker, anticipating the inevitable
finale.

Cicero gives examples of perfect prose, in which it is impossible to
vary the order without destroying the rhythm.   He also attempted
to give rules for composition, distinguishing between good and bad
endings.   Here he was not so successful.   His examples agree but
imperfectly with his own practice, and he has no coherent theory
to propose.   The one statement which is really fruitful, and which
tends to emerge more and more clearly in subsequent writers, is that
the chief ingredient in prose rhythm is the cretic.   He laboured under
the same difficulty as we do to-day.   We know that, when we write,
we choose a word or a collocation, because our ears tell us that it
is right.   Also, when we read a piece of perfect English, we are con-
scious of a bewitching rhythm, but we cannot tell wherein the charm
resides.   It is necessary to insist on this point, since many writers
assume that the last word on Latin rhythm was said by Cicero, and
turn deaf ears to all the results of modern analysis.   They say, ' I will
go as far as Cicero went, and not one step further.   The modern
method is not that of Cicero.'   The answer is, ' Quite true, but
Cicero failed.'

The secret of ancient prose was discovered recently, and that
in a curious manner.   The inquiry was started in 1880 by Noel
Valois in a tract upon the art of letter writing in France in the Middle
Ages.   He drew attention to certain texts in which the use of three
methods of ending a clause or sentence is inculcated.   These are
termed *cursus planus*, *cursus tardus*, *cursus velox*.   Fresh contributions
were made by a number of scholars.   It was shown that the three
forms of the *cursus* were not peculiar to letter writing, but were

---

[1] *Cursus*, p. 5.   [2] *Fontes Prosae Numerosae*, p. 35.

employed in a vast body of literature. In the eleventh and twelfth centuries the *cursus* was adopted by the Roman *curia*, and rules for its use were laid down by various Popes. The *planus* consists of five syllables with accents on the first and fourth, e. g. *vóces testántur*; the *tardus* of six syllables, also with accents on the first and fourth, e. g. *méa curátio*; and the *velox* of seven syllables with accents on the first and sixth, e. g. *gáudia perveníre*. Modern writers would attribute to the last a minor accent on the fourth syllable. The English equivalents for these forms would be, e. g. *sérvants depárted, pérfect felícity, glórious ùndertáking*. The next step was to show that these accentual clausulae were already used in writers of the fourth and fifth centuries, and were preceded by a system in which quantity, not stress, played the chief part. Thus *vóces testántur* is preceded by *vōcĕ tēstātur, méa curátio* by *nōstră cūrātĭo*, and *gáudia pèrveníre* by *gāudĭŭm pērvĕnīrĕ*. This metrical system was shown to go back to classical Latin prose, and to be present in the writings of Cicero himself. Meanwhile patient workers had been tabulating the endings of Cicero's sentences, and arrived independently at the result that his favourite forms were exactly those which correspond to the three forms of the *cursus*. These may be reduced to a single formula, viz. a cretic base with a trochaic cadence of varying length.[1] This, however, was no new invention of Latin writers: like everything else it came from Greece. The prose of Demosthenes, like that of Cicero, is 'winged' with numbers, and Roman writers quote as examples of his severe rhythm μηδὲ τοξεύῃ and τοῖς θεοῖς εὔχομαι, which are examples of the *planus* and *tardus*. The Asiatic writers chiefly affected the ending with a double trochee, which corresponds to the mediaeval *velox*. Before Demosthenes we find the same favourite forms in the prose of Isocrates, which already exhibits the same rhythms as those which pervade the prose of Cicero. We are thus dealing with a development which extended over a period of nearly 2,000 years. I do not, of course, imply that the favourite rhythms were at first so frequent as they became subsequently. There was originally a rich variety of cadences. In course of time the three special forms became increasingly common, until finally, like Aaron's rod, they swallow up their competitors. The final result was that prose composition became stereotyped.

I have tried to state the case as simply as possible, since this is not the occasion for a minute discussion of the ancient clausula. I must add that various licences are allowed. The commonest of these is the

---

[1] The last syllable is always *anceps* as in verse.

substitution of two short syllables for one long, e. g. *ĕssĕ vĭdĕārĕ* in Form i : so also *ĕssĕ vĭdĕāmĭnī* in Form ii.[1] These varieties survive in the *cursus*. Thus for *esse videatur* the accentual equivalent is *mála nocuísset*, and for *ésse videámini* we find e. g. *míssae celebrátio*. Another frequent licence is the prolongation of the trochaic cadence by another syllable (Form iv), e. g. *spíritum pèrtiméscere*, which in the *cursus* becomes *cúriae véstrae scríbere*. There is also a very interesting variation, viz. the substitution for special purposes of a spondee for the trochee in the cadence, which did not pass into the *cursus*. Of this I will speak shortly.

The remarks of the ancients on prose rhythm have naturally led various inquirers to ask if similar phenomena are to be found in our own tongue. Saintsbury tells us that Bishop Hurd wrote on the rhythm of Addison, and John Mason, a Nonconformist minister, in 1749 published an essay on the 'Power and Harmony of Prosaic Numbers'. These writers tried to apply to English prose the rules laid down by Cicero and Quintilian. The task was one in which success was impossible. In the first place, there is the essential difference that Latin rhythm depends on quantity and English rhythm on stress. Secondly, there is the fact that Latin is a polysyllabic language, while English is largely monosyllabic. Lastly, it has been shown that Cicero and Quintilian did not grasp the secret principles by which they were themselves influenced. Their disciples, therefore, were following blind guides.

In spite of all the obscurities which surround the subject, no one has doubted that there are principles at work, if only we could grasp them. Thus various friends have suggested to me that regular rhythms are to be found in Gibbon and Macaulay. I had myself some two years ago amused myself by tabulating forms of the *cursus* to be found in the speeches of that very rhythmical orator, Mr. Lloyd George.

The question was put on a fresh basis by a paper written by Mr. John Shelly, which appeared last year in the *Church Quarterly Review*. In this he shows that the writers of the Prayer Book adopted in the Collects and in other parts of the liturgy rhythms identical with those which they found in their copy, viz. the Missal and Breviary. This throws light upon a remark which I have heard more than once, that it seems impossible now for any one to write a good Collect. Mr. Shelly goes on to show that these rhythms passed into current use and have persisted to the present time. Thus he quotes from a sermon of Newman, in which twelve clauses in one sentence end

[1] These varieties are known as i[2] and ii[2]. In both of them the second long syllable is replaced by two shorts. So also other resolutions, e. g. iii[2].

with some form of the *cursus*. He thinks that Newman's style must
have been influenced by his prolonged study of the Fathers.

Saintsbury refers to Mr. Shelly's paper, which was published after
his own book was in type. He says, however, 'I doubt whether
Latin cadences are patient of exact adjustment to English. I also
doubt the possibility of effectually introducing, with us, the so-called
cursus.' The method which he follows himself is the traditional one,
that founded on Cicero and Quintilian. He used quantitative symbols
throughout, marking stressed syllables long and unstressed syllables
short. There are various points in his system which may be criticized,
but I do not propose to deal with these now, and would only refer
to some objections which I have raised in the *Oxford Magazine*
(April 24, 1913). The most disconcerting feature in his book is
the lack of positive results. He professes himself unable to give any
rules by which fine effects are to be attained, 'any prose-forms corresponding to the recognized forms of verse.' So also he remarks,
'I disdain, detest, abominate, and in every other English and classical
form renounce the attempt to show how a prose-harmonist should
develop his harmony.' Here he is a little inconsistent, since elsewhere
he relents in favour of a particular combination.[1] His final judgement,
however, is that 'as the essence of verse-metre is its identity, at least
in equivalence and recurrence, so the essence of prose rhythm lies in
variety and divergence'. When commenting on the finale of Browne's
Urn Burial, he notes that in his scansion 'no two identical feet ever
follow each other, not so much as on a single occasion'. The reader
cannot but suspect that there must be some flaw in a method which
produces such small results.

While I venture to criticize Saintsbury's method, I am full of admiration for his fine taste, which is shown not only by felicitous criticisms
expressed in striking phrases, but also his selection of passages from
the greatest authors, which, in his judgement, are perfect examples of
prose rhythm. He has formed a collection of what he calls 'diploma
pieces'. This is a contribution of the greatest value, since on this
subject he speaks with authority. He has the advantage of a sensitive
and highly trained ear, and if he says that the rhythm is flawless, we
have no alternative save to accept his judgement. Saintsbury, therefore, has performed the great service of focussing the question. If
his diploma pieces do not reveal the nature of English prose rhythm,
it is idle to search elsewhere.

I cannot but think that Saintsbury pushes the principle of variety

---

[1] Dochmiac, third paeon, and amphibrach.

too far. I do not for one moment dispute that it is one of the ingredients in prose rhythm. The essence, however, of rhythm both in prose and verse is regularity of beat. As Dionysius says, prose is εὔρυθμος, since διαπεποίκιλταί τισιν ῥυθμοῖς, but not ἔρρυθμος, since οὐχὶ τοῖς αὐτοῖς οὐδὲ κατὰ τὸ αὐτό. This, he remarks, is true of all prose which exhibits τὸ ποιητικὸν καὶ μελικόν, e.g. that of Demosthenes.

That in English rhythmical prose is closely allied to verse is shown by the extreme ease with which we drop into blank verse. Saintsbury remarks that Chaucer, whom he calls the Father of English prose, although in his prose works he eschews rhyme, cannot avoid metre. Thus the tale of Melibee 'opens with a batch of almost exactly cut blank verse lines'.

> A young man called Melibeus, mighty and wise begat
> Upon his wife, that callèd was Prudence
> A daughter which that callèd was Sophie.

Saintsbury gives several instances where a skilful writer avoids blank verse by various devices. Thus Malory writes

> And so Sir Lancelot and the damsel departed,

where *maid* for *damsel* would produce blank verse.

So de Quincey says

> Among the lovely households of the roe-deer,

where the addition of *roe* breaks the measure.

The most striking *tour de force* is the dream of Amyas Leigh in Kingsley's *Westward Ho*, which Saintsbury arranges as a piece of continuous blank verse, pointing out that 'from time to time words are inserted which break the regularity of the rhythm and remind the reader that after all it is not meant to be metre'. He considers it a successful experiment, but applies to such an experiment a remark of the late Professor Bain on the subject of kissing, that 'the occasion should be adequate and the actuality rare'.

I would now call attention to two statements made by Saintsbury. The first is that in Old English or Anglo-Saxon the rhythm is mainly trochaic. He speaks of a 'continuous trochaic roll which at the énd of línes is práticálly ómniprésent'.[1] This 'trochaic hum' is said to be due to the character of the language, which, being 'largely monosyllabic and at the same time inflected, necessarily begets trochees ready made in still larger quantities'. The second statement is, that in Middle English the 'trochaic tyranny' was mitigated by the disuse

---

[1] Here he employs six consecutive trochees, a good example of this 'roll'.

of inflection and the introduction of a more polysyllabic vocabulary taken from the Romance languages and from Latin. This process begins with Chaucer and is consummated by the writers of the Prayer Book and the Authorized Version who had Latin models before them. The rhythm of Middle English, we are told, is 'composite', i.e. partly native and partly Latin.

This is an observation of the highest importance, and suggests a method of attacking the problem, which is, so far as I know, new. It is briefly this. If we take passages which Saintsbury considers perfect—and here his judgement seems to me infallible—and mark those rhythms which are Latin in character, the probability is that the residue, and especially those effects which are wholly alien to the Latin system, are native. We are dealing with two quantities, one of which is known. This being so, we ought to be able to discover something about the unknown quantity.

Before I go further, it is necessary to say something on the subject of word division, or *caesura*. In the examples which I have given previously, I have for the sake of clearness made the clausula begin with a word. This, however, is not necessary. Thus *vultusque moverunt, iactabit audacia, nefarium concupisti* are just as good as *voce testatur, nostra curatio, gaudium pervenire*. So also in English the rhythm of *obéy thy commándments* and *keép thy commándments* is the same. The caesura within the clausula requires special attention, since here a difference between English and Latin becomes visible.

In order to make the point clear, we must go back to Latin. Here in Form i there are five possible varieties, which have been distinguished thus: [1]

1 α   bālnĕātōrī.
1 β   nōn ŏpōrtērĕ.
1 γ   vōcĕ tēstātŭr.
1 δ   cāllĭdē fēcĭt.
1 ε   rēstĭtūtī sūnt.

The favourite caesura in Form i, in classical Latin, is γ, and in the *cursus* this becomes normal. This is also true of Form ii, but in Form iii the δ type is usual in classical Latin and normal in the *cursus*. The exact equivalents, therefore, in English are e.g. *sérvants depárted, pérfect felícity, glórious ùndertáking*. Since, however, English is chiefly disyllabic and monosyllabic, the *cursus* becomes modified in the process of naturalization. Thus in i the favourite type is γδ, e.g. *dúty and sérvice, hónour and glóry*. This combination, it may be noticed,

[1] Zielinski, *das Clauselgesetz*, p. 27.

emphasizes the trochaic rhythm which is natural to the language. We find many other varieties, e. g.

βγ   thése our misdóings, praíse and thanksgíving.
βγδ   déw of thy bléssing, síght of the heáthen.
γε   mércy upón us.

So also in ii,[1] e. g.

βγ   jóy and felícity.
γδ   Cána of Gálilee.
δεζ   cómeth to júdge the earth.
βγδεζ   shíne for thy líght is come.

Also in iii, e. g.

γδ   pásseth all ùnderstánding.
γδζ   sérvice is pérfect freédom.

It may be noticed that other varieties of the *cursus* are represented in English. Thus Form iv, e. g. *spīrĭtŭm pērtĭmēscĕrĕ* ($=$ *cúriae véstrae scríbere*) corresponds to *boúntiful lïberálily, heávenly bènedíction, plénary àbsolútion*. Also, Cicero's *esse vïdeare* (1^2), which in the *cursus* is succeeded by *mála nocuísset*, is paralleled in English by e. g. *glóry everlásting*. We find modifications of this with more than one caesura, e. g. *glóry of the Fáther, wrítten for our leárning, índustry and lábour*.

The scansion *glóry everlásting* is in accordance with the rules followed in accentual Latin. Here, if a word like *videátur* is preceded by one unaccented syllable, e. g. *míhi*, the first two syllables are not accented. Thus *míhi videátur* is the successor of Cicero's *ēssĕ vĭdēātŭr*. If, however, it is preceded by two unaccented syllables, e. g. *plúrima vïdeántur*, then the first syllable receives a minor accent. Thus *glóry everlásting* corresponds to *míhi videátur* and *glórious, èverlásting* to *plúrima vïdeántur*.

So also we find parallels for other resolutions, e. g. *sílly agitátion*, which corresponds to *ēssĕ vĭdĕ̄imĭnī*. This is to be contrasted with *fúrious àgitátion*.

I am aware that in chants the usual accentuation is *glóry èverlásting*. This, I take it, is due to the 'trochaic roll', inherent in the language, which has mastered the Latin cadence.

---

[1] The exact equivalent with the γ caesura only is rare, except when the last word is of Latin origin, e. g. óther aɗvérsity, sérvant Victória, etérnal salvátion, pérfect contrítion. In modern English such words as *salvation* are pronounced as trisyllables, in the Prayer Book they are quadrisyllables. Thus *etérnal salvátion* is equivalent to *aetérna salvátio* (*tardus*).

Mr. Shelly points out that out of ninety-five cases in the Collects which do not belong to forms of the *cursus* no less than seventy-one end with an accented syllable, e. g. *ármour of líght, contémpt of thy wórd.* This is wholly alien to Latin. The Latin accent is never on the last syllable of a word, and accented monosyllables were carefully avoided at the end of a sentence. Such an ending was felt to be bizarre, as in Horace's line—

parturiunt montes, nascetur ridiculus mus.

Here, therefore, we have a clear case of a native rhythm as distinct from the *cursus.*

In several examples where an accented monosyllable comes at the end, there is a marked trochaic cadence, e. g. *fórty dáys and fórty níghts, pléase thee bóth in wíll and deéd, thiévish córners óf the streéts.* The most striking instance which I have noticed is in the *Te Deum,* viz. —

We, thérefore, práy thee, hélp thy sérvants, whóm thou hást re-deémed wíth thy précious bloód.

We find similar prolongation of the trochaic movement when the last word is a disyllable, e. g. *máke thy chósen peóple jóyful ; fíre and brímstone, stórm and témpest.* In Latin this would be very bad ; in English our ears tell us that it is good. Here, also, again we have something which is not Latin. The trochaic hum rises above the soft music of the *cursus.*

Saintsbury quotes a passage from Bishop Fisher to illustrate the development of harmonious prose in the time of Henry the Eighth. The sentence begins as follows :[1]

No creature may express how jóyful the sínner is (2), when he knóweth and ùnderstándeth (3) himself to be delivered from the great búrden and heáviness (2).

Here the influence of the *cursus* is clearly visible.

When discussing the *A. V.,* he selects the sixtieth chapter of Isaiah as one of the highest points touched by English Prose :

Arise, shíne, for thy líght is cóme (2) and the glory of the Lord is rísen upón thee (1). For, behold, the darkness shall cóver the eárth (*) and gróss dárkness the peóple (1), but the Lórd shall aríse upón thee (3) and his glóry sháll [2] be seén upón thee (*) and the Gentiles shall cóme to thy líght (*) and kings to the bríghtness of thy rísing (1[2]).

---

[1] In this as in other citations I add the stress-accents where they appear to cast light on the rhythm. Asterisks mean that there is no Latin equivalent.

[2] Saintsbury scans *glōrÿ shăll bĕ*. It seems to me that there is a stress on *shall*. If so, we have a succession of trochees. If, however, there is no stress, then the form is the Latin iii[2].

Here two clausulae, viz. *cóver the eárth* and *cóme to thy líght*, both of which end in a stressed monosyllable, are clearly not Latin in character.

Saintsbury draws attention to the effect produced by the monosyllable *shíne* at the beginning of the sentence. This is made more emphatic by the fact that it is preceded by another stressed syllable, viz. *aríse*. He also points out the fine effect of the adjective in *gróss dárkness*. Here also there is a similar clash of accents. We are now face to face with a fundamental difference between the *cursus* and the native rhythm. The main object in the *cursus* is to secure an interval between stressed and unstressed syllables. In the *planus* and *tardus* there is an interval of two unstressed syllables between the two stresses, and in the *velox* of four, or if we allow the minor accent on the fourth syllable, two also. The same rule prevails in Greek Prose of the Byzantine period. This collision of accents appears to introduce sublimity in English Prose.[1] Further on in this paper I shall give other examples : here I would merely call attention to the effect in the Confession of the conflicting accents in

We have erred and strayed from thy wáys, líke lóst sheép.

Here the stressed monosyllables produce the effect of a wail.

No author is treated by Saintsbury with more enthusiasm than Sir Thomas Browne. He gives a long quotation from *Urn Burial*, which he pronounces to be a 'spaced and rested symphony'. It begins with the famous sentence :

Nów since thése deád bónes have alreády outlásted (1) the living onés of Methúsaleh (2) and in a yárd únder groúnd (*) and thín wálls of cláy (*) oútwórn áll the stróng and spécious buíldings abóve it (1) and quíetly résted (1) under the drúms and trámplings of threé cónquésts.

Saintsbury very happily compares the opening five monosyllables to 'thuds of earth dropping on the coffin-lid'. The passage is remarkable for the collision of stress accents, viz. *yárd únder, thín wálls, threé cónquésts*. It will be noticed that it contains two disyllables with a stress accent on each syllable, viz. *oútwórn* and *cónquésts*. The clausula *trámplings of threé cónquests* is of special interest since it may be illustrated by parallels in classical Latin.

We find from time to time in Cicero and other authors a striking deviation from the ordinary trochaic cadence, viz. the substitution of a spondee for the trochee. This is most common in Form iii, which thus becomes $-\cup- \mid -- \mid -\veebar$, e.g. *includuntur in cárcěr.'m*

---

[1] Cf. For the Lórd is a greát Gód, and a greát Kíng abóve áll góds.

cŏndēmnāti, commōtŭs ēst, sūdāt, pāllēt, but is also found in Form ii,
e. g. *ēbrŭs sērvīrĕ, lībĕrī sērvi ōdērŭnt*. This harsh rhythm is reserved for passages in a major key. I have examined all the occasions
in the Philippics where it occurs, and find this true almost without
exception. Zielinski says of such rhythms, 'then comes the hammer
stroke'.

Here *trámplings of threé cónquests* appears to be the English
equivalent of *ēbrŭs sērvīrĕ*.

I would compare Saintsbury's remark upon a sentence of Thomas
Hobbes, viz. :

In great difference of persons the greater have often fallen in love
with the méaner, but nót cóntráry.[1]

He remarks, 'every time of reading—at least I have found it so for
some half-century—the penetrating, but not clangorous dirge-sound
will be heard more clearly.'

Meáner but nót cóntráry is an English parallel for *carcerem con-
demnati*. Saintsbury's dirge-sound corresponds to Zielinski's hammer
stroke.

Browne in this passage varies his rhythms. Thus a sentence
which Saintsbury singles out for special praise is purely Latin, viz. :

According to the ordaíner of órder (1) and mýstical màthemátics (3)
of the cíty of heáven (1).

The mixed rhythm of English prose was now fixed, and its general
character appears to be the same in passages quoted from various
authors. The style of Addison is interesting, since a contemporary,
Bishop Hurd, tried to find in it observance of the rules laid down by
Cicero and Quintilian. In this connexion a criticism of Hurd is
quoted. He says :

'Oŭr sīght ĭs thĕ mōst cŏmplēte ănd mōst dĕlīghtfŭl sēnse wĕ hāve.'
Here, except the second foot, which is an anapaest, the rest of them
are all of one kind, i. e. iambics. Read now with Mr. Addison—
'Oŭr sīght ĭs thĕ mōst pērfĕct ănd mōst dĕlīghtfŭl ŏf āll oŭr sēnsĕs '—
and you see how the rhythm is varied by the intermixture of other
feet, besides that short redundant syllable *-ses* gives to the close
a slight and negligent air, which has a better effect, in this place, than
the proper iambic foot.

[1] Saintsbury scans *cŏntrăry̆*, but the old pronunciation seems to have been
contrár̆y, corresponding to the Latin *contrārius*. In modern English the accent
has shifted, with the result that the long syllable has been shortened.

Here *delíghtful of áll our sénses* is Form iii, while *delíghtful sénse we háve* is an example of the trochaic roll to which attention has been called. *Our síght is the móst compléte* is Form ii, while *our síght is the móst pérfect*, which Hurd prefers, is an example of S 2, the spondaic rhythm which I have just discussed.

The first sentence in Saintsbury's extract from Gibbon is :

The protection of the Rháetian fróntier (1) and the persecution of the Cátholic Chúrch (*) detained Constántius in Ítaly (2²) above eighteen months after the depárture of Júlian (2).

The clausulae here are Latin except *Cátholic Chúrch*.

Saintsbury's remarks upon *depárture of Júlian* are suggestive. After stating that 'Gibbon's everlasting irony is assisted by rhythm ', he says that ' for actual cadences some have noted a recession or rescission towards trochaic ending as in *ăftĕr thĕ dĕpārtŭre ŏf Jŭliăn*'. He prefers to arrange it ' āftĕr | thĕ dĕpārtŭre | ŏf Jūliăn, thus giving that juxtaposition of paeon (chiefly third) and amphibrach which will be found almost omnipresent in Gibbon and which may be a proximate cause of his peculiar undulation'. This statement is noticeable in view of Saintsbury's insistence upon variety as the chief factor in prose rhythm. I would remark in the first place that *Julian* appears to be a trisyllable, not a disyllable. If so, the clausula is an example of No. 2. If not, then it is No. 1.

Saintsbury's third paeon and amphibrach give us the sequence ∪∪ − ∪ ∪ − ∪, i. e. ~ ~ ∠ ~ ~ ∠ ~. Here the first two syllables, according to my view, do not affect the rhythm, and the other five, viz. ∠ ~ ~ ∠ ~, are the ordinary formula for the *cursus planus*.

Saintsbury notices that ' the word values are arranged with evident cunning' in the following extract from Coleridge :

The woody Castle Crag between mé and Lodóre (*) is a rich flower-gárden of cólours (1), the brightest yéllows with the deépest crímsons (3²) and the ínfinite shádes of brówn and greén (4) . . . Little woól-packs of whíte bríght vápour (S 3) rest on different súmmits and declívities (2²).

He remarks : ' In *the brightest* | *yellows* | *with the deepest* | *crimsons* (amphibrach, trochee, third paeon, trochee) I almost dare to say we glimpse one of our panthers, a common prose combination corresponding to a verse.' I scan *yéllows with the deépest crímsons* as 3². Cf. the Latin *frōnde căpŭt ōbvŏlūtŭm*.

He calls attention to ' the familiar-unfamiliar word *woolpacks*, the parts of which might have no sense at all—it is so perfectly expressive, in sound, of what it means'. The rhythm would rather seem to reside in the collision of accents, viz. *white bright vápour. Wool-packs of white bright vápour* is the English equivalent for Cicero's *mōtŭs ēst, sŭdāt pāllēt* (S 3).

De Quincey supplies 'a perfect type in miniature of rhythmed prose', viz.:

And her éyes, if they were éver seén (*), would be neíther sweét nor súbtle (*); no mán could reád their stóry (*): they would be found fílled with périshing dreáms (*), and with wrecks of forgótten delírium (2).

The interest of this short sentence, which Saintsbury terms 'a magazine of the secrets of its kind', is that it contains only one Latin rhythm, viz. *forgótten delírium,* and that in the clausula, where tune is most required. The other effects appear to be indigenous. Here we recognize the prolonged trochaic run in *neíther sweét nor súbtle* and *mán could reád their stóry* and the accented monosyllable at the end of the clauses *éver seén* and *périshing dreáms,* for which Latin has no parallel.

De Quincey can also write in the Latin style, as in the following extract, which Saintsbury calls beautifully rhythmical:

Out of the darkness . . . uprises the héavenly fáce of Fánny (3). One áfter the óther (1) like the antiphónies in the chóral sérvice (3²) rise Fánny and the róse in Júne (2²), then báck agaín the róse in Júne and Fánny (*). Then cóme both togéther (1), as in a chorus, róses and Fánnies (1), Fánnies and róses (1), without end, thick as blóssoms in Páradise (2).

Fanny here is the musical unit, which lends itself admirably to the different combinations. In one case we have the trochaic rhythm of Anglo-Saxon, viz. *báck agaín the róse in Júne and Fánny*: the other clausulae are Latin.

From Landor I would take two passages, the first of which is put by Saintsbury beside de Quincey's gem in the *Mater Suspiriorum* as 'unsurpassed since the renaissance of numerous prose':

There is a gloom in deép lóve as in deép wáter (S 2): there is a silence in it which suspénds the foót (*), and the fólded árms (*) and the dejécted heád (*) are the ímages it reflécts (*)[1]. Nó voíce shákes its súrface (*): the Muses thémsélves approách it (*) with a tárdy and

---

[1] Possibly *it* should here be stressed. If so, we have Form ii.

a tímid stép (2²), and with a low and tremulous and mélanchóly[1] sóng (∗).

Here the rhythms seem due to indigenous factors, the collision of accents, viz. *deép lóve, deép wáter, nó voíce shákes, Múses thémsélves,* the stressed monosyllable at the end of the clauses, *suspénds the foót, fólded árms, dejécted heád, tímid stép, mélanchóly sóng,* and the trochaic run which pervades the passage. The only clauses for which Latin affords any parallel are *lóve as in deép wáter,* and *tárdy and a tímid stép.* Of the mediaeval *cursus* there is no trace.

Another passage which Saintsbury terms ' a little more rhetorical ' yields different results :

Thére are nó fiélds of ámaranth (4) on thís síde of the gráve (∗), there are no voíces O Rhódope (2) that are nót soón múte (∗), hówever túneful (1), thére is nó náme (∗), with whatever emphasis of pássionate lóve repeáted (3), of which the écho is not faínt at lást (2²).

Carlyle's prose is said by Saintsbury to be essentially Wagnerian, containing ' rhythm fragments of extreme beauty, united by a master harmony which pervades the jangle '. He quotes a description of Spanish soldiers marching to Chile :

Eách sóldier láy at níght (∗) wrápped in his póncho (1), with his knápsack for píllow (1) under the cánopy of heáven (1²), lúllabied by hárd trávail (∗) and súnk soón enough ínto steády nòse-mélody (2), ínto the foólishest roúgh cólt dánce of unimáginable Dreáms (∗).

Here the collision of stressed monosyllables is noticeable, viz. *eách sóldier, hárd trávail,* and *roúgh cólt dánce,* also the stressed monosyllable *dreams* at the end of the sentence. The rhythm *steády nòse-mélody* deserves especial attention. This is exactly similar to the metrical Form ii used in classical Latin, e. g. *nōstră cūrătĭō,* i. e. a cretic followed by a trochee. In the *cursus,* e. g. *méa curátio* or *bóna remédia,* the third syllable is shortened by the tug of the accent, which shortens unstressed syllables, as in modern Greek or English. Consequently, while Terentianus Maurus assigns to the cretic a *beata sedes* in the clausula just before the end, Pope Gregory VIII (A. D. 1187) says, ' *finales dictiones debet quasi pes dactilus antecurrere.*' Now in *steády nòse-melody* the dactyl has become a cretic again. This, I take it, is due to the fact that the monosyllable *nose* resists the tug of the accents in *steády* and *melody.* If, therefore, a stressed monosyllable occupies this place in English, the base is a cretic rather than a dactyl. It is for this

---

[1] Saintsbury scans *mēlănchŏlў* according to the present pronunciation.

reason that in the previous extract from Landor I treat *thére are nó fiélds of ámaranth* as an example of Form iv. Carlyle continues:

Canópus and the Soúthern Cróss (2^2) glítter dówn and áll snóres steádily begírt by gránite déserts (*), looked on by the constellátions in that mánner (1^1).

Saintsbury notices that rhythm is here the determining factor, and says that ' Cănōpŭs | ănd thĕ Soūthĕrn | Crōss are chosen from the Host of Heaven to look down on the incongruous snorers because of the desirable combination of amphibrach, third paean, and mono-syllable'. I take the clause to be 2^2 ending with a stressed mono-syllable, and would draw attention to the trochaic movement in *begírt by gránite déserts*.
Macaulay's rhythm is very classical, e. g.

And there the ladies whose lips more persuásive than thóse of Fóx himsélf (4) had carried the Westmínster eléction (1) against pálace and treásury (2) shóne roúnd Geórgiána (? 3), Dúchess of Dévon-shire (2).

Geórgiána here is a beautiful double-trochee, and I am rather sur-prised that Macaulay did not complete the rhythm by writing *shóne aroùnd*, in which case the clausula would have been wholly Latin. Wherever we get a double trochee, it is easy to construct perfect specimens of the *velox*, e. g. *beaútiful Píccadílly, Látin and Ánglo-Sáxon.*
Saintsbury notices Macaulay's fondness for trochaic endings, and says that ' the staccato style undoubtedly invites them and so in very modern work gives a throw-back to the most ancient'. This is a very suggestive remark. The cadences to which he refers are simply those of classical and mediaeval prose.
Newman is pronounced to have been one of the greatest masters of quietly exquisite prose. This statement is interesting in view of the facts pointed out by Mr. Shelly, to which I have already alluded. The prose of Ruskin hardly falls within the scope of this discussion, since frequently it transcends the limits of prose and becomes poetry. Saintsbury notices in one extract successions of eight, ten, and thirteen blank verses, while in another place Ruskin actually drops into rhyme.
Pater is said to have been the most remarkable writer belonging to the last division of the nineteenth century. While Ruskin may be charged with absence of quiet, quietude is the chief feature of Pater. ' On this apex of English Prose, if on no other, there is rest.' Pater's

composition as a whole inclines to the non-Latin type, as may be seen from the sentence :

Through his strange veil of síght (2) thíngs reách him só (∗): in no órdinary níght or dáy (2²), but as in faínt líght of eclípse (∗), or in sóme briéf ínterval (∗) of fálling raín at dáybreak (∗), or thróugh deép wáter (∗).

Here we notice the strings of stressed monosyllables and the resultant clash of accents : also the predominant trochaic roll. Of Latin influence there is little to find.

I now venture to put together some reflections which present themselves to the mind after this discussion.

Rhythm in poetry depends upon the recurrence of longs and shorts, or stressed and unstressed syllables, in a regular order. In prose the effect is produced by the same means, but the metre is not complete. We have to deal with two principles, viz. that of recurrence and that of variety. Saintsbury appears to attribute too much importance to variety, which, if not modified by some sort of system, however loose, results in chaos.

The rhythm natural to a language depends upon its vocabulary. Here there is an obvious difference between Latin and English. Latin is essentially a polysyllabic language, while most words in English are disyllables and monosyllables. This difference is fundamental and must always be borne in mind. On the other hand there is a striking point of similarity, namely the trochaic cadence which is a characteristic of both languages. This was modified in Latin by the cretic base which precedes the trochaic movement, and the use of harsher measures in the middle of the clauses. The trochaic rhythm is chiefly found in the *clausula*, and does not generally extend further than over a few syllables. In English the trochaic movement pervades the whole sentence and frequently produces the effect of blank verse.

The three forms of the *cursus* came into English from Latin and from the Romance languages. When Latin words were naturalized, they brought with them the cadences in which the genius of the Latin tongue found best expression. The introduction of such words was largely due to their occurrence in the liturgy of the Church, and to their consequent adoption by the authors of the Prayer Book and the translators of the Bible. These cadences, however, were modified when they became anglicized, owing to the lack of polysyllables. The English *cursus* presses monosyllables into its service with the result that, although the scheme of accentuation is the same, the caesuras are more numerous and more varied. No attempt was made to make the *cursus* universal. This would have been to force the language into a bed of Procrustes. The native elements, viz. the trochaic roll and the stressed monosyllable, were combined with the exotic. The rhythm of English is mixed, like the nation itself, and the mixture constitutes its charm. In this respect English differs from mediaeval prose and frequently presents analogies to the freer system of Cicero and Demosthenes. We have won our way back from monotony and servitude to variety and liberty.

It would appear that the sublimest effects in English prose are produced by the native not the exotic rhythm. The two chief means employed appear to be the collision of accents which is alien to the binary movement [1] of mediaeval prose and the prolongation of the trochaic roll with its tendency towards blank verse. The object of the *cursus* was to procure a smooth ending, or, as its name implies, a 'run'. It produces harmony, not grandeur, and imparts to prose an element of tune.

[1] *Cursus*, p. 22.

THE ART

OF

POETRY

Inaugural Lecture delivered before

the University of Oxford

5 June 1920

by

WILLIAM PATON KER

Fellow of All Souls ; Professor of Poetry

THE ART OF POETRY

I wish I could say how deeply I feel what I owe to the generous and sanguine friends who have elected me to this most honourable Chair. It would be less difficult to find words for the danger of the task; this is the Siege Perilous. But I will not attempt to say in full what I think and feel most sincerely with regard to the honour you have done me; as for the hazards of the place, they must be manifest to every one who has spent any time at all in thinking of the Art of Poetry. But you will allow me to say as much as this, that I find the greatest encouragement and the best auspices in those who have held this Chair before me; and I ask leave in this place to thank Mr. Bradley, Mr. Mackail, and the President of Magdalen for their good wishes.

Drummond of Hawthornden, writing his sentiments about a new fashion in poetry which displeased him, begins with some old-fashioned sentences which may afford a text here; in a letter addressed 'to his much-honoured friend M. A. J., Physician to the King'. His friend is the poet Arthur Johnston, 'who holds among the Latin poets of Scotland the next place to the

A 2

elegant Buchanan'.   Drummond is writing to a man of the highest principles, as follows :

'It is more praiseworthy in noble and excellent things to know something, though little, than in mean and ignoble matters to have a perfect knowledge.   Amongst all those rare ornaments of the mind of Man *Poesie* hath had a most eminent place and been in high esteem, not only at one time, and in one climate, but during all times and through those parts of the world where any ray of humanity and civility hath shined. So that she hath not unworthily deserved the name of the Mistress of human life, the height of eloquence, the quintessence of knowledge, the loud trumpet of Fame, the language of the Gods. There is not anything endureth longer : Homer's Troy hath outlived many Republics, and both the Roman and Grecian Monarchies ; she subsisteth by herself, and after one demeanour and continuance her beauty appeareth to all ages.   In vain have some men of late (transformers of everything) consulted upon her reformation, and endeavoured to abstract her to metaphysical ideas and scholastical quiddities, denuding her of her own habits, and those ornaments with which she hath amused the world some thousand years. *Poesie* is not a thing that is in the finding and search, or which may be otherwise found out, being already condescended upon by all nations, and as it were established *iure gentium* amongst Greeks, Romans, Italians, French, Spaniards. Neither do I think that a good piece of *Poesie* which Homer, Virgil, Ovid, Petrarch,

Bartas, Ronsard, Boscan, Garcilasso (if they were alive and had that language) could not understand, and reach the sense of the writer.'

If they had that language! Here is the difficulty, so obvious that it escapes notice in many panegyrics of the Muses. In the other arts there is nothing like the curse of Babel; but the divine Idea of Poetry, abiding the same with itself in essence, shining with the same light, as Drummond sees it, in Homer and Virgil, Ronsard and Garcilaso de la Vega, is actually seen by very few votaries in each and all of those several lamps. The light of Poetry may be all over the world and belong to the whole human race, yet how little of it is really available, compared with the other arts! It is broken up among the various languages, and in such a way that not even time and study can always be trusted to find the true idea of Poetry. It is not merely that you are required to spend on the tongues the time that might be given to bear-baiting (as Sir Andrew discovered, ancestor of so many old gentlemen whose education has been neglected, so many seekers of culture), but even when you have mastered the grammar and dictionary you may find in the foreign poets insuperable difficulties of thought and sentiment. For poetic melody is not the same thing as music; it is much more deeply idiomatic and national. French is better understood in this country, more widely read than any foreign language; yet even the poets in this country, some of them, have spoken dismal things in disparagement of French poetry. It is no uncommon thing for ingenuous youth, lovers of poetry in England, to be made unhappy by the difficulty and strangeness, as it seems to them, of French verse. Mr. John Bailey and Mr. Eccles have helped them, and you remember how our friend, M. Émile Legouis, came here nine years ago and dealt faithfully with the English poets and critics who boasted of their deafness. They were refuted and confounded, their injustice exposed with logical wit, their grudging objections overborne simply by the advocate's voice, as he read the songs of Musset's *Fortunio* and Victor Hugo's *Fantine*.[1]

But the difficulties remain, and English readers have to be taught that the French Alexandrine is neither 'our four-footed verse of the triple cadence' nor yet what the Northern languages made of it in the seventeenth century, High Dutch or Low Dutch, and Danish; and Drayton in *Polyolbion* :

Through the Dorsetian fields that lie in open
    view
My progress I again must seriously pursue.

The peculiar idiom of the French tongue is diffused through all French poetry, and if this makes it hard for us, what becomes of the uni-

---

[1] *Défense de la poésie française, à l'usage des lecteurs anglais.* (Constable, 1912.)

versal pattern which Drummond holds up as the same for all nations—'like the Ancients, and conform to those rules which hath been agreed unto by all times'? What is the use of all times agreeing, if each nation hears nothing but its own tune?

On the other hand, Drummond's worship of the Muses is not to be dismissed as fashionable rhetoric or conventional idealism. He knew what he was talking about, and he is thinking naturally of his own well-studied verse, his own share in the service of true poetry, along with Petrarch, Ronsard, Boscan, and Garcilaso. The names are not chosen at random, they are not there for ornament, like historical allusions of the popular preacher gabbling 'Socrates, Buddha, and Emerson', or like the formula of 'Goethe, Kant, and Beethoven', that used to pester us in the enlightened journalism of the War. When Drummond names Petrarch, Bartas, Ronsard, Boscan, and Garcilaso, he means the poets whom he knows and follows; more particularly in the Italian and Spanish names he means an art of poetry which he has made his own. For Drummond of Hawthornden belongs, like Spenser and Milton, to the great tradition of the Renaissance in modern poetry, the most comprehensive and vitally effective school of poetry in Christendom after the mediaeval fashion of Provence which it succeeds and continues. Drummond knows that he belongs to the great company of artists in poetry who get their instruction from Italy, and he is right : his sonnets and madrigals are part of that Italian school which transformed the poetry of France and England, Portugal and Spain ; which gave to England the music of Spenser's *Epithalamion* and of *Lycidas*.   The difficulties of the curse of Babel are not abolished ; but it is matter of historical fact that Italian poetry got over those obstacles in the sixteenth century ; in some places even earlier.   The Italian measures and modes of thought are adopted in other countries.   Garcilaso and Camoens are Italian poets writing Castilian and Portuguese.   Their names are found together in that pretty scene near the end of *Don Quixote* ; the shepherdesses who took Don Quixote out of their silken fowling-nets were going to act eclogues of Garcilaso and Camoens. Drummond's madrigals, Milton's verses *On Time*, are pure Italian form.   The poets of that tradition or school, or whatever it may be called, are not talking wildly, they are not hypocrites, if they speak as Drummond does of Poetry and say 'she subsisteth by herself, and after one demeanour and continuance her beauty appeareth to all ages'.   At any rate they have proved in their own practice that they agree in different languages, drawing the same pattern, following the same rules of thought and melody.

With this reality in their mind they are justified to themselves in arguing that Poetry has not to be invented anew and is not to be trifled with.

Drummond in his respect for authority is quite different from the mere critics who preach up the Ancients. Any one can do that. We know their dramatic unities, and their receipts to make an epic poem. But the poet who belongs to a great tradition of art, transcending local barriers of language, is in a different case altogether. Even though he may not be, as Drummond was not himself, one of the great masters, and though the forms of his poetry be no more varied than those of Petrarch, still he has the reality of his own poems. The merely intellectual scheme of the critic turns to reality in the practical reason of the poet. His poetic life is larger than himself, and it is real life. Abstract and ideal in one way, no doubt, if you think of a bodiless Petrarchian form, identical in all the imitators of Petrarch. But the empty abstract Italian form of verse, the unbodied ghost of sonnets and *canzoni*, is itself real and a source of life :

> Small at first, and weak and frail
> Like the vapour of the vale :

but 'thoughts sprang where'er that step did fall', in the dance of the Italian syllables. The life of the poet is real in the poems he composes ; through them he knows where he is.; his praise of universal poetry is what he has made true for himself in the moments of his life, which he shares somehow with Petrarch and the other poets. Drummond has not had as good fortune as they, though before we leave him let us remember that Charles Lamb has put Drummond among the best-loved names. Drummond is in the great tradition, and this is what he makes of it :

Rouse Memnon's mother from her Tython's bed,
That she thy carrier may with roses spread,
The nightingales thy coming each where sing,
Make an eternal spring,
Give life to this dark world which lieth dead.

And again :

This world is made a hell
Depriv'd of all that in it did excel;
O Pan, Pan, winter is fallen in our May,
Turn'd is in night our day.

It is the tune of Petrarch, Garcilaso, and Camoens, of the prevalent Italian school. It is poetry, as the art of poetry was understood for two or three centuries, in Italy and wherever the Italian poets found an audience.

What is there in it ? When one looks into it to find the common element, to abstract the quintessence of the Italian school, is there anything more important than their favourite form of verse ? Namely, that harmony of their longer and shorter lines which Dante explained in his essay on the principles of Italian poetry—the harmony of our ten-syllable and six-syllable line, which in Italian is eleven and seven. Of which Dante says (with strange enthusiasm over a very simple metrical formula, you will think) :

' The most noble verse, which is the hendeca-syllable, if it be accompanied with the verse of seven, yet so as still to keep the preeminence, will be found exulting higher still in light and glory.'

Et licet hoc (i.e. endecasyllabum) quod dictum est celeberrimum carmen ut dignum est videatur omnium aliorum, si eptasyllabi aliqualem socie-tatem assumat, dummodo principatum obtineat, clarius magisque sursum superbire videtur; sed hoc ulterius elucidandum remaneat.

Whatever else there may be in the Art of Poetry, there is this mysterious power of certain formulas, abstract relations of syllables; of all these frames of verse in modern poetry there is none of greater dignity and at the same time more widely spread, more generally understood than this measure of the Italian *Canzone*. A bodiless thing; in itself you would say as abstract as a geometrical diagram and of not much more worth for poetry.   Yet read the great lyrical poems of Spenser and Milton, read the *Ode to a Nightingale*, *The Scholar Gipsy*, *Thyrsis*, and you will hear how the abstract harmony takes pos-session of the minds of poets, and compels their thought and imagination to move in the same measure.   The noblest thoughts have gone to this tune:

Fame is no plant that grows on mortal soil
Nor in the glistering foil
Set off to the world nor in broad rumour lies.

Our own poet of *Thyrsis* makes a contrast between his world, the Cumnor hills, the Wytham
flats, the upper river, and the Sicilian fields of
the old pastoral poetry :

When Dorian shepherds sang to Proserpine.

Yet his Oxford verse is derived from Italy, from
the poetry that began at the court of the Norman
kings in Sicily : ' Flowers first open'd on Sicilian
air '.

In Drummond's praise of poetry we can detect
two modes of thought, equally true but not equally
effective.   One is regard for the Ancients, which
we can all share as readers of poetry.   The other
mode is adherence to a certain noble tradition of
verse which is a living influence much nearer to
the mind of the artist. Looking at Homer and
Virgil, he is in a theatre along with innumerable
other spectators.   But at the sound of Petrarch's
verse, he leaves the benches and takes his place
in the orchestra. The infinite riches of Homer
and Virgil he appreciates as a man of taste and
a scholar ; but the simple Italian metrical formula
—11 : 7— makes a poet of him.

I have long thought of writing a book on the
measures of modern poetry, from about the year
1100, when it begins in Provence. Whether it
would do for lectures, I am not sure. It might
possibly be useful if not entertaining. You will
allow me a quotation, which I hope is not imper-
tinent ; a passage from the life of Dr. William

Crowe, of New College, who was Public Orator a hundred years ago; a poet of whom Wordsworth thought well, and the author of a treatise on versification. 'Writing to Rogers in February, 1827, to ask him to negotiate with Murray for the issue of a new edition of his poems, in which he wished to include a treatise on English versification, Crowe says:

'If he is willing to undertake the publishing I will immediately furnish more particulars and also submit the copy to your inspection. If the part on versification could be out before the middle of April it would find a present sale in Oxford, for this reason: there are above four score young poets who start every year for the English prize, and as I am one of the five judges to decide it they would (many of them) buy a copy to know my doctrine on the subject. The compositions are delivered in about the beginning of May.'[1]

My treatise will, I think, bring out some curious things, not generally known, of the same sort as the well ascertained and widespread influence of the Italian *Canzone* on the solemn odes of many languages. The same magical life of the spirit of verse is found everywhere. The best in this kind are echoes, and they travel over prodigious distances. My story will begin with the Venerable Bede, the first Englishman to write on prosody. Ages before the English took to the measures of modern verse Bede explained in Latin how it

[1] Clayden, *Rogers and his Contemporaries*, ii. 29.

would be done. He shows the difference between learned and popular, metrical and rhythmical verse ; how without respect for quantity the measure of strict verse may be imitated, and how the rustic licence of popular poets may be used by artists in poetry. He gives the rule (e. g.) of the trochaic tetrameter ; trochaic and tetrameter still, he reckons it, even when the rules of metrical quantity are neglected :

Apparebit repentina dies magna Domini.

A thousand years later the tune of it takes the mind of Dr. Johnson, and he sings :

Long-expected one and twenty,
   Ling'ring year, at length is flown :
Pride and pleasure, pomp and plenty,
   Great *Sir John*, are now your own.

Loosen'd from the minor's tether,
   Free to mortgage or to sell,
Wild as wind and light as feather,
   Bid the sons of thrift farewell.

It appears first in modern poetry in William of Poitiers. His authorship of Burns's favourite stanza is well known. He also uses this, the verse of *a Toccata of Galuppi*, combined with the verse of *Love among the Ruins*.

When Captain Scott Moncrieff the other day translated the *Song of Roland* in the verse of the original, he found the measure recognized as that of the old Scottish version of the 124th Psalm :

Now Israel may say and that truly
If that the LORD had not our cause maintained.

THE ART OF POETRY 15

The reason is that the Scottish poet was translating from the French Psalter of Marot and
Beza; he wanted the French tune for his congre-
gation of 'Gude and godlie ballads', and of course
he had to keep the measure with the sharp pause
at the fourth syllable, just as in *Roland* :

>Halt sunt li pui e tenebrus e grant

and

>En Rencesvals mult grant est la dulur.

For a thousand years in Christendom the Art
of Poetry has lived on the old forms of rhythmical
verse, derived, some of them obviously, others
otherwise, from the metres of Greek and Latin,
with the help of musical tunes.

Now this seems to bring out a considerable
difference between the art of poetry and the other
arts, at any rate in modern times. We talk of
schools of poetry; but the beginners in poetry do
not work through their apprenticeship in schools
of art and offices like students of painting, music,
and architecture. They are not taught; they
have much to learn, but they learn it in their own
way; the rudiments are easily acquired. Even
a momentous discovery like that of which Dante
speaks, the Italian harmony, as I have called it,
is a trivial thing in appearance; it has been the
life of very glorious poems, but there is nothing in
it that needs to be explained to a working poet.

Is it true, or not, that the great triumphs of
poetical art often come suddenly? Art like that
of Pindar would seem to be impossible without

long preparation; but the Drama in Athens, England, and Spain, does it not seem to come very suddenly by its own, and attain its full proportions almost at once when once it has begun? The speed of the victory in England has been rather obscured for the popular mind through the conspiracy of Shakespeare's friends and admirers to praise him in the wrong way for native uncorrected genius, not at all for art.   Yet is there anything more amazing in Shakespeare's life than his security in command of theatrical form?   One of the first things he does, when he has a little leisure, is to invent the comedy of idle good manners in *Love's Labour's Lost*; in *A Midsummer Night's Dream* he raises and completes the finest and most varied structure of poetical comedy: where did he learn it all?   There had been nothing on earth like it; what had Plautus or Terence to contribute to that entertainment of Theseus and Hippolyta?   Did Shakespeare get anything from classical comedy except the *Errors* and that fardel of baby things which proves the parentage of Perdita?   That eternal bag of evidences—πηρίδιον γνωρισμάτων—it was a disappointment lately to observe that Menander could not leave it behind him when he was brought up from underground in Egypt.   Shakespeare and Molière (in *Scapin*) have no scruples about the bundle of tokens at the end of the play, identifying the female infant. Yet to wait centuries for Menander in the original Greek, and then to find him dwelling with zest on this old fardel—it did not add to the gaiety of nations. Shakespeare did not need this mis-adventure of Menander to bring out the contrast. Where did he learn his incomparable art?

On the other hand, there may be convention and long tradition leading to a sudden stroke of genius. Two of the most original of English poets, Chaucer and Burns, are the most indebted to their poetical ancestors. Burns has been injured in the same way as Shakespeare, by the wrong sort of admiration. Unlike Shakespeare, he began this himself, with the voluntary humility of his Edinburgh dedication to the Caledonian Hunt: 'I tuned my wild artless notes as she inspired'. 'She' is 'the Poetic Genius of my country'. But the Muse of Scotland had estab-lished for Burns a convention and tradition full of art; his book is the result of two or three generations of poetical schooling, and 'wild artless notes' are as unlike the perfect style of Burns as the sentiment of his preface generally is unlike the ironical vision of the *Holy Fair*.

The Art of Poetry is much more free than the other arts, in the sense that the right men do not need such steady training. Perhaps it is easier for the right men to work miracles, such as Burns did, in bringing the appearance of novelty and freshness out of old fashions. Also the essence of poetry is such that often much smaller things, comparatively, tell for success than in painting or music. Eight lines beginning 'A slumber did my spirit seal ' may be larger in imagination than earth's diurnal course. Eight lines lately addressed to a mercenary army were enough to tell how the sum of things was saved :

> Their shoulders held the sky suspended,
>   They stood, and earth's foundations stay.

Often single lines and phrases seem to have the value of whole poems. In the old English song ' Bitwene Mershe and Averill when spray ginneth to springe' the opening words are everything ; though one is glad to have more. Herrick has put the whole meaning of the pilgrim's progress into two lines of his *Noble Numbers* :

> I kenn my home, and it affords some ease
> To see far off the smoaking villages.

Quoniam advena ego sum et peregrinus, sicut omnes patres mei. It is the English landscape too, as you come down the hill at the end of the day.

Gavin Douglas, Bishop of Dunkeld, is praised for his descriptions, particularly the Summer and Winter in two of his prologues. He is not often quoted for his great discovery in a line or two of the thirteenth prologue of *Eneados*, where he tells how he watched the midsummer midnight in the North, and finds not only the right word for what he sees, but the right word for his own poetry :

> Yondir down dwinis the evin sky away,
> And up springis the bricht dawing of day
> Intill ane uthir place nocht fer in sunder
> Quhilk to behald was plesance and half wonder.

He sees a new thing in the life of the world—no poet that I know of (except Homer) had thought of it before—and in naming it he gives the interpretation also, the spirit of poetry : plesance, and half wonder.

This sort of miracle, this sudden glory, is an escape from the fashion of the time, and the fashions of poetry, the successive schools are such that escapes are not so difficult as in the other arts. The history of poetry must be the history of schools and fashions. But the progress of poesy does not mean simply the refutation of old schools by new fashions. The poets have sometimes thought so; like Keats in *Hyperion*, possibly; like Dante when he speaks of the older lyric poetry as distained by comparison with the sweet new style, *dolce stil nuovo*, of his own masters and fellows. But apart from the grace that you may find in the older fashion as a whole, taking it as an antiquarian curiosity, there is the chance, the certainty, that here and there among the old songs you will come upon something new, independent, a miracle. In the old lyric poetry of Provence, which has been made a byword for conventionality and monotonous repetition, there are poems that seem to start afresh, worth dwelling on and remembering. This is true also of the other similar school of the German minnesingers, which has been equally maligned.

Mnemosyne, Mother of the Muses, has allowed many things to pass into oblivion. But the

Memory of the World in poetry keeps alive everything that is kept at all, and in such a way that
at any time it may turn to something new. The
simplest measures of verse, the best known
stories, you can never be sure that they are out
of date. The stories of the Greek mythology
have long ago been indexed. I have an old
Dutch Ovid in prose, the *Metamorphosis* translated 'for the behoof of all noble spirits and
artists, such as rhetoricians, painters, engravers,
goldsmiths, &c.' Nothing could be more business
like : a handy book of suitable subjects then ;
now long abandoned, you would say, in the
march of intellect. Yet we know how the old
tragic legend of Procne and Philomela turned
into the *Itylus* of *Poems and Ballads* :

O sweet stray sister, O shifting swallow
    The heart's division divideth us ;
      Thy heart is light as leaf of a tree,
But mine goes forth among seagulfs hollow
    To the place of the slaying of Itylus,
      The feast of Daulis, the Thracian sea.

There is no need for me to say more of this :
Who hath remembered, who hath forgotten?
For the present, I have spoken long enough.

Printed in England at the Oxford University Press.

Dante Gabriel Rossetti and German Literature

A PUBLIC LECTURE
DELIVERED IN HILARY TERM, 1912, AT THE
TAYLOR INSTITUTION, OXFORD

BY

L. A. WILLOUGHBY, M.A., Ph.D.
Fellow of University College, London
Taylorian Lecturer in German

1912

DANTE GABRIEL ROSSETTI AND GERMAN LITERATURE

To one well versed in the numerous biographical and
critical studies on Rossetti, the title of my lecture may
have come somewhat as a surprise. He will have but the
most distant reminiscences of any connexion of Rossetti's
with German literature, for the space allotted to the
subject by his biographers is but small indeed. They
either do not take his German studies into account, or
they pass them over with a few cursory and deprecatory
remarks. Yet the importance of these interests for
Rossetti's literary and artistic development would seem
to warrant a closer acquaintance with this phase of his
career. It was with a view to filling in some details in
the earlier chapters of Rossetti's biography that the
present essay was undertaken.[1]

Rossetti's boyhood, we should note first, falls just

[1] Of the vast Rossetti bibliography, I have found the following
works especially useful :

The Collected Works of Dante Gabriel Rossetti, 2 vols., 1886.

William M. Rossetti, *Ruskin, Rossetti, Pre-Raphaelitism*, 1899.

D. G. Rossetti : His Family Letters, 2 vols. With a Memoir by
W. M. Rossetti, 1895.

Letters of D. G. Rossetti to William Allingham. Ed. by G. B.
Hill, 1897.

W. M. Rossetti, *Pre-Raphaelite Diaries and Letters*, 1900 ;
Some Reminiscences of William Michael Rossetti, 1906.

T. Hall Caine, *Recollections of D. G. Rossetti*, 1882.

E. Wood, *D. G. Rossetti and the Pre-Raphaelite Movement*, 1894.

H. T. Dunn, *Recollections of D. G. Rossetti*, 1904.

A. C. Benson, *Rossetti*. English Men of Letters, 1904.

W. Waldschmidt, *D. G. Rossetti, der Maler und der Dichter*, 1905.

Kurt Horn, *Zur Entstehungsgeschichte von D. G. Rossettis
Dichtungen*, Königsberg, 1909. [Reprinted in Normannia, vol. v,
Berlin, 1909.]

within that period when the influence of German literature was paramount in England.[2] Under the enthusiastic partisanship of Mme de Staël's *De l'Allemagne*, and of the untiring efforts of English men of letters like De Quincey, Henry Crabb Robinson, Robert Pearce Gillies, William Taylor of Norwich, and Thomas Carlyle, of ardent supporters like Mrs. Sarah Austin and Mary Howitt,[3] German literature was gradually recovering from the

[2] On the subject of the general indebtedness of English to German literature, see E. Koeppel, *Deutsche Strömungen in der englischen Literatur* (Kaisersgeburtstagsrede), Strassburg, 1910, to which a very complete and valuable bibliography is appended. On the German influence during the last quarter of the eighteenth and the beginning of the nineteenth centuries, cf. Theodor Süpfle, *Beiträge zur Geschichte der deutschen Literatur in England im letzten Drittel des* 18. *Jahrhunderts* : Kochs Zeitschrift für vergleichende Literaturgeschichte, neue Folge vi, 305; E. Margraf, *Einfluss der deutschen Literatur auf die englische am Ende des* 18. *und im ersten Drittel des* 19. *Jahrhunderts*, Leipzig, 1901 ; Leslie Stephen, *The Importation of German*: Studies of a Biographer, vol. ii, London, 1899 ; Theodor Zeiger, *Beiträge zur Geschichte der deutsch-englischen Literaturbeziehungen*: Kochs Studien zur vergleichenden Literaturgeschichte, i, 239 und 273.

[3] W. A. Dunn, *Thomas de Quincey's Relation to German Literature and Philosophy*, Strassburg, 1900; W. Y. Durand, *De Quincey and Carlyle in their Relation to the Germans*: Publications of the Modern Language Association of America, xxii, 521 (1907) ; *Diary, Reminiscences, and Correspondence of Henry Crabb Robinson*, edited by T. Sadler, 1872: cf. G. Herzfeld, *Aus Henry Crabb Robinsons Nachlass*: Herrigs Archiv, cxx, 25. On Robert Pearce Gillies see Zeiger, l. c. ; Georg Herzfeld, *William Taylor von Norwich*, Halle, 1897 ; W. Streuli, *Thos. Carlyle als Vermittler deutscher Literatur und deutschen Geistes*, Zürich, 1895 ; H. Kraeger, *Carlyles Stellung zur deutschen Sprache und Literatur*: Anglia, xxii, 145. For further studies on Carlyle and his relations to German literature see Koeppel, l. c., p. 25 ; *Three Generations of Englishwomen : Memoirs and Correspondence of Mrs. John Taylor, Mrs. Sarah Austin, and Lady Duff Gordon*, by Janet Ross, 1888 ; *Mary Howitt : An Autobiography edited by her daughter*, Margaret Howitt.

felon blow dealt it at the close of the eighteenth century by the parodies of the *Anti-Jacobin* and the *Meteors*.[4] The critical reviews of the twenties and thirties of last century, the *Edinburgh*, the *London Magazine*, *Blackwood's*, the *Foreign Review*, are full of references to German literature, of critical surveys of German books. And translations and adaptations of German works now followed fast one upon the other. Not only were the masterpieces of Goethe and Schiller translated, but the Romantic writers came into even a greater vogue. The works of Tieck, to judge from the numerous translations which appeared, were great favourites, but men like Fouqué, Müllner, J. P. Richter, Novalis, the two Schlegels, Klingemann, were accorded a share of attention.

If now we turn to the list of books referred to by Mr. William Michael Rossetti as having been read by his brother as a boy, we shall not be surprised to find amongst them many of the names we have just mentioned. First and foremost was Goethe's *Faust*, which Dante Gabriel read again and again in Filmore's translation,[5] supplemented by the study of the famous outlines to Goethe's *Faust* of the German artist, Retzsch,[6] which were a never-failing source of joy. Two other German classics, with illustrations by the same artist, were two ballads of Schiller : *Fridolin* (*Der Gang nach dem Eisenhammer*) and *The Dragon of Rhodes* (*Der Kampf mit dem Drachen*).[7] 'The former', says Mr. W. M.

[4] See C. H. Herford, *The Age of Wordsworth*, p. 138 ; T. Rea, *Schiller's Dramas and Poems in England*, 1906, p. 13 seq.

[5] L. Filmore, *Faust*, part i. London, 1841.

[6] Retzsch's *Outlines to Goethe's Faust*. London, 1827.

[7] *Fridolin, or the Road to the Iron-Foundry*, with a translation by J. P. Collier, Esq., illustrated with eight engravings by Henry Moses from the designs of Retzsch, London, 1824; *The Fight with the Dragon*, a romance by F. Schiller, with a translation by J. P. Collier, &c. (as above), London, 1825.

Rossetti with some show of justice, ' we thought feeble stuff.' More to the taste of the youthful circle were Chamisso's *Peter Schlemihl* and De la Motte-Fouqué's *Undine*, two of the most delightful stories which German Romanticism has produced. The interest in the morbid and supernatural stories of E. T. A. Hoffmann, which Rossetti read in a French translation,[8] is still more characteristic of his future development. Of a similar character was the famous supernatural novel of Matthew Gregory Lewis, *The Monk*, which itself is founded, at least in part, on German sources.[9] Then, also, there were *Sidonia the Sorceress* and *The Amber Witch* by Meinhold,[10] both stories of witchcraft and magic. Nor must we forget the *Tales of Terror and Wonder* [11] of M. G. Lewis ; adaptations of Norse and German ballads, chosen for the gruesomeness of their contents, and original poems by the editor, which surpass their models in grotesque horror. Yet amongst the absurdities of *Grim, King of the Ghosts*,

[8] *Contes fantastiques de E. T. A. Hoffmann.* Traduction nouvelle par Henry Egmont, Paris, 1836, 4 vols. ; or the edition by P. Christian, Paris, 1843.

[9] ' *Ambrosio* ' or *The Monk*, 1795, and many times since. On the sources of *The Monk* see Max Rentsch, *Matthew Gregory Lewis. Mit besonderer Berücksichtigung seines Romans ' Ambrosio ' or The Monk*, Leipzig, 1902 ; O. Ritter, *Studien zu M. G. Lewis' Roman ' Ambrosio ' or The Monk*: Herrigs Archiv, cxi, 106 ; G. Herzfeld, *Die eigentliche Quelle von Lewis' ' Monk* ': Archiv, cxi, 316 ; O. Ritter, *Die angebliche Quelle von M. G. Lewis' ' Monk* ': Archiv, cxiii, 56 ; G. Herzfeld, *Noch einmal die Quelle des ' Monk* ': Archiv, cxv, 70.

[10] *The Amber Witch* [' *Maria Schweidler die Bernsteinhexe* '], by W. Meinhold, translated from the German by E. A. Friedländer, 1844 ; *Sidonia the Sorceress*, by W. Meinhold, translated by Mrs. W. R. Wilde, 1847.

[11] M. G. Lewis, *Tales of Terror*, 1799 ; *Tales of Wonder*, written and collected by M. G. L., 2 vols., 1801 ; the two republished by Professor Morley in 1887.

or *The Little Grey Man*, we also find such masterpieces of ballad-poetry as the *Erl-King*, the *Fisherman* of Goethe, and the *Wild Huntsman* and *Lenore* of Bürger. The latter is of special interest to us in view of Rossetti's subsequent adaptation of the poem, and we must return to it presently. This collection of Lewis may be held in no small measure responsible for the development of Rossetti's genius. In the supernatural elements which abound here, as they do also in the novels of Meinhold, we must seek the origin of that fascination which the occult exercised over Rossetti during the whole of his life, and which found its supreme literary expression in his *Sister Helen*, in what he terms in a letter to Allingham 'the pitch of brutal bogyism'.

It is significant that Rossetti's first efforts in original composition were inspired by his German reading. This was the fragment of a novel entitled *Sorrentino*, written in August 1843. The manuscript was probably destroyed by its author before he came of age, but it left such a powerful impression on the mind of his brother, that, some fifty years afterwards, he was able to recollect some details of the plot. It was apparently a fantastic story in the manner of Hoffmann's *Elixiere des Teufels*, in which love-potions, and duels, and the Evil One (a favourite personage of young Dante's since his early acquaintance with Goethe's *Faust*), played a prominent part. Mr. W. M. Rossetti describes the work as 'spirited, effective, and well-told', and we can only echo his lament at its destruction. The 'spirit of *diablerie*' seems to have entered into the Rossetti children generally; we hear also of a prose story by Christina bearing some resemblance to *Peter Schlemihl*, but which, also, met with a similar fate as her brother Dante's early efforts.

Rossetti's German studies were not, however, to be

confined to translations in English or French ; owing to
fortunate circumstances he was soon able to turn to the
originals themselves. One day, about the beginning of
1842, just before Dante Gabriel left school, Dr. Adolf
Heimann, then professor of German at University College,
London, presented himself at the Rossettis' house, with
the request that the father should give him Italian lessons,
whilst he, in return, would teach the children German.
The proposition was joyfully accepted, and from this
time onwards, until about 1848, the two families (for
Dr. Heimann had married about 1843) were on terms of
the greatest intimacy. Thus it came about that our
poet, along with the other three children, was introduced
into the intricacies of German accidence. Although
Dante Gabriel acquired a creditable knowledge of the
language, he seems never to have mastered it thoroughly,
for we have his brother's testimony that, by the age of
25–30, he had forgotten four-fifths of what he had learned.
We have also evidence of his own from later years which
corroborates this statement : ' I do not know that
language,' he writes in a letter to Mr. Hall Caine, referring
to German. In his library, too, German authors were
conspicuous by their absence, the only ones he possessed
being Goethe's *Faust* and Carlyle's translation of *Wilhelm
Meister*. These statements, however, all date from 1880
or thereabouts, or some forty years after the events here
discussed. And that he should have forgotten German
at that distance of time proves nothing as to his previous
knowledge of the language. We know ourselves, only too
well, how a foreign language, once neglected, will vanish
utterly.

In Dr. Heimann, Rossetti, no doubt, had an able
teacher. It may appear not uninteresting to state about
him such particulars as I have been able to collect.

Adolf Heimann was born at Posen on August 17, 1809, of Jewish parents. He studied philosophy and classical and Germanic philology at the universities of Berlin and Leipzig under authorities like Gans, Hegel, von Savigny, Karl Lachmann. He took his doctor's degree at Berlin in 1833 with a dissertation on the Orations of Thucydides. Such is the information one gathers from the usual *Curriculum vitae* appended to the dissertation in question.[12] For the next ten years, until the date of his appointment to the chair of German at University College, his life is a blank. From 1842 onwards, as we saw, he was on an intimate footing with the Rossettis, and it is to the family letters of Dante Gabriel Rossetti that one turns for further information. Towards 1843 he married Amelia Barnard, ' a very pleasant young English Jewess,' as William M. Rossetti terms her, whilst Mrs. W. Ross (Lucy, the daughter of Ford Madox Brown) seems to have entertained a strong dislike for her. But whatever reason Mrs. Ross may have had for her antipathy to Mrs. Heimann, the fact is that from 1843 Dr. Heimann and his wife were the Rossettis' ' most constant and kindly friends, well known to the entire household '.

Of Professor Heimann's activities at University College there is little record. Unfortunately, the Calendar of the College was not regularly printed until a much later date, so that we have no information as to the subjects on which the professor lectured during the course of these years of intimacy with the Rossettis.[13] We hear on one occasion the echo of a complaint of the educational

---

[12] Heimann (Adolphus) Posnaniensis, *De Thucydidis Orationibus dissertatio*: Berolini, 1833.

[13] Nor has any record been preserved in the archives of University College, London. I have to thank Mr. W. W. Seton, Secretary of the College, for the above information.

methods of University College. The authorities, it
seems, insisted on his arranging his lectures with a view
to examinations, with the result that they often disturbed
the course of instruction Dr. Heimann would have
pursued on his own account.

Dr. Heimann must have been a man of some literary
ability, to judge from a translation into German of
Henry Taylor's drama, *Philip van Artevelde*, which
appeared at Leipzig in 1852.[14] This is the only work of
any permanent value mentioned by the catalogue of the
British Museum.   Besides, Dr. Heimann edited a number
of text-books and a dictionary.   He died in 1874.

If I have gone into some details about Professor
Heimann, it is because the close relations in which he
stood to the Rossetti family, and to Dante Gabriel during
the most impressionable years of his boyhood, warrant
the attempt to form some idea of his personality.   From
his translation of Henry Taylor's drama it is evident that
Heimann's literary sympathies were for a drama which
should unite reason with imagination.   From an early
letter of Dante Gabriel's, we learn that he had a great
admiration for Keble's *Christian Year*.   From such scanty
data it is obviously impossible to draw any very serious
inference of his attitude to poetry generally.   But we
can easily understand that a certain sympathy must
have existed between Heimann and his pupils : the one,
Christina Rossetti, to become one of the finest exponents
of deep religious feeling, tinged with a romantic colouring; the other, Dante Gabriel, the very quintessence
of Romance poetry.   We must beware of overrating
Dr. Heimann's influence, but it is not to be passed over
in silence.

[14] *Philipp van Artevelde's Tod.*   Ein Drama von Henry Taylor.
Aus dem Englischen übersetzt von A. Heimann. Leipzig, 1852.

It was entirely owing to the interests awakened by Dr. Heimann that Rossetti was induced to attempt the first of his translations from the German. This was a version of Bürger's *Lenore*, which he made in or about June 1844, at the age of 16. Subsequently, with the loss of his German interests, Rossetti banished the subject from his thoughts. For years no more was heard of it, and at the date of his death in 1882 the manuscript was not in his possession. In his introduction to his brother's *Family Letters*, written in 1895, Mr. W. M. Rossetti speaks of the translation as having perished. In November 1899, however, one of the copies made by Rossetti in 1844 turned up unexpectedly at a sale at Sotheby's. It was bought by Mr. G. T. Ellis, the publisher, and edited separately with a preface by Mr. W. Rossetti in 1900. It has also been included in the new complete edition of Rossetti's works which has just appeared.

It is significant that Rossetti's first poetical work should have been a translation from the German, and, above all, an adaptation of Bürger's famous ballad. One feels tempted to apply to Rossetti the remark made by Scott to Mrs. Barbauld, viz. that it was William Taylor's translation of *Lenore* which made him a poet. Rossetti could not have opened his poetic career with a more suitable work.

The weird and fascinating ballad is so well known that I can be brief in its description. Of all the soldier lads in the village, Lenore's sweetheart alone has not returned from the war. He has fallen in the battle of Prague, fighting for King Frederick against the Austrians. Lenore rebels against the decree of Providence, and, in her soul's anguish, utters reckless words of complaint against God's goodness and mercy. At the dead of night, a ghostly rider gallops up to Lenore's door. It is William, her dead

lover, who comes to bear her off to the bridal bed. She
mounts behind him, and they speed in a mad gallop over
meadow-land and heather, past ditches and hedges,
through towns and villages :

> Tramp, tramp across the land they speed,
> Splash, splash across the sea !

until they arrive at the churchyard where William lies
buried. And the phantom rider changes into a skeleton
with scythe and hour-glass, whilst the spirits dance round
the graves in the moonlight as they chant Lenore's dirge :

> Be patient, though thine heart should break,
> Arraign not heaven's decree.

This ballad, which was inspired partly by a German
Volkslied and partly by one of the ballads in Percy's
Reliques, was written by Bürger in 1773. Within a few
years it had spread from one end of Europe to the other,
and had called forth innumerable translations and
adaptations. Nowhere was it more popular than in
England, where, from 1796 to 1799, no less than seven
different versions appeared.[15] The best were those by
William Taylor and Sir W. Scott, the latter being inspired
by Taylor's version, which he had heard recited, and of
which the famous lines,

> Tramp, tramp across the land they speed,
> Splash, splash across the sea !

were in the nature of a direct reminiscence.

Rossetti found Taylor's version in the *Tales of Wonder* ;

[15] On *Lenore* in England see A. Brandl, *Lenore in England*,
in Erich Schmidt's *Charakteristiken*, Berlin, 1886, p. 244 ; W. W.
Greg, *English Translations of Lenore* : Modern Quarterly of
Language and Literature, 1899, No. 5, and 1900, No. 1 (a note
on Rossetti's version) ; G. Herzfeld, *Zur Geschichte von Bürgers
Lenore in England* : Herrigs Archiv, cvi, 354 ; W. B. Colwell, *An
Eighteenth-Century Translation of Bürger's Lenore* : Mod. Lang.
Notes, xxiv, 1909, p. 254 f.

we also have his brother's affirmation that he knew the translation by Scott.[16] Rossetti's version will compare very favourably with any of these for accuracy both of form and spirit. Literal it certainly is not, but, in spite of a few misunderstandings, it is moderately faithful, and is a marvellous performance for a young boy of 16. One of these mistakes is worthy of special attention. In strophe 6 he substitutes for the ' Vaterunser ' of the original an ' Ave Marie '. Whether this change was intentional or not, it is an interesting instance of an inclination to catholicize the atmosphere of the poem, which in the original is essentially protestant.[17] Thus, in his earliest works, Rossetti displayed those Catholic sympathies which are entirely in harmony with the nature of Romanticism in literature and art.

Bürger's ballad is written in the old ' Common Metre ', which is the customary metre of English ballad poetry. Rossetti has allowed himself certain deviations from the metre of the original: he leaves lines 1 and 3 of each stanza unrhymed, and has lengthened the last two lines

[16] In view of his interest in the drawings of Retzsch, Rossetti may also have been attracted by a reprint of the version of J. Beresford in Retzsch's *Outlines to Bürger's Ballads*, Leipzig, 1840, although there is no internal evidence to show that he made use of this edition. On the other hand, there are distinct traces of borrowing from Scott's *William and Helen*, Edinburgh, 1796. Cf. Rossetti's ' she busked her well ' (str. 19) with Scott's ' she busks, she bounces ', and in the same strophe both translators have ' hurry ' for ' hurre '.

[17] Mr. W. Rossetti alludes to this in his ' prefatory note '. He also points out that ' zur Wette ' (str. 17) does not mean ' 'Tis for a wager ', but ' I wager you '. He might have added that ' Küster ' (str. 22) is not a ' chorister '. On the other hand, he is unjust in laying to his brother's charge the contradiction between strophes 15 and 17. Rossetti followed Bürger literally ; here, too, midnight is mentioned as past, whilst the clock subsequently strikes eleven.

to four instead of three beats.[18]   Whilst we are examining the form of the poem, let us also consider the rhyme technique for a moment.   Rossetti has been constantly blamed for his imperfect rhymes, and especially for his fondness for rhyming a fully stressed vowel with an unaccented derivative syllable.   This fault was very aptly parodied by Robert Buchanan in *The Fleshly School of Poetry* :

> When winds do roar and rains do pour,
> Hard is the life of the sailor,
> He scarcely, as he reels, can tell
> The side lights from the binnacle :
> He looketh on the wild water.[19]

Now it is interesting to trace this unfortunate propensity to this early translation of *Lenore* ; we find here not only more legitimate specimens like tenderly : thee,

[18] The following scheme will afford the best comparison between the metres of Rossetti and his original :

$$\text{Bürger,} \quad a_4 \, b_3 \, a_4 \, b_3 \, c_4 \, c_4 \, d_3 \, d_3 \,;$$
$$\text{Rossetti,} \quad a_4 \, b_3 \, c_4 \, b_3 \, d_4 \, d_4 \, e_4 \, e_4.$$

The above is the most common form of Rossetti's stanza.   We find it in strophes 6, 7, 8, 9, 10, 11, 15, 22, 26, 29, 30.   Or this normal type is varied by the introduction of an extra rhyme into one or more of the lines of four beats.   Examples of this are stanzas 14, 17, 20, 23, 24, 27, 28, 31, where line 2 is thus split up.   Graphically this would be expressed :

$$a_4 \, b_3 \, c_3 \, c_2 \, b_3 \, d_4 \, d_4 \, c_4 \, c_4.$$

Or, again, both lines 1 and 2 are thus divided :

$$a_2 \, a_2 \, b_3 \, c_2 \, c_3 \, b_3 \, d_4 \, d_4 \, e_4 \, e_4 \,;$$

so in verses 3, 12, 13, 19, 21, 25.

The other stanza forms are but variations of the above three :

$$\text{Verses 4 and 18 :} \quad a_2 \, a_2 \, b_3 \, c_4 \, b_3 \, d_2 \, d_2 \, d_4 \, e_4 \, e_4,$$
$$\text{Verse 1 :} \quad a_2 \, a_2 \, b_3 \, c_4 \, b_3 \, d_4 \, d_4 \, e_4 \, e_4,$$
$$16 : \quad a_2 \, a_2 \, b_3 \, c_2 \, c_3 \, b_3 \, d_2 \, d_3 \, d_4 \, e_4 \, e_4,$$
$$32 : \quad a_2 \, a_2 \, b_3 \, c_2 \, c_3 \, b_3 \, d_4 \, d_4 \, c_2 \, e_2 \, e_4,$$
$$2 : \quad a_3 \, b_3 \, c_4 \, d_2 \, d_2 \, d_4 \, e_2 \, e_2 \, e_4 \,;$$

whilst strophe 5, the metrical scheme of which is $a_4 \, b_3 \, a_4 \, b_3 \, c_4 \, c_4 \, d_4 \, d_4$, is exactly the stanza of Bürger, except for the added beat in lines 7 and 8.

[19] Robert Buchanan, *The Fleshly School of Poetry and other phenomena of the day*, p. 52.

speedily : free : eternally, but monstrosities like skull :
horrible—which is truly horrible.[20]   In palliation it has
been suggested that Rossetti's fondness for these weak-
ending rhymes was due to his foreign upbringing, to the
influence of the sonorous Italian endings.   It seems to
me much more probable that it was entirely owing to his
early acquaintance with old English ballad poetry, where
rhymes like me : bodie are quite common, and that Rossetti,
in his early translation from the German, made use of them
as a device to reproduce a supposed mediaeval colouring,
and was afterwards unable to rid himself of the trick.

On the other hand, Rossetti has been very fortunate in
his rendering of Bürger's numerous onomatopoeic expressions, which play such an important part with him, in
evoking the spirit of vigour and bustle which pervades the
poem.   One example must suffice as typical of the rest : [21]

> Und aussen, horch ! ging's trapp, trapp, trapp,
> Als wie von Rosses Hufen.

which Rossetti renders :

> But hark to the clatter and the pat, pat, patter !
> Of a horse's heavy hoof !

[20] Very bad are also the following : war : afar, calm : warm,
driven : eleven, bed : lid, driven : heaven, wonder : tinder.

[21] Cf. also the following :
Stanza 2 :

> Und jedes Heer, mit Sing und Sang,
> Mit Paukenschlag und Kling und Klang—

which Rossetti renders :

> And the martial throng, with laugh and song,
> Spoke of their homes as they rode along,
> And clank, clank, clank ! came every rank,
> With the trumpet-sound that rose and sank.

Or, again, strophe 19 :

> And hurry, hurry ! ring, ring, ring !
> To and fro they sway and swing ;

which is not equal, however, to the original :

> Und hurre, hurre, hopp, hopp, hopp !
> Ging's fort im sausenden Galopp.

In stanza 21 Rossetti has inserted an onomatopoeic line which is

Another point to which I would draw attention is that Rossetti, in several instances, endeavours to tone down the plain-spokenness of Bürger's language. Thus:

> Komm, Pfaff', und sprich den Segen,
> Eh' wir zu Bett uns legen!

becomes:

> Come, friar, come,—let the blessing be spoken,
> That the bride and the bridegroom's sweet rest be unbroken.

This fastidiousness strikes us as strange in the future poet of the sonnets of *The House of Life*, whose lack of reticence brought down upon him the not altogether undeserved attack of *The Fleshly School of Poetry*.

But when we turn from these details to a more general consideration of the poem, we cannot fail to endorse William Rossetti's views: that the version Dante Gabriel made at the age of 16 is, if not the best, certainly among the best of the numerous translations of *Lenore*. Rossetti has thoroughly caught the spirit of the original and has reproduced most admirably the eeriness of the poem. And yet there is in Rossetti's rendering trace of the mystic, spiritual evolution, through which Romanticism had passed since the days of Bürger. It is no longer the mere supernatural which pervades Rossetti's version; the supernatural element is tempered by an intense feeling for beauty, is tinged with a delicate colouring, which is wanting in the crudity of the original. There is the deep

---

not in the German:

> Horch, Glockenklang! Horch, Totensang!
> Ding dong! ding dong! 'tis the sound, 'tis the song.

There is a slight inaccuracy in rendering the German ' husch ! ' an onomatope suggestive of haste and hurry, by the English ' hush'. Strophe 26:

> Und das Gesindel, husch, husch, husch!
> —And hush, hush, hush! the dreamy rout.

tenderness, the fervour which characterizes Rossetti's later poems. We seem to catch an echo of *Rose Mary* in such lines as

> Oh ! mother, mother ! gone is gone !
> I reck no more how the world runs on.

There is a world intervening between these lines and Bürger's :

> O Mutter, Mutter ! Hin ist hin !
> Verloren ist verloren.

Or again :

> Spark of my life ! down down to the tomb
> Die away in the night, die away in the gloom.
> What pity to me does God impart ?
> Woe, woe, woe ! for my heavy heart.[22]

The crux of any rendering of *Lenore*, and it is here where most of the translators come to grief, is in the reproduction of the magnificent description of the ghostly ride, in which the heavens and stars overhead seem to fly past in the mad rush of the gallop. Bürger might well claim that here he had achieved something Shakespearian in its sublimity.

> Wie flog, was rund der Mond beschien,
> Wie flog es in die Ferne !

[22] Cf. Greg, l. c. Instances of this kind might easily be increased : Cf. strophe 8 :
> Despise the fickle fool, my girl,
> Who hath ta'en the pebble and spurned the pearl.

Strophe 12 :
> Wringing her hands and beating her breast,—
> Tossing and rocking without any rest ;—
> Till from her light veil the moon shone thro',
> And the stars leapt out on the darkling blue.

Strophe 15 :
> Hark to the winds, how they whistle and rush
> Thro' the twisted twine of the hawthorn-bush.

Strophe 29 :
> The tombs around looked grassy and grim,
> And they glimmered and glanced in the moonlight dim.

Wie flogen oben überhin
Der Himmel und die Sterne ! —
' Graut Liebchen auch ? . . . Der Mond scheint hell !
Hurra ! die Toten reiten schnell ! —
Graut Liebchen auch vor Toten ? '—
' O weh ! Lass ruhn die Toten ! '

As an example of the way in which Rossetti has
acquitted himself of his task, let me quote the following
translation of the above stanza of Bürger :

How flew the moon high overhead,
    In the wild race madly driven !
In and out, how the stars danced about,
    And reeled o'er the flashing heaven !
' What ails my love ? the moon shines bright :
Bravely the dead men ride thro' the night.
Is my love afraid of the quiet dead ? '—
    ' Alas ! let them sleep in their dusty bed.' [23]

From *Lenore* Rossetti's ambition led him to make
a similar venture with the *Nibelungenlied*. About 1845
the old German epic seized hold of his imagination, and
his enthusiasm was aroused to such a pitch that he set
himself to translate the poem. This was a much more
ambitious venture than *Lenore*, and it is doubtful
whether Rossetti was sufficiently equipped for the task.
His knowledge of Middle High German can never have
been very accurate, and even with the help of the
illustrated edition of Pfizer [24] and the explanations of

[23] Rossetti has rendered admirably Bürger's skilful use of the
thrice repeated question and answer between her lover and
Lenore, in which her vague uneasiness at her uncanny surround-
ings grows into terror, which culminates in

' Is my love afraid of the quiet dead ? '—
' Alas ! let them sleep in their dusty bed ! '

[24] *Der Nibelungen Noth*, illustrirt mit Holzschnitten nach
Zeichnungen von Julius Schnorr von Carolsfeld und Eugen
Neureuther. Die Bearbeitung des Textes von Dr. Gustav Pfizer.
Stuttgart und Tübingen, 1843.

Dr. Heimann, Rossetti could hardly have done more than make out the general gist of the narrative. His brother informs us that the translation progressed up to the end of the fourth ' aventiure ', where Siegfried first meets Chriemhild. Rossetti was apparently discouraged by the magnitude of the task he had set himself, and abandoned it at this juncture. Even this fragment has disappeared without a trace, although it is not impossible that it may turn up again some day, just as *Lenore* has done.[25]

The third and last of Rossetti's translations from the German was *Henry the Leper*, a rendering of Hartmann von der Aue's *Armer Heinrich*, which was undertaken about 1846. It remained amongst the poet's papers until 1871, when Rossetti revised the work and ' cut out some juvenilities '. Although, as we know from his brother, Rossetti thought well of the poem, it was not published during his lifetime. In 1886 Mr. W. M. Rossetti included it amongst the *Collected Works*. An autograph

[25] Had this translation been preserved it would have had the distinction of being, in point of time, the first translation of the poem into English. We must except the few versified extracts contained in H. W. Weber's account of the poem in the *Illustrations of Northern Antiquities*, 1814, and Thos. Carlyle's essay in the *Westminster Review* of 1831. It is not improbable that Rossetti may have heard of the above accounts. They are not likely to have escaped the attention of Dr. Heimann, whose interest in the *Nibelungenlied* must have dated from his student days in Berlin, when he sat at the feet of Karl Lachmann. Whatever the incentive may have been which induced Rossetti to attempt the translation, the loss of the fragment is much to be deplored, for, according to his brother, it was ' a fine translation with rolling march and a sense of the heroic '. Actually the first complete rendering into English was that by Birch, published at Berlin in 1848. It was possibly the appearance of this version which induced Rossetti to abandon his. On English renderings of the *Nibelungenlied* cf. F. E. Sandbach, *The Nibelungen and Gudrun in England and America*, London, 1904.

manuscript of the poem subsequently found its way into the auction-room, and was sold to an American collector. It was published in facsimile for the Bibliophile Society of Boston in 1905.[26]

How Rossetti's attention was first drawn to this work of the twelfth-century German poet is purely a matter of conjecture. The interest in the *Nibelungenlied* would naturally lead him to the wider field of mediaeval German literature ; and the influence of Professor Heimann is, again, to be borne in mind. There is nothing more natural than that Rossetti should have read the *Armer Heinrich* as an introduction to Middle High German. It is the usual work chosen for that purpose even to-day, by reason of its inherent charm, its brevity, and the comparative simplicity of its language. It is almost impossible to determine Rossetti's exact sources, in view of the very freedom of the translation. From an examination of the variant readings, and the comparison with Rossetti's translation, it would appear that he used as the basis of his version the text of Haupt's edition of 1842.[27]   No

[26] *Henry the Leper (Der arme Heinrich)*, paraphrased by D. G. Rossetti, with an introduction by W. P. Trent.   Printed for members only.   The Bibliophile Society, 1905.   2 vols.

[27] The editions of *Der arme Heinrich* which Rossetti might have used are : Grimm 1815, Lachmann 1820, Müller 1842, Haupt 1842, supplemented by the translation of Simrock 1817, of Büsching 1816, or by Chamisso's paraphrase of 1839.   I base my assertion that he relied above all on Haupt on the following facts. In lines 225 and 447 of the original, the MSS. and editors vary in their reading between *erbaere, vriebaere, manbaere, hibaere.*   The only editor who reads *erbaere* in both instances is Haupt.   Rossetti translates the passage in question,

... eine maget
diu vollen erbaere,

in the first instance (p. 425) by :

An innocent virgin for to find,
Chaste, and modest, and pure in mind,

doubt Dr. Heimann rendered him every assistance, and the library of the British Museum, which was a favourite haunt of his at this period, afforded him every facility for study.

Der arme Heinrich, by Hartmann von der Aue, is one of the most charming poems of the Middle Ages. The good knight Henry has, for his worldliness and pride, been punished by Heaven with leprosy. Not all the wisdom of the most famous medical faculties of the day, Montpellier and Salerno, has been able to cure him : there is only one remedy, the blood of a virgin who should give her life for his. In despair, the

and in the second (p. 430) by : ' a virtuous maid,' both being obviously a rendering of *erbaere* = honourable, beyond reproach.

Again, after line 852 most editors and translators (e. g. Grimm, Lachmann, Müller, Simrock) insert the reading of MS. B :

> Da sol uns viere der tot lôsen
> Von der hellen und von den geisten bôsen,

whilst Haupt relegates the passage to the notes. Nor is there any trace of it in Rossetti, p. 440.

I have no idea whence Rossetti derived his reading, p. 428 :

> It chanced the peasant and his wife,
> And his *two* little daughters sate—

when the original l. 355 only mentions *one* daughter :

> nu saz der meiger und sin wip
> unde ir tohter, diu maget—

unless Rossetti took the feminine article ' diu ' for a neuter plural. He could hardly, by some curious lapse, have mistaken ' diu ' for the numeral two, led astray by an outward resemblance to the Italian ' due ' !

In line 303 all editors, except Simrock, accept the reading of MS. A, ' ein kint von ahte jaren,' as against that of B, ' wol von zwelf jaren.' Rossetti renders the passage by : ' Whose tenth year was just passing her,' apparently a fanciful reading of his own. Simrock reads, ' ein Kind, das kaum im zwölften Jahr,' whilst the brothers Grimm, in a note to p. 53, suggest that ' zwelf ' would be the better reading. Had Rossetti used Simrock or Grimm he would surely have chosen the more advanced age.

lord Henry returns to Germany. He is cut off from the society of his equals, divides up his broad lands amongst the poor and the Church, and takes up his abode on the farm of one of his poorer tenants. Now, indeed, is he ' der arme Heinrich '. Henry wins the affections of the farmer and his wife by his gentleness and submission to God's will. They do their utmost to soothe his sufferings. He becomes a great favourite with their children, and one of these, a little girl of eight, is devoted to him, and ever anxious to minister to his few wants. In jest he often calls her *trutgemahele*, ' dear little wife '. Three years have elapsed, when, one day, the child over-hears a conversation between her father and the lord Henry, and learns the possibility of his recovery. That night her parents are awakened by the sobs of the little maiden, as she lies at the foot of their bed, weeping for the cruel fate which has befallen her lord. She tells them of her firm resolve to offer up her life for his. Neither tears nor threats can shake her resolution. The fervour and the eloquence of her pleading at last convince the simple folk that her utterances are inspired. With a heavy heart they give their consent. Henry, too, wearied out by her entreaties, and under the sway of his natural desire for life, declares himself willing to accept the sacrifice.

Thus they set out together for Salerno. Arrived at their journey's end, the maiden is obdurate against all attempts to shake her decision. Even the pleas of the leech are of no avail, and sad that one so young and beautiful should suffer death, he leads her into his chamber, and prepares to take her life. Poor Henry stands without, in an agony of fearful suspense. Hearing the sound of the knife being whetted, he peers through a chink in the partition and sees the maiden lying bound on the slab in her naked beauty. The thought that this pure, innocent creature should die for him strikes him now in all its monstrosity. He resolves rather to submit to the divine will, and bear his sickness in patience and humility. In spite of the maiden's tears and reproaches, he insists that the enterprise be abandoned.

Together they journey homeward : he sorrowful and expecting naught but mockery from the world, she wasted almost unto death with weeping and complaining. When, lo ! God's merciful goodness was so made manifest in Henry, that, of a sudden, he was pure and cleansed from the leprosy. He is restored to his possessions and dignities.

His friends and relations now urged him to take a wife. Having assembled them, he told them it was his intention, they willing, of wedding the maid to whom he owed health and life. And, as she was a freeman's daughter, the retainers all approved the suggestion, in spite of the difference in rank, so that his *gemahele* became his wife in very deed.

This story is familiar from Longfellow's *Golden Legend*, in which it lies buried under a mass of extraneous and sentimental additions. Longfellow drew his inspiration from the same source.[28]

The belief in the efficacy of human and, especially, children's blood, against leprosy, is as old as the illness itself. It was a common superstition amongst the ancient Egyptians and, through the Romans, found its way into the West. It is a favourite motive in mediaeval literature, where the sickness is described with nauseous details.[29]

[28] Cf. Friedrich Münzner, *Die Quellen zu Longfellows 'Golden Legend'*. Dresden, 1898.

[29] On leprosy see the account in W. Wackernagel's edition of *Der arme Heinrich* (neu herausgegeben von Ernst Stadler), 1911, p. 189 seq.

Hartmann von der Aue was too great an artist to mar his works by such faults.[30] His *Armer Heinrich* in its directness, its earnestness, its *naïveté*, stands side by side with *Aucassin, et Nicolette*, as one of the gems of mediaeval literature.

In Hartmann, the leading idea of the poem was essentially a religious one. It is that of the forgiveness and mercy which may be won by a contrite heart ; it is that of *triuwe*, of renunciation and compassion.[31]. But what appeals to the modern world is rather the idea of the all-redeeming power of a woman's love. It is in this spirit that most of the modern renovations of the old legend have been undertaken.[32]

Apart from mere translations, there are no less than eight modern German dramas on the subject, excluding one by Gerhart Hauptmann, which is much the finest of the series. The story reappeared in novel form by Ricarda Huch in 1899—a decidedly modern, half romantic, half realistic version, in which all mystical elements of sacrifice are eliminated. The legend has also formed the subject for two musical works : one a musical drama by Hans Pfitzner, first performed at Mainz in 1895 ; the other a cantata by Sullivan, based on Longfellow's *Golden Legend*.

If now we turn to the consideration of Rossetti's paraphrase, the first point that strikes us is a breadth and a diffuseness of the narrative, which are absent from the original, in spite of the fact that the latter is some hundred lines longer. Often Rossetti has imparted a romantic

---

[30] Goethe's harsh condemnation of the poem, as contaminated by the terrible disease of the hero, is most unjust. Hartmann never allows the thought of the illness itself to obtrude upon the listener. Goethe, *Tag- und Jahreshefte 1811* (Werke, 32, 73).

[31] Cf. G. Ehrismann, *Die Treue in Hartmanns Armem Heinrich*. Prager Deutsche Studien viii [Festgabe für J. v. Kelle], 1908, p. 317.

[32] Cf. H. Tardel, ' *Der arme Heinrich* ' *in der neueren Dichtung*, Munckers Forschungen zur neueren Literaturgeschichte, xxx. 1905.

glamour by the addition of a line or two of vivid colouring.
The following twelve lines will illustrate this tendency
sufficiently, and must also serve as an example of Rossetti's
style. They correspond to eight lines of the original :

> With favour which to blessings ran,
> God looked upon the worthy man :
> He gave him strength to aid his life,
> A sturdy heart, an honest wife,
> And children such as bring to be
> That a man's breast is brimmed with glee.
> Among them was a little maid,
> Red-cheeked, in yellow locks arrayed,
> Whose tenth year was just passing her ;
> With smiles most innocently clear,
> Sweet smiles that soothe, sweet tones that lull ;
> Of gracious semblance wonderful.

The above description is Pre-Raphaelite in its vivid
colouring, in its truthfulness of detail. These characteristics in this early poem are worthy of note.

No doubt one of the chief sources of attraction to
Rossetti was the mysticism underlying the doings and
utterances of the farmer's little daughter. He has
reproduced her lengthy speeches with evident relish, even
improving upon them occasionally. At other times his
diffuseness is mere diffuseness and nothing more ; as, for
instance, when the perfect simplicity and artlessness of
the four lines which tell of the miraculous healing are
expanded by pious, philosophical reflections of Henry
and the maiden to no less than forty-seven lines !

At other times the *modern* poet betrays himself. It is
quite a modern touch that Rossetti should introduce
ten lines of explanation, in order to palliate Henry's
acceptance of the child's offer.[33] It is a modern sense

---

[33] p. 444. Cf. also from this point of view p. 449. The leech
makes a final report to Henry and informs him that he cannot
shake the maiden's determination to die for her lord. He asks

of the fitness of things, which makes him add two years
to the child's age ;[34] it is purely from early Victorian
prudishness that he cuts out the naïvely effective
lines where Henry looks through a chink in the door
and discovers the maiden lying naked on the table ;[35]
it is modern sentimentality which induces the omis-
sion of the passage in which the farmer threatens his
daughter with a sound beating, unless she desists from
her importunities.[36]

From the metrical point of view, the poem again leaves
much to be desired as regards the rhymes.[37]   Nor do
Rossetti's lines of four beats bear much resemblance to the
original metre, by reason of the numerous dactyls introduced.   Whether the latter be a serious blemish or not, it
is difficult for one who knows and loves the original to join
whole-heartedly in the unqualified praise bestowed upon
Henry the Leper by Mr. William Rossetti.   In spite of
many poetic passages and felicitous renderings, there
can be no doubt that Rossetti's lengthy philosophic
reflections, the diffuseness, the somewhat florid style, even
the heightened romantic colouring, all tend to detract
from the pure, naïve simplicity of Hartmann's story.

With *Henry the Leper*, Rossetti's German studies
practically come to an end.   Before we endeavour to sum
up the importance of such studies for Rossetti, let us first

for final instructions.   Rossetti makes Henry sunk in thought,
and thus spares him the necessity of speaking the fatal command :

> But Henry was full of troublous thought ;
> Peradventure he hearken'd not,
> For he answer'd not that which was sain.
> So the leech turn'd, and went out again.

[34] Line 303.   See note 27 above.
[35] Line 1228 seq.   [36] Line 586.
[37] Cf. the following examples : ruffian : man, sepulchre : fear,
ago : through, smoke : rock, conclusions : once, merciful : dule,
hast : chaste, excellent : went, crown : put on.

examine what traces of direct German influence are to be found in Rossetti's works.

Although German soon became to Rossetti a forgotten language, one book, Goethe's *Faust*, remained firmly fixed in his memory. *Gretchen in the Chapel* was one of the few sketches that he contributed to the common portfolio of the Pre-Raphaelite coterie. The picture of Lady Lilith is possibly not intended as a representation of the supernatural Lilith of rabbinical mythology. But as the incarnation of sensual beauty, entirely free from any moral restraint, the Lady Lilith of the picture is inspired by the recollection of Goethe's quatrain on Lilith from the *Walpurgisnacht*. This is proved by a transcript of the lines, which Mr. W. Rossetti made for his brother in 1866, and which Rossetti translated.[38] It is not these lines, however, which are much inferior to Shelley's, but rather the sonnet of *The House of Life*, entitled *Body's Beauty*, which affords the best commentary on the picture, and at the same time the finest paraphrase of Goethe's lines.

Of Adam's first wife, Lilith, it is told
(The witch he loved before the gift of Eve,)
That, ere the snake's, her sweet tongue could deceive,
And her enchanted hair was the first gold.
And still she sits, young while the earth is old,
And, subtly of herself contemplative,
Draws men to watch the bright web she can weave,
Till heart and body and life are in its hold.

The supernatural Lilith exerted a peculiar fascination

---

[38] *Faust*, i. 3764 :
    Nimm dich in Acht vor ihren schönen Haaren,
    Vor diesem Schmuck, mit dem sie einzig prangt !
    Wenn sie damit den jungen Mann erlangt,
    So lässt sie ihn so bald nicht wieder fahren.
Rossetti renders this (vol. ii, p. 469) :
    Hold thou thy heart against her shining hair,
      If, by thy fate, she spreads it once for thee ;
    For, when she nets a young man in that snare,
      So twines she him he never may be free.

over Rossetti during the whole of his life. She reappears
in his *Eden Bower*, that most sensuous of his sensuous
poems :

> It was Lilith the wife of Adam :
>> (*Sing Eden Bower !*)
> Not a drop of her blood was human,
> But she was made like a soft sweet woman.

Lilith, once a snake herself, was given human form after
the creation of Adam, and was beloved of him. At the
creation of Eve she is turned out of Eden and, with the
serpent, plots the downfall of the first human lovers,
and exults at the thought that Adam will return to her
embrace. Besides the above-mentioned influence of
Goethe's *Faust*, there is here a reminiscence of a story of
E. T. A. Hoffmann, which Rossetti had probably read
in early youth. It is entitled *Der goldene Topf*, and is a
fantastic tale of the young student Anselmus, and his love
for the snake woman Serpentina, for whom he forsakes
his blue-eyed betrothed Veronika. *The Golden Pot* is one
of the best of Hoffmann's stories, and it was the only one
which Carlyle included in his *German Romance*.[39]

In a remark made to Hall Caine, Rossetti has explained
his *Blessed Damozel* as an answer to Edgar Allan Poe's
The Raven. ' I saw ', he said, ' that Poe had done the
utmost it was possible to do with the grief of the lover on
earth ; and so I determined to reverse the conditions,
and give utterance to the yearnings of the loved one in
heaven.' It has always struck me that there was, if not
a reminiscence, an interesting parallel with the second
part of Goethe's *Faust*.[40] As Faust's soul is borne up to

---

[39] *German Romance : Specimens of its chief authors*, by the
translator of *Wilhelm Meister*. 4 vols. Edinburgh, 1827. *The
Golden Pot*, vol. ii, p. 200.

[40] Hardly more than a parallel, for there is no evidence that
Rossetti ever read the second part of *Faust*. Filmore's transla-

heaven by the angels, Margaret, who has awaited his coming with ardent longing, has a distinct foreboding of his approach. She nestles up to Our Lady, and tells her of her undying love for him. ' Grant me to teach him,' she begs of the Mater gloriosa, and the latter answers :

> Come, soar to higher spheres ! Divining
> Thee near, he'll follow on thy way.

This reminds one of

> We too, she said, will seek the groves
> Where the lady Mary is.

And then, again, the famous lines of the ' Chorus mysticus' might serve as a motto for Rossetti's poem :

> Alles Vergängliche
> Ist nur ein Gleichnis ;
> Das Unzulängliche,
> Hier wird's Ereignis ;
> Das Unbeschreibliche,
> Hier ist's getan ;
> Das Ewig-Weibliche
> Zieht uns hinan.

A further parallel between the *Blessed Damozel* and Goethe's *Faust* has already been pointed out. Strophe 6 has been referred to the Prologue in Heaven, to the paean of the archangel Gabriel. Exigencies of time prevent my pointing out wherein the resemblance lies.[41] That the

tion was only of Part I. On the other hand, the second part had been translated four times before 1847. First, anonymously, in 1838, then by Bernays 1839, Gurney 1842, Birch 1842 ; see W. F. Hauhart, *The reception of Goethe's Faust in England in the first half of the nineteenth century*, New York, 1909. Rossetti's interest in the second part of *Faust* may have been awakened by some outlines of Retzsch, *Umrisse zu Goethes Faust*, zweiter Teil, 1836.

[41] Strophe 6 :

> Beneath the tides of day and night
> With flame and darkness ridge
> The void, as low as where this earth
> Spins like a fretful midge.

Cf.

> Und schnell und unbegreiflich schnelle
> Dreht sich umher der Erde Pracht ;

influence of *Faust* should be so apparent in the *Blessed Damozel* need not surprise us when we remember that it was written early in 1847, at a time when Rossetti was still under the sway of his German studies.

If time did not press, and it were not outside one's province, it would be interesting to attempt a study of Rossetti's indebtedness as a painter to German art.   The Pre-Raphaelite movement, we are told, had its origin in a meeting at Millais' house one evening in 1848, when a circle of friends were looking over a book of engravings of the Campo Santo at Pisa.   This statement has been made and re-made so often that, through sheer repetition, it has almost gained the force of an infallible dogma. And yet, to any one who takes the trouble to look over Lasinio's book of engravings [42] for himself, it will be a matter of great astonishment that any work so imperfect, so uninteresting in subject-matter, should ever have been a source of inspiration for one of the most potent art-movements of the century.   Now, if we turn up the sources of this tradition, and especially if we look into the biography of Holman Hunt,[43] who was himself present on the occasion, the matter will appear in quite another light.   We shall find that the frescoes of the Campo Santo are put more in the background, and that, on

Es wechselt Paradieseshelle
Mit tiefer, schauervoller Nacht.

Quoted by Horn, l. c., p. 40.

[42] There are apparently two editions of these engravings : *Pitture a fresco del Campo Santo di Pisa intagliate da Carlo Lasinio,* Firenze, 1812, and another *disegnate da G. Rossi ed incise dal Prof. Cav. G. P. Lasinio Figlio,* Firenze, 1832.   This latter, by Lasinio's son, is the finer of the two.

[43] *Pre-Raphaelitism and the Pre-Raphaelite brotherhood,* Holman Hunt, 1905, vol. i, p. 130.

the other hand, a prominent position is given to a set of illustrations (those inspired by Tieck's *Genoveva*) by the Austrian painter Joseph Führich.[44] The name of Moritz Retzsch is also mentioned in this connexion. The latter, through his illustrations to *Faust*, to Schiller's and Goethe's ballads, to *Hamlet*, was well known to Rossetti from his earliest boyhood. So, too, were the engravings of Schnorr von Carolsfeld to the *Nibelungenlied*. All the above-mentioned artists were enthusiastic exponents of the German romantic ideals. Führich himself had sat at the feet of Overbeck in Rome, and had listened to the dictums on art which fell from the lips of the great Romantic critic Friedrich Schlegel. And when we remember that Ford Madox Brown, the father of Pre-Raphaelitism, had, on a journey to Italy, himself been introduced to the survivors of the German Pre-Raphaelite brethren,[45] we can have but little doubt as to whence the English movement drew its inspiration. Not that I would suggest that there is much connexion, except the name, between the early representatives of the Nazarenes and the English school. They were in no repute, we hear, with the young British artists. Cornelius and Overbeck represented essentially the Catholic religious side of Romanticism. Yet they had this in common with Rossetti and his circle, that they, too, sought their models amongst early Italian painters; they, too, had started out with the idea of freeing painting from pseudo-classical conventions ; they, too, sought a more intimate connexion with nature. But whilst Overbeck and Cornelius represent the religious tendency of Romanticism,

[44] *Bilder zu Tiecks Genovefa*, von J. Führich. Berlin, G. Reimer, no date.
[45] In 1845. See F. M. Hueffer, *Ford Madox Brown*, 1896. Cf. H. W. Singer, *Dante Gabriel Rossetti*, 1906.

the tendency which induced men like Schlegel and Overbeck to embrace the Catholic faith, which brought about in England the Oxford Movement, the younger generation, of which Führich and Schnorr are typical examples, represent the mediaeval, the poetic, and chivalrous aspect. It was this side of German Romantic art which appealed to Rossetti and his brethren, and which they found present in the illustrations of Führich on the memorable evening in 1848.

If we would now sum up the influence of German literature and art on Rossetti, we must agree that it played a very prominent part in his poetic development. In it he found the mysticism, the romantic colouring, the sensuousness, the supernatural element, the deep religious feeling, which were all essential characteristics of his own art. And if he absorbed these elements so thoroughly, if he found in them a source of inspiration, it was because they were congenial to his own nature. German poetry was the incentive he needed to start him on that search for beauty in art, literature, and life, which will ever render his memory glorious to all times and to all peoples.

THE STUDY
of
ANGLO-NORMAN

Inaugural Lecture delivered

before the University of Oxford on

6 February 1920

by

PAUL STUDER

Taylorian Professor
of the Romance Languages

1920

THE STUDY OF ANGLO-NORMAN

THIS lecture is long overdue and I apologize for the delay. When I had the honour to be elected to the Professorship of Romance Languages in the University of Oxford, it was my intention to deal with the Study of Anglo-Norman in an Inaugural Lecture, but owing first to the War, and then to ill health, I have been hindered until now from carrying out my intention.

I must further apologize for the choice of my subject. Modern thoughts and modern studies are the fashion of the day, and it requires a little courage, even in this ancient seat of learning, to urge the claims of mediaeval lore. I hope, however, that my motive will not be wrongly interpreted, for I need hardly say how sincerely I welcome the establishment of a Chair of French Literature [1] in this University. Thanks to the benefactions of Sir Basil Zaharoff and Mr. Heath Harrison [2], our students will have exceptional facilities for acquainting themselves with the intellectual and social movements of Modern France, and I trust that increasing numbers of them will avail themselves of these advantages. But I would plead that the Middle Ages should be better known, especially that period of the Middle Ages in which France and England shared a common language and a common literature, and took part in the same social and religious activity. The study of Anglo-Norman,

[1] The Marshal Foch Chair of French Literature was endowed by the munificence of Sir Basil Zaharoff.

[2] Mr. Heath Harrison bequeathed the sum of £20,000 for the creation of Travelling Scholarships and the promotion of Modern Language Studies in the University of Oxford.

revealing, as it must, the points of contact as well as the differences between the two nations, will lead to surer knowledge and greater mutual appreciation. Above all it will throw much light on English history, social and constitutional, on Middle-English, one might even say pre-Shakespearian literature, and particularly on the growth and evolution of the English language.

I ought at the outset to explain why I have retained the old-fashioned name of 'Anglo-Norman' in preference to that of 'Anglo-French', which has been proposed by many scholars. My first consideration has been one of expediency. 'Anglo-French' has a distinctly modern flavour; at all events it is ambiguous, and cannot be used without further qualification. The term 'Anglo-Norman' is, however, quite definite. It is universally applied to the period which extends from the Conquest to the time when the two races, with their respective languages and characteristics, blended into *one* homogeneous nation. I do not think that it has ever been challenged by historians, although some philologists have taken exception to its use. They urge that the French introduced by William the Conqueror was ' in its origin a mixture of various Norman and other Northern French dialects'[1] or 'that the characteristics of all the Northern French dialects were reflected in various regions of England'[2]. In short, that among the invaders and their descendants there prevailed a confusion of tongues, a very Tower of Babel, which might be labelled ' French' but could not be called ' Norman'. Such a conclusion is, however, contrary to facts. Indeed there is considerable evidence to show that at no period before the close of the fourteenth

---

[1] J. A. H. Murray, *New Engl. Dict.*, general explanation, p. x.
[2] H. A. Sturmfels, *Anglia*, viii (1885), p. 212. A similar view has been expressed by Miss Pope in her *Étude sur la langue de Frère Angier*, Paris, 1903, pp. 4-5.

century did any great divergence of speech exist among those who naturally used French in this Island. The erroneous conception can, however, be accounted for to some extent, especially if we bear in mind that continental Norman was not a homogeneous dialect, and that in phonetic development it lay across the border line of Western and North-Eastern French. Even to-day French *chat* is pronounced *ka* (for older *kat*) in the greater part of Normandy; whereas Fr. *chant* is pronounced *kã* (older *kant*) only along the eastern fringe. On the other hand for Fr. *chasse*, the pronunciations *kash* (older *kache*) and *shas* (older *chace*) are very evenly distributed. In the same way Fr. *cerise* is pronounced *shriz* or *sheriz* (older *cherise*) in the greater part of the province, but for Fr. *cercle* the pronunciation *shekl* or *sherkl* (older *chercle*) is confined to a few isolated areas.[1] From these examples we can infer that, as a rule, the pronunciation more widely spread in Normandy alone survived in England; or if the rarer pronunciation was also retained, it was restricted to a special meaning, e.g. Engl. 'cant' by the side of 'chant'. It is interesting to note that the form *chace* (*chase*) alone occurs in literary texts and became fashionable, while *cache* continued to find favour among the menial classes; hence the double pronunciation and double meaning in Modern English.

Although the spelling of scribes is a poor guide, there is reason to suppose that the pronunciation soon became more uniform in England than it ever was in Normandy. The phenomenon is not without parallel in European history. At home the Romans spoke a variety of dialects—the divergence of Italian dialects is notorious and in many cases goes back to great antiquity—but they imposed on their vast dominions a language which was practically uniform. Recent history furnishes us with an example not less

[1] Cf. Gilliéron et Edmont, *Atlas linguistique.*

striking. Men from various parts of the British Isles have taken to the Colonies their peculiarities of speech, but they in their own lifetime, or at all events their descendants, have gradually discarded those peculiarities, and adopted the characteristic pronunciation and phraseology which enables us to tell the Australian from the Anglo-Indian, the Cape Colonist from the Canadian. In the same way as British settlers, with their Scottish, Irish, or Welsh accents, their local drawls and intonations, and their varied colloquialisms, have created in each foreign region a fairly uniform standard of speech, the Normans of the eleventh and twelfth centuries introduced into this country a language which was practically uniform. In both cases the determining factors were essentially the same, namely, the influence of literature and the existence of an official language.

In the tenth and eleventh centuries Paris did not possess the prestige it was destined to acquire during the following age. On the ruins of the Carolingian Empire the descendants of Hugh Capet were laying the foundations of the new kingdom of France, but their task was beset by many difficulties; some of their feudatories were in open rebellion; others, like the Dukes of Normandy, professed allegiance, but wielded greater power and influence than their nominal overlords. Thanks to superior statesmanship the Normans, within their own borders, mitigated the evils of feudalism and set up an efficient government. Nay more, the sons of those who ruthlessly pillaged and destroyed the monasteries to such an extent that 'in Normandy scarcely a church survives anterior to the tenth century ',[1] became the protectors of the Church, and the champions of art and learning. The schools of Bec and Caen rose to fame before those of Paris. Latin was *par excellence* the language of

[1] C. H. Haskins, *The Normans in European History*, London, 1916, p. 35.

scholars, and was carried by them in the eleventh and twelfth centuries to a degree of perfection seldom equalled in later periods of the Middle Ages.   But the Nobles, who contributed materially to this Early Renaissance, and began to feel the fascination of intellectual pursuits, were as a rule ignorant of Latin.   To enlist their support and sympathy scholars must needs address them in French.   Thus arose in Normandy a literary language which, thanks no doubt to the fruitful influence of the revival of classical studies, revealed itself in the first two masterpieces which Northern French can boast of, the *Vie de S. Alexis* and the *Chanson de Roland*, as an instrument of power and promise.   This language differed little from that of educated Parisians, and underwent few changes until about the year 1160.[1]   It produced the most abundant harvest of masterpieces witnessed in any period of mediaeval French, the epic songs of *Roland* and *Guillelme*, romances of classical inspiration, the love story of *Tristan*, the *Lays* which Marie de France tuned to Celtic melodies, and the remarkable *Chronicles* of Wace.   That literary language, which was taught in the schools and spoken at the Court, could not fail to imprint a lasting character on the speech of all those who laid any claim to refinement and education.

Of greater importance, perhaps, than the influence of poets and schoolmasters, was the existence of a strong and fairly centralized government, first in Normandy and later

---

[1] Cf. G. Paris: 'Au XIe siècle il est impossible de dire ce qui sépare le normand du français pur,' *Vie de S. Alexis*, Paris, 1872, p. 65 ; and again, ' Ce n'est qu'à une période qui n'est pas antérieure au XIIe siècle que se sont manifestées entre le langage des Français et celui des Normands certaines différences,' *op. cit.*, p. 42.   The year 1160, as marking the end of the first A.-N. period, was suggested by Suchier, and has recently been confirmed by Tanquerey, cf. *Évolution du verbe en anglo-français*, Paris, 1915, p. 858.   See also C. de Boer, *La Normandie et la renaissance classique dans la littérature française du xiie siècle*, Groningue, 1912.

in England, using Latin in permanent records, but Norman
French in councils, courts of justice, and baronial courts of
all kinds.[1]   Even the Merchant Guilds, which sprang up in
England under the influence of foreign settlers, drew up
their statutes and conducted their proceedings in a language
which differed little from that used at Westminster or in
contemporary literature.[2]   In the eleventh century the
Normans had lost nothing of the adventurous spirit of their
Scandinavian ancestors.   As pilgrims, merchants, or soldiers,
or a combination of all three, they found their way into
many parts of France and Spain, and visited every Mediterranean port.   While their Duke was securing his hold
over England, other bands of Normans established a
powerful kingdom in the south of Italy.   But the high-
water mark of Norman power was reached in the twelfth
century, when the dominions of Henry II extended from
Scotland to the Pyrenees, and the clever diplomacy of the
monarch seemed on the point of bringing all western
Europe under his sway.   Henry was Angevin by birth,
but, as Haskins has forcibly urged in his recent history of
the Normans, it was as Duke of Normandy that he rose to
power, and it was thanks to Norman organization and
statesmanship that he was able to consolidate his vast
dominions.   'No Angevin influence is traceable in the field
of finance, and none seems probable in the administration
of justice.'[3]   His subjects belonged to many races and

---

[1] The publications of Maitland furnish the proof that even when the
court was presided over by an ecclesiastical lord, the pleading was
done in French, although the enrolment of it was in Latin. *Court
Baron* (Selden Soc.), p. 15.

[2] Many of the Guilds, those of London, Ipswich, Winchester,
Southampton, &c., were doubtless in existence in the twelfth century,
but their Laws have generally reached us in thirteenth- or even in
fourteenth-century versions. Cf. C. Gross, *The Gild Merchant*,
Oxford, 1890.   [3] Haskins, *op. cit.*, p. 100.

tongues, but 'over the various languages and dialects ran the Latin of the law and government, and the French of the court and affairs.'[1] The theory, that under the Plantagenets the language received a strong admixture of Angevin, does not rest on sufficient evidence.[2] The empire which the Normans had built up so rapidly was preeminently a maritime power. The sea-borne trade with Gascony soon became a source of wealth to the monarch and to the community, and furnished the Normans with an opportunity to show their genius for organization. The relations between skippers and merchants on the one hand, between captains and their crews on the other, were regulated; the duties and obligations of all concerned were clearly defined; and for the first time since the days of the Romans, law and order was introduced into a realm where anarchy and violence had long reigned supreme. These old sea-laws, known under the name of *Rolls of Oléron* were drawn up in Anglo-Norman about the time of King Richard I.[3]

Thus literature and education on the one hand, government and trade on the other, contributed powerfully to mould the speech of the Frenchmen, who streamed into this country in the wake of the Conqueror, into one homogeneous language. But this language once established in England developed independently. For reasons still

---

[1] Haskins, *op. cit.*, p. 88.

[2] It has been held by Miss Pope: 'La langue ordinaire qui avait cours était d'une nature composite, car au normand-picard du XIe siècle, qui en formait probablement la base, s'était ajouté au cours du XIIe siècle, un fort élément angevin (poitevin).' *Op. cit.*, p. 5.

[3] Some years ago I made a careful comparison of the oldest versions of the *Rolls of Oléron*, both Continental and English, and showed that they came from a common source *x*, written in A.-N. (*Oak Book of Southampton*, vol. ii, p. lxiv). But, as M. Ch. Bémont pointed out in a very generous review of my work (*Revue Historique*, cix (1912), p. 395), my further contention that *x* was probably derived from a Gascon original is based on evidence altogether too slight.

imperfectly known, it changed somewhat more rapidly
than the dialects of the Continent.   This was due, in some
measure at least, to the constant contact with another
language.   Increasing numbers of Englishmen learnt to
speak it.   'Uplondisshe men wil likne thymself to gentil
men and fondeth with greet besynesse for to speke Frensce,
for to be i-tolde of', says Trevisa[1], and some of them, like
Thomas Becket, rose to the highest dignities in Church
and State.   On the other hand, the Normans who at first
despised the language of the vanquished, and compared it
to the bark of dogs,[2] began from necessity or through
mere curiosity to familiarize themselves with it, and even
with the literature.   Marie de France and Denis Piramus
both assure us that they used English models, the one for
her *Fables*,[3] the other for his *Vie Seint Edmund le Rei*:[4]
and Geffrei Gaimar, in his *Estorie des Engleis*, borrowed
several points from the Anglo-Saxon Chronicle.[5]   By the
thirteenth century most of the Norman English and many
of the Saxon English were bilingual, but the contention of
Schreibner[6] that 'to both classes of the population French
was now an acquired language', is not supported by facts.
It is based largely on a mistaken interpretation of the anti-
foreign feeling which manifested itself in the reign of
Henry III.   The movement was directed, not against the
French language, but against the king's policy which

[1] Trevisa's translation of Higden's *Polychronicon*, lib. i, cap. 59.

[2] Wace, *Roman de Rou*, iii. 8094-5.

[3] The English original has left unmistakable marks on the work of
Marie de France.   Cf. *Die Fabeln der Marie de France*, ed. Warnke,
p. xliv.

[4] Cf. 'Translaté l'ai desqu'a la fin E de l'engleis e del latin' 3267-8,
Corolla Sancti Eadmundi, ed. Lord Francis Hervey, London, 1907.

[5] Cf. M. Gross, 'Geffrei Gaimar, die Komposition seiner Reimchronik
und sein Verhältnis zu den Quellen,' *Roman. Forschungen*, xvi (1904), I.

[6] O. Schreibner, *Über die Herrschaft d. franz. Sprache in England*,
Annaberg, 1880, p. 28.

tended to supplant Norman barons by foreigners more
amenable to royal authority ; and the *Provisions of Oxford*,
which marked the triumph of the barons, were drawn up
in French.

Until the middle of the fourteenth century Anglo-
Norman remained in every sense of the term a 'living'
language, and the natural medium of expression of a considerable portion of the population, of the king's household,
the nobility, the clergy, and even the merchants.[1] Nay
more, it was steadily gaining ground. A recent investigation[2] has shown that before 1300 few letters were written
in Anglo-Norman except by members of the aristocracy,
but fifty years later all but the lowest classes of the community conducted their correspondence in that language.
But bilingualism, the severance of intimate intercourse with
Normandy (after 1204), and the gradual absorption of the
Norman element in the population accelerated the decay of
Anglo-Norman. For a long time, however, it maintained
itself as the language of the aristocracy. In the fourteenth
century it was used by William Twich in his *Art de
Venerye* (a treatise on hawking), by Sir Thomas Gray in his
Scalacronica (1355), and in many satires and political
songs. The regulations of this University were drawn up
in Latin and French,[3] and students were forbidden to converse in any other language ;[4] and when Bishop Stapeldon

---

[1] It has been pointed out that the vernacular of English Jews
remained French up to the time of their expulsion, 1290 (cf. Schofield,
English Literature, p. 64). In Southampton, French remained the
official language of the Guild Merchants until the middle of the fifteenth
century (cf. Studer, *Supplement to Oak Book*, pp. 8, 9).

[2] F. J. Tanquerey, *Recueil de lettres anglo-françaises*, Paris, 1916.

[3] *Munimenta Academica*, 437 'Item diligenter debent attendere
quod Scholares sui regulam observent in Latinis vel in Romanis,
prout exigunt status diversi, et non observantes bene puniantur'.

[4] Cf. Statutes of Oriel Coll. (1328) and Exeter Coll. (1330), quoted by
Warton, *The Hist. of Engl. Poetry*, 2nd ed., vol. i, p. 5.

wished the nuns of Polsloe Priory fully to understand his
meaning, he drew up his injunctions not in English but in
Anglo-Norman.[1] When native production began to run
thin, continental writers lent their good offices. The exploits of the Black Prince were told by a Walloon for the
benefit of an English audience,[2] and for generations the
chronicles of Froissart continued to find appreciative readers
in this country. Although pleading in English was allowed
after 1362, French remained the official language of the
law down to the reign of Henry VIII, and lingered on until
the eighteenth century.[3] Even to-day the Royal assent to
a Bill is still expressed in French. But notwithstanding
these late survivals, Anglo-Norman was a dead language
by the middle of the fourteenth century.

Between the Norman tongue of the eleventh century and
the French spoken in England at the close of the fourteenth,
the difference is obviously enormous, but there is considerable evidence that, in spite of rapid changes, the language
was at all periods substantially the same in every part of
the country. No doubt, writers of continental birth, like
Marie de France, Denis Piramus, or Frère Angier, retained
some of the idiosyncrasies of their native dialect. Hesitation
prevailed in the pronunciation of certain sounds for which
English had no exact equivalent, e.g. French *u*. Investigations in this field are very complicated on account of the
notorious inconsistency of Anglo-Norman scribes. The

[1] *The Register of Walter de Stapledon, Bishop of Exeter,* ed.
F. C. Hingeston-Randolph, 1892 (A.D. 1319), p. 316.
[2] *Life of the Black Prince,* ed. M. K. Pope, and E. C. Lodge, Oxford,
1910. Tanquerey, however, questions Miss Pope's conclusion that the
author was a Walloon and claims the work for the A.-N. literature.
Cf. *Évolution du verbe,* pp. 818–19, 840.
[3] *The Reports of Cases* by E. Lutwyche († 1709) are drawn up half
in French, half in Latin. Cf. Vising, *Franska Språket i England,* iii,
p. 34.

spelling became even more confused when the revival of Middle-English writing introduced into French various peculiarities of Anglo-Saxon orthography (e.g. the spellings *ea* and *eo*). Allowance must be made also for those 'uplondisshe men' who, like William of Wadington, were reared in the country, where there was neither *burg ne cité*, and wrote a language of which they readily admitted they had but an imperfect knowledge. The rise of Paris as a seat of learning and the home of a brilliant court finally established for all times the superiority of Parisian French over other dialects, even over Provençal and Anglo-Norman, and made it the literary language of the whole of France. The vocabulary, and especially the spelling, of Anglo-Norman was bound to be affected to some extent. Later writers, like Gower, even endeavoured to write Parisian French.[1] But on the whole, the uniformity of the dialect was very little, if at all, impaired. From the twelfth century onward, Anglo-Norman was and remained a distinct language. Foreigners like Garnier, the biographer of Thomas Becket, might pride themselves on the superiority of their speech, because it was acquired abroad;[2] Welshmen like Walter Map[3] might poke fun at 'Marlborough French'; the fact remains, that 'Marlborough French' or French 'after the scole of Stratford atte Bowe' was the language current throughout the country. It is true that Luces de

---

[1] Tanquerey (*op. cit.*, pp. 828 sq.) has also detected the influence of N.-E. and E.-French on verbal endings, after 1250. This influence is chiefly noticeable in non-literary texts, and would seem to have affected the spelling rather than the pronunciation.

[2] 'Mis languages est buens; car en France fui nez,' v. 5820.

[3] Referring to a certain Gaufridus, bishop elect of Lincoln, Map says: 'Cessit igitur apud Merleburgam, ubi fons est quem si quis, ut aiunt, gustaverit, Gallice barbarizat, unde cum viciose quis illa lingua loquitur, dicimus eum loqui Gallicum Merleburge,' *De Nugis Curialium*, ed. M. R. James (Anecdota Oxoniensia), 1914, p. 246.

Gast [1] and the anonymous author of the *Poème sur l'Antéchrist* [2] blushed to confess, like Madame Eglentyne, that
'Frensh of Paris was to hem unknowe'. But the majority
of their countrymen were quite content with the knowledge
of what was still a fashionable and aristocratic language.
John Peckham (†1292), a distinguished Oxford teacher,
afterwards archbishop of Canterbury, continued to write
his letters in Anglo-Norman, although he had studied and
taught many years in the University of Paris. [3] Even in
the fourteenth century, when Parisian French had long
outdistanced other dialects as a literary medium, the French
language spoken in England was still fairly uniform. The
testimony of Higden (*c.* 1350) has often been cited, but has
hardly been sufficiently appreciated. In his *Polycronicon*
(lib. i, cap. 59) he says: 'Ubi nempe mirandum videtur,
quomodo nativa et propria Anglorum lingua, in unica
insula coartata, pronunciatione ipsa sit tam diversa; cum
tamen Normannica lingua, quae adventitia est, univoca
maneat penes cunctos.' Which John of Trevisa quaintly
renders (after 1385): 'Hit semeth a greet wonder how
Englische, that is the burthe tonge of Englisshemen and
her owne langage and tonge, is so dyverse of sown in this
oon ilond, and the langage of Normandie is comlynge
(imported) of another londe, and hath oon manere soun
among alle men that speketh hit aright in Engelond.' And
he further adds: 'Nevertheless there is as many dyvers
manere Frensche in the reem of Fraunce as is dyvers manere
Englische in the reem of Engelond.' Which shows that he
was well able to tell one dialect from another. He was an
educated man and remarkably well informed. Above all he

---

[1] Cf. E. Löseth, *Le roman en prose de Tristan*, Paris, 1891, p. 2.

[2] Mr. A. Rowlands of Jesus College has in preparation an edition of
this poem.

[3] F. J. Tanquerey, *Recueil de lettres anglo-françaises*, Paris, 1916,
p. xvi.

was an Oxford man and a fellow of my own college (Exeter).
Surely we could not desire a more trustworthy witness.
The tradition of a homogeneous Anglo-Norman speech
was still alive in 1415 when an enterprising (Oxford?)
teacher produced his *Dialogues Français*[1] for the benefit
of young gentlemen who desired to acquire a knowledge of
Parisian (?).   When asked for his name, the pupil is made to
answer : ' J'ai a noun Johan bon enfant, beal et sage et bien
parlant engleys, fraunceys et bon normand.'   'Good' Norman
still ranked as an independent language by the side of
English and Parisian French.   Modern scholarship, too, has
greatly strengthened our case.   A careful study of the
vocabulary of Middle-English led Professor Behrens[2] to the
conclusion that the French words taken up by the English
language before the end of the fourteenth century point,
almost without exception, to a Norman origin.   This view
has been confirmed by recent investigations, e.g. those of
J. M. Booker on *The French inchoative suffix in Middle-
English*,[3] and of Zachrisson on the *Anglo-Norman influence
on English Place-Names*.[4]   For a final solution of the
problem we must of course wait until Anglo-Norman has
been more systematically studied; but two points at least
seem fairly established : (1) That Anglo-Norman was not
a jargon but an independent language, as homogeneous in
character as the majority of French dialects.[5]   (2) That it

---

[1] P. Meyer, *Romania*, xxxii, pp. 49 sq.

[2] *Französische Studien*, v, pp. 105 sq., 309 sq., and Paul's *Grundriss*, i, pp. 960 sq.

[3] Dissertation, Heidelberg, 1912.

[4] R. E. Zachrisson, *A contribution to the Study of A.-N. Influence on
English Place-Names*, Lund, 1909.

[5] This view has been greatly strengthened by Tanquerey's masterly
study of the A.-N. verb, to which reference has already been made.
He sums up his results as follows : ' Ces quelques idées a priori laissent
donc supposer que l'anglo-français a été autre chose qu'une mauvaise
manière de parler et d'écrire le français ; ce sont des preuves véritables

was closely related to continental Norman, from which it derived its phonetic system and the bulk of its vocabulary. No one will deny that it also borrowed from other sources, but even Francien (Parisian French) includes in its vocabulary elements from almost every province of France. The statement of Paul Meyer[1] that 'il y avait en Angleterre plusieurs espèces de français comme il y a maintenant en Grèce plusieurs espèces de grec' must therefore be revised, or at least qualified; and with it disappears the strongest argument of those who urge that 'Anglo-French' is a more appropriate term than 'Anglo-Norman'. Gröber[2] was, I believe, the first to use 'Anglo-French' in this sense, but American and German scholars have almost without exception retained 'Anglo-Norman'. In France and England usage has varied, and many have, like myself, made confusion worse by using both terms indiscriminately. The desirability of arriving at an agreement must be obvious to every one, and I trust I have given adequate reasons for preferring 'Anglo-Norman'.

In my attempt to show that Anglo-Norman was a homogeneous language with distinctly Norman characteristics, I have broadly outlined its history down to the close of the fourteenth century. There remains the more difficult and delicate task of forming an estimate of the value (literary or linguistic) of the records which have been preserved. So many works are accessible only in MSS. or in faulty

que nous en trouvons dans l'étude que nous avons faite sur le verbe. Celle-ci met en évidence quatre points, que révélerait également toute étude générale sur l'anglo-français: d'abord l'unité de la langue dans un ouvrage donné; puis l'unité de la langue à un moment donné; ensuite l'évolution réelle qu'on peut observer pendant les trois siècles de son existence; enfin l'influence restreinte exercée sur elle par l'anglais,' p. ii.

[1] *Romania*, xxiv, p. 362.
[2] *Zeitsch. f. rom. Phil.*, vi (1882), p. 486.

editions that a final verdict cannot yet be passed. But from the material already available we may infer that, apart from the masterpieces of the twelfth and thirteenth centuries, there is little that bears the mark of superior talent. When the *élan* of the premature Renaissance had spent itself, the neglect of form and style became increasingly evident. The Normans established in England never again caught the true epic spirit so conspicuous in the *Chanson de Roland*; although their delight in lives of saints showed no sign of waning, they produced little that can bear comparison with *La Vie de Saint Alexis*. They were a people intensely practical, caring more for facts and ideas than for beautiful phrases. Their thirst for knowledge was unquenchable, their curiosity knew no bounds, but they had no stomach for pure sentimentality, and lyric poetry is feebly represented. In spite of the personal influence of Queen Eleanor and that of her sons, the songs of the troubadours found little echo in this country. On the other hand scientific works—as science was then understood—were in great demand. It was among the Normans of England that the *Physiologus*, the mediaeval text-book on natural history, was first translated into the vernacular (*Bestiaire* of Philippe de Thaun). The earliest French versions of Lapidaries appear also to be the result of their efforts.[1] Almanacs, prophecies, charms, medical recipes, cookery-books were plentifully supplied in prose and verse. Encyclopaedias, running to thousands of lines, were specially written for those unskilled in Latin. They can hardly be reckoned as specimens of literature, but they give us a comprehensive view of the beliefs and superstitions which were current in their days, and of the naïve theories which

[1] A final opinion must, however, be deferred until the question has been more fully investigated. In collaboration with Miss Joan Evans I am preparing an edition of all the extant A.-N. Lapidaries.

accounted for natural phenomena, and explained their inner and higher significance. History proved equally attractive to the Normans. Whilst in France, with a few notable exceptions, it continued to be written in Latin down to the time of Froissart, England was flooded with a mass of chronicles rhymed in French. Some of the earliest, those of Wace in particular, reveal fine workmanship and a real desire to supply trustworthy information. The later products are generally much inferior, in point both of style and of trustworthiness ; but even they can be turned to useful account by the modern historian.

The Renaissance of the eleventh and twelfth centuries was to some extent the outcome of a religious revival, which received its strongest impulse from Cluny, but found nowhere a wider scope than under the aegis of the Norman Rulers. Their people, although too deeply engrossed in the affairs of this world to be much given to mysticism, were nevertheless keenly interested in religion. As Jusserand puts it, ' The real religious poems we owe to the Normans are those poems in stone, erected by their architects at Ely, Canterbury, York, and Durham.'[1] Not content to provide stately buildings for monks and clerks, they claimed a share of their knowledge. The earliest translation into French of any section of the Bible, that of the Books of Kings,[2] was made in this country. Versions of the Psalter, the Gospel of Nicodemus, the Book of Revelation, &c., followed in course of time. Poems based on Biblical stories are numerous and still imperfectly known, but they are surpassed in number by treatises on the Deadly Sins, the follies of mankind, poems on the Love of God,

[1] J. J. Jusserand, *A Literary History of the English People*, 2nd ed., London, 1907, vol. i, p. 124.

[2] Cf. *Li quatre livres des reis*, ed. E. R. Curtius, *Gesell. f. rom. Lit.*, 26. Bd., Dresden, 1911 ; and the review by A. Stimming, *Zeitsch. f. rom. Phil.* xxxvi, p. 743.

exhortations to saintly life, dull reading when judged by modern standards, but not devoid of interest as the source of some of the earliest Middle-English writings. But the real value of Anglo-Norman civilization lies in the new orientation it gave to human thought. By breaking down racial barriers it fostered an active interchange of ideas between nations which had kept aloof from one another. It engendered a true cosmopolitan spirit, a catholicity of taste, which yielded a plentiful harvest. Men and ideas were esteemed for their intrinsic value, or their personal qualities. Italians, Bretons, Frenchmen from every province were given equal opportunities to display their talents in State and Church. The court of Henry II and Eleanor of Aquitaine was a centre of learned men and poets, as well as of warriors and knights. The gain was immeasurable. 'Geographically belonging, with the Scandinavian countries, to the outlying lands of Europe, the British Isles', it has been said, 'had been in serious danger of sharing their remoteness from the general movement of European life and drifting into the backwater of history. The union with Normandy turned England southward, and brought it at once into the full current of European affairs.'[1] A spirit of adventure and enterprise, sound statesmanship and business capacity, an appreciation of art and literature, and above all a lively curiosity were grafted upon a nation which had grown effete and unnerved.

Norman literature, which had begun on the Continent with works of the highest promise, continued productive in England. *La Chanson de Roland* and *Le Pèlerinage de Charlemagne* have been preserved in Anglo-Norman MSS., and both were translated or imitated in English. Richard Cœur-de-Lion, Fulk Fitz Warin, King Dermot became the heroes of new epic legends. But under a more peaceful

---

[1] Haskins, *op. cit.*, p. 82.

sky and more settled conditions, epic songs lost their war-like spirit and grew into romances of chivalry and adventure; and the stories of *Otinel* and *Fierabras* retained their popularity till well into the fifteenth century. So thoroughly did the Normans find themselves at home in this country, that by the end of the twelfth century they began to cele-brate the exploits of their former foes. Guy of Warwick, the Saxon champion who overcame Colbrand the Dane, and the legendary Boeve of Hampton became epic figures as. famous as Roland and Oliver, and won applause far beyond the compass of these Islands. It is less surprising to find Havelok and Horn extolled in similar manner, for they were after all of viking blood and the kinsmen of Ralph the Ganger.

Running through Norman literature there is a note of seriousness and piety. Boeve converts the giant Escopart and has him duly baptized. Guy of Warwick spends the evening of a boisterous life in the quietude of a monastery. If many warriors were sung in verse, they were as the grain of sand in the desert, compared with the multitude of saints who were similarly honoured. The legends that gathered round the names of saints are often very strange: orthodox teaching blends with ill-concealed pagan worship; true Christian piety and crude superstition are inextricably mingled. They hardly commend themselves as food for the soul, but as a rich mine of myth and folklore they would repay more careful study.[1] Closely connected with the Church was also the incipient Drama. The honour of producing the oldest extant play [2] in the vernacular belongs

---

[1] Prof. A. T. Baker, of Sheffield University, has facilitated such a study by his editions of the Lives of S. Richard (*Rev. Lang. Rom.* liii, 1910), S. Panuce (*Romania*, xxxviii), S. Paul l'Hermite (*Mod: Lang. Rev.* vi), S. Osith (*Mod. Lang. Rev.* vi–vii), and especially of S. Marie l'Égyptienne (*Rev. Lang. Rom.* lix, 1916–17).

[2] *Le Mystère d'Adam*, ed. P. Studer, 1918.

to an Anglo-Norman poet endowed with real dramatic skill and instinct. Religious spectacles with their impressive display could scarcely fail to become popular and were continued in English when French went out of use. The *Mystère d'Adam* has been preserved in a single MS., likewise the *Anglo-Norman Resurrection*, and many links connecting the English Miracles with the Norman drama must have been irretrievably lost.[1]

But the Normans did more than endow England with epic literature, legends of saints, and the elements of dramatic art. They brought the country once more into contact with Latin civilization. Many classical themes, the story of *Troy*, that of *Thebes*, the Romance of *Eneas* penetrated into this Island through the medium of French; together with tales from the distant East, of *Alexander*, of *Prester John*, of the *Sleepers of Ephesus*, to mention but a few at random; and when they ceased to be read in French, they retained their popularity in English adaptations.

By imparting to England something of the spirit of the classics and preparing the way for the greater Renaissance, the Normans have done a service which has hardly been adequately appreciated.[2] But from the point of view of literature their greatest merit has been to open to Western Europe the treasure-house of Celtic imagination. For centuries Saxons had lived side by side with Celts, as foes or peaceful neighbours, without even suspecting that any good might come from Wales or Ireland! No sooner had the

---

[1] Miss Foster has recently shown that the *Towneley Plays* were derived to a considerable extent from the *Northern Passion*, the ME. adaptation of an A.-N. poem, illustrating incidentally another channel through which A.-N. contributed to the development of the English drama. Cf. *Northern Passion*, E.E.T.S., original series, 145 and 147 (1913-16).

[2] The problem has been ably discussed by J. E. C. de Montmorency in the *Edinburgh Review*, Jan., 1919.

Normans settled in this country than new and wonderful tales began to stir the imagination of high and low. They told of travels to those enchanted islands in the Western Seas, whither Abbot Brendan journeyed with his forty monks; or they told of castles peopled with invisible hosts, of boats steered by invisible hands, of fairies who sought the love of mortal men, of maidens changed into white harts, of magic bows and swords, of sorcerers and seers. Other tales there were of a mysterious passion which the world had never before experienced. It was not the sensuous love of the Frenchman, nor the elemental passion of the Saxon, neither was it the lip-worship proffered by the troubadours, nor yet the fateful spell known to the ancients. It was the irresistible but complex feeling, mystical yet sensual, which united Tristan and Iseult, caused them to disregard all conventions, yet never lowered them in their own estimation. The manner in which these new themes penetrated into French literature is still to some extent a matter of dispute. But whether bilingual Bretons or Welsh bards equipped with sufficient French served as intermediaries between Celts and Normans, whether the contact was established through serious scholars or through strolling minstrels, in England or on the Continent, one thing seems certain, namely, that these themes in the hands of Anglo-Normans acquired a fecundity which they never possessed in Welsh or in Irish. Blending with religious aspirations they yielded the most beautiful of Christian legends, the *Holy Grail*. Exposed to the vivifying influence of the chivalry of Northern France and to the refinement of Provence, they grew into those exquisite stories of *Arthur* and his knights, which permanently endowed English literature with a most powerful source of inspiration.

Although Anglo-Norman means so much to England, it has been little studied and appreciated in this country.

'On s'étonne que l'Angleterre, pour qui l'ancien français est une langue nationale presque autant que pour la France, ne l'étudie pas avec plus d'ardeur et ne consacre pas, notamment, plus de travaux à la langue et à la littérature anglo-normande'.[1] Thus wrote a distinguished French Scholar some twenty-five years ago, and, sad to relate, his words have fallen on deaf ears. Interest in the subject would seem to have waned rather than increased. A century and a half ago Warton did not think that a correct estimate of Middle-English poetry could be formed if Anglo-Norman works were left out of consideration. Thomas Wright shared the same conviction and laboured unceasingly to secure a proper appreciation of Anglo-Norman writers.[2] More recent critics have seldom followed their good example. *The Cambridge History of English Literature* devotes special chapters to Anglo-Saxon and to the Latin literature produced in England, but refers only incidentally to Anglo-Norman production. Jusserand,[3] it is true, pays more attention to the subject, but almost confines himself to an analysis of French influences in England.

Continental text-books refer to Anglo-Norman writers in so far only as they fit into the great literary movements of France. G. Paris indeed attempted to do them justice in his *Littérature française au moyen âge*.[4] H. Suchier in his *Geschichte der französischen Literatur* made them the object of a separate study which can still be consulted with

[1] *Romania*, xxiv (1895), p. 158.
[2] The name of Francisque Michel, the indefatigable editor of A.-N. texts, should also be mentioned in this connexion.
[3] J. J. Jusserand, *op. cit.*, 1st ed., 1894.
[4] G. Paris has also contributed a number of useful articles, e.g., a review of Suchier's work (*Mélanges de littérature française*, pp. 21 sq.), 'La Littérature normande avant l'annexion' (*Mélanges*, pp. 71 sq.), 'L'Esprit normand en Angleterre' (*Poésie au moyen âge*, 2ᵉ série, pp. 45-74).

profit. J. Vising has devoted to the subject a life-long
interest and published some able monographs,[1] but it is
a matter of regret that his best work (*Franska Språket
i England*, Göteborg, 1900–02) is written in Swedish and
not accessible to the average English student. The fullest
account of Anglo-Norman literature is from the pen of
W. H. Schofield, a Harvard Professor. His *English Literature from the Norman Conquest to Chaucer* (London,
1906; reprinted, 1914) gives an excellent bird's-eye view of
the whole subject, and lays due stress upon the dependence
of Middle-English upon Anglo-Norman. But the work,
while it is well suited to the needs of the average reader,
is not sufficiently detailed, nor provided with adequate
bibliographical information to meet the requirements
of scholars. A ' Manual ' is wanted which will give an
account of what is still in MS., and will co-ordinate the
information scattered in periodicals, monographs, bulletins,
&c., by such a prodigious worker as the late Paul Meyer.
I have collected a considerable amount of material which
might form the basis of such a Manual, but nothing of
permanent value can be attempted before the libraries of
this country have been thoroughly investigated.[2]

A true appreciation of Anglo-Norman literature is hardly
possible until more texts have been edited, and several of
the existing editions revised and corrected. Here is a great
opportunity for young philologists desirous of acquiring
useful experience. The careful editing of a text affords an
excellent exercise. It stimulates the initiative and sharpens
the critical faculties. Moreover the field is wide and

---

[1] *Étude sur le dialecte anglo-normand du xii° siècle*, Upsala, 1882;
Sur la versification anglo-normande, Upsala, 1884, &c.

[2] For MSS. containing texts of a scientific nature, this investigation
is being carried on with admirable thoroughness by Dr. Singer of
Exeter College. It is earnestly to be hoped that he will ultimately
turn his attention to the remaining MSS. also.

provides for a variety of tastes. Some texts offer a purely linguistic interest; others can best be studied in connexion with the Middle-English works derived from them. Typical examples of the latter kind are the *History of the Holy Rood tree* by the late Professor Napier (E. E. T. S. No. 103, 1894) and the *Northern Passion* by Miss Foster (see above). In his book on *Gawain and the Green Knight*[1] Professor Kittredge has recently shown how much a practised and subtle critic can extract from the comparative study of these early texts.

A comprehensive 'Grammar' of Anglo-Norman is another desideratum. The work of Menger[2] contains a useful collection of facts, but lays no claim to completeness or critical treatment. Tanquerey's study of the evolution of the verb in Anglo-Norman[3] is more exhaustive. It is a praiseworthy attempt to solve a most intricate problem. Although some of the conclusions may have to be revised in the light of fuller knowledge, a great part of the work will prove of permanent value. The comparative study of Middle-English and Anglo-Norman philology has already yielded interesting results,[4] but there is ample room for

---

[1] G. L. Kittredge, *A Study of Gawain and the Green Knight*, Harvard Univ., 1916.

[2] L. E. Menger, *The Anglo-Norman Dialect*, Columbia Univ., 1904.

[3] F. J. Tanquerey, *L'Évolution du verbe en anglo-français (xii*-xiv* siècles)*, Paris, 1915.

[4] I refer especially to works like the following: Sturmfels, 'Der altfr. Vokalismus im Mittelenglischen bis zum Jahre 1400' (*Anglia*, viii), 1885; Einenkel, *Streifzüge durch die mittelengl. Syntax*, 1887; Behrens, 'Zur Lautlehre der französischen Lehnwörter im Mittelenglischen' (*Franz. Studien*, v), and 'Die französischen Elemente im Englischen' (Paul's *Grundriss*, i, pp. 799 sq.); Brinkmann, *Syntax des Französischen und Englischen*; Burghardt, 'Über den Einfluss des Englischen auf das Anglonormannische' (*Studien zur engl. Phil.* xxiv, Halle, 1906); Zachrisson, *Anglo-Norman Influence on English Place-names* (Lund, 1909); Bødtker, *Critical Contribution to Early English Syntax* (Christiania, 1910); Gadde, *On the History and Use of the Suffixes -ery, -age*

further investigation. The abundant material supplied by
Professor Wright's *Dictionary of English Dialects* should
be carefully explored.[1] Some use might be made also of
local records. Many boroughs have a considerable number
of documents in Anglo-Norman and Middle-English which
would repay examination.[2]

Finally, every student of Anglo-Norman has felt the need
of a trustworthy ' Dictionary '.[3] Kelham's work is notori-
ously incomplete and unreliable. Godefroy records Anglo-
Norman forms and meanings to a very limited extent.
Tobler's Dictionary, now in course of publication, is equally
incomplete in this respect.[4] Brüll's list[5] is necessarily of
limited value. The *New English Dictionary*, especially
in the later volumes, contains a mass of valuable material
but, like Brüll's list, confines its attention to words which
actually occur in English texts. I would humbly suggest
that an *Oxford Dictionary of Anglo-Norman* would constitute a worthy sequel to the *English Dictionary*.

The programme which I have outlined is so vast that it
calls for the friendly rivalry and collaboration of scholars in
every country. Nothing is further from my mind than the
suggestion that Oxford should monopolize these studies.

and -ment in English (Lund, 1910) ; Booker, *The French inchoative
Suffix -ss and the French -ir conjugation in ME.* (Heidelberg, 1912).

[1] J. Derocquigny, *A contribution to the study of the French Element
in English* (Lille, 1904), lays stress on the valuable information that
could be derived from that source.

[2] I have devoted considerable attention to the records of Southampton
(cf. my edition of *The Oak Book of Southampton*, 3 vols., 1910-11,
The Port Books of Southampton, 1913), and I hope at some future
date to complete my investigation.

[3] The want of such a dictionary was particularly emphasized by the
late Prof. Maitland.

[4] See my review of the first part of Tobler's Dictionary in *Mod.
Lang. Rev.*, xii (1917), p. 100.

[5] H. Brüll, *Untergegangene und veraltete Worte des Französischen
im heutigen Englischen*, Halle, 1913.

But I hope that we shall rise to the occasion, and not let others do *all* the work. For, let me ask, 'Is there a more fitting place for the study of Anglo-Norman than Oxford?' It was in the priory of St. Frideswide that Frère Angier wrote the legend of St. Gregory. It was in Oxford, too, that Peter of Peckam completed his *Lumiere as Lais*, the most successful Anglo-Norman encyclopaedia. The chronicler Nicholas Trivet was proud of his Oxford training, and the University still cherishes the memory of its first Chancellor, Robert Grosseteste—even though it may have forgotten that this distinguished teacher and divine was perhaps the ablest Anglo-Norman writer of his day.[1] More names could be quoted, and who could tell how much of the anonymous literature of the age emanated from scholars of this University. But we have much more than vague memories or venerable traditions. We possess in our libraries the products of their labour, the books which they wrote, numerous manuscripts which have been thumbed by compilers of catalogues or foreign palaeographers, but which have never been adequately studied. Like the ancient buildings that house them they are a rich legacy of the past, which it is our privileged duty not only to hold in trust, but to utilize for the benefit of sound learning.

The revived interest in Modern Languages, which is very evident in Oxford to-day, cannot fail to react favourably on the study of Anglo-Norman. Already we see hopeful signs of greater activity in this long neglected field.[2]

---

[1] His principal work in A.-N. is *Le Château d'amour*. The great popularity of this fine allegorical poem is attested by the large number of MSS. still extant, and by the English translations which appeared in the course of the thirteenth and fourteenth centuries. Cf. ed. J. Murray, Paris, 1918.

[2] The following editions are in active preparation:

(1) *A Year-Book of Edward II* (for the Selden Soc.), by Miss M. K. Pope (to whose valuable *Étude sur la langue de Frère Angier*

and edition of *The Life of the Black Prince* reference has already been made); Miss Pope is also contemplating an edition of the *Horn Romance*.

(2) *Le Voyage de Saint Brendan*, by E. G. R. Waters, Taylorian Lecturer in French.

(3) *The Treatise of Walter de Bibbesworth*, by C. T. Onions, Joint-Editor of the *Oxford English Dictionary*.

(4) *Poème sur l'Antéchrist et le Jugement dernier*, by A. Rowlands, Jesus College.

(5) *Anglo-Norman Lapidaries*, by Miss Joan Evans and Paul Studer.

The Taylorian Lecture

1920

MALHERBE

and the

Classical Reaction

in the

Seventeenth Century

By

EDMUND GOSSE, C.B.

1920

MALHERBE AND THE
CLASSICAL REACTION

In contemplating the chart of literary history we are
confronted by phenomena which more or less closely
resemble those marked on the geographical map. The
surface is not uniform, but diversified by ups and downs
of the feature that we call taste or fashion. A special
interest attaches to what may be described as the water-
sheds of literature, the periods which display these
changes of direction in thought and language. I propose to bring before you briefly some characteristics of
one of the most saliently marked of all these points of
alteration, that which led irresistibly and imminently to
the classical school, as it is called, in France, and from
France ultimately to the whole of Europe. Before doing
so, I must draw your attention to the fact that while
most of us are led to give special heed to movements
which tend, like the Romantic renaissance of poetry in
England two centuries later, to the emancipation and
even the revolution of literature, that of which I am
about to speak was deliberately introduced in the
interests of law and order, and was in all its features
conservative, and, if you choose to call it so, retro-
gressive. It did not aim at enlarging the field of
expression, but at enclosing it within rules, excluding
from it eccentricities and licentious freaks, and rendering it subservient to a rigorous discipline. In
this University, where the practice of poetry is now

conducted with so much ardour and with such audacity of experiment, you may or may not, as you please, see any parallel between the condition of France in 1595 and our own condition to-day.   My purpose is, with your leave, to describe the former without criticizing the latter.

The sixteenth century had been a period of great activity in the literature of France, where the interaction of two vast forces, the Renaissance and the Reformation, had introduced wholly new forms of expression into the language.   Prose had started from its mediaeval condition into full modernity in Calvin, and then in Montaigne. In poetry, with which we are concerned to-day, there had existed since 1550 the brilliant and feverish army of versifiers who accompanied Ronsard, 'the Prince of Poets', and claimed with him to have created out of the rude elements of the Middle Ages a literary art which linked modern France directly with ancient Greece. While England was still languishing under the early Tudors, and Italy had grown weary of her burst of chivalrous epic, France gave the world the spectacle of a society palpitating with literary ambition.   Ronsard's magnificent audacity had conquered for poetry, an art which had hitherto enjoyed little honour in France, the foremost position in the world of mental activity.   Verse, which had been treated as a butterfly skipping from flower to flower, was now celebrated by the Pléiade as a temple, as a sunrise, as the apotheosis of the intellect. Immensely flattered by being suddenly lifted to the status of a priesthood, all the budding versifiers of France, who a generation earlier would have withered into insignificance, expanded into affluent and profuse blossom.   By the year 1560 it was 'roses, roses all the way', but the misfortune was that the flowers were foreign, had been transplanted from Greece and Rome and Italy, and were not really native to the soil of France.

During the next generation, under conditions with which we have no time to occupy us to-day, there was a steady, indeed an almost precipitous decline in the quality of French verse. If we turn to our own litera-ture of half a century later, we see a parallel decline in the drama down from Shakespeare to Shirley and the later disciples of Ben Jonson. We all know how dis-concerting it is to pass from the sheer beauty of the great Elizabethans to the broken verse and the mixture of flatness and violence of the lesser poets of the Commonwealth. But in France the decadence had been still more striking, because of the extremely high line adopted by Ronsard and Du Bellay in their prose manifestos. The doctrine of the Pléiade had been as rigorous and lofty as a creed in literature could well be, and it rose to an altogether higher plane than was dreamed of by the English critics half a century later. No dignity, no assurance of high and pure poetic reso-lution could surpass the apparent aim of the manifestoes of 1549. Frenchmen, it seemed, had nothing to do but follow these exalted precepts and to produce the most wonderful poetry which the world had seen since the days of Pindar and Sappho. We cannot to-day enter into the question why these high hopes were almost immediately shattered, except so far as to suggest that excellent principles are sometimes insufficient to produce satisfactory practice. We have to look abruptly this afternoon into the conditions of French poetry in the last years of the sixteenth century, and to realize that those conditions had brought French literature to a point where reform was useless and revolution was inevitable.

There was no slackening—and I ask your particular attention to this fact—there was no slackening in the popularity of the poetic art. There existed, in 1595, as great a crowd of versifiers as had been called forth fifty years earlier by the splendour of the Pléiade. A feature of poetic history which is worthy of our notice is that an extreme abundance of poetical composition is by no means necessarily connected with the wholesomeness and vigour of the art at that moment. There was a crowd of poets in France during the reign of Henri IV, but they were distinguished more by their exuberance and their eccentricity than by their genius. I shall, in a few moments, endeavour to give you an idea of their character. In the meantime, let us be content to remark that the exquisite ideals of the Pléiade had degenerated into extravagant conventionality, into which an attempt was made to infuse life by a spasmodic display of verbal fireworks. The charm of sobriety, of simplicity, was wholly disregarded, and the importance of logic and discipline in literature ignored and outraged. The earlier theory, a very dangerous one, had been that poetry was the language of gods rather than of men, that it was *grandiloquentia*, an oracular inspiration. Being above mankind in its origin, it was not for mortal men to question its authority. It possessed a celestial freedom, it was emancipated from all rules save what it laid down for itself. Let us see what was the effect of this arrogance.

The scope of imaginative literature as practised by the Pléiade had been curiously narrow, so much so that it is difficult to distinguish the work of different hands except by the dexterity of the technique. The odes and pastorals of the lesser masters are just like those of Ronsard, except that Ronsard is very much more skilful.

But by the close of the century there was a wide divergence between the various poets in their themes and their points of view. Two of them greatly excelled their contemporaries in eminence and popularity, and these two were as unlike each other in substance as it was easy for them to be. The elder of these two was Salluste du Bartas, a writer whose quartos are now allowed to gather dust on the shelves, and who, when he died in 1590, was, with the exception of Tasso, the most eminent European writer of verse. His influence on English poetry in the next generation was immense. Translations of his works by Joshua Sylvester and others had begun to appear before his death, and were extremely popular. Du Bartas possessed qualities of intellect and art which are by no means to be despised, but his taste was execrable. He wished to create a national religious poetry on a large scale, and he has been called the ' Milton manqué de la France'. Du Bartas is all relinquished to evangelical and moral ex-hortation, and his immense *Les Semaines*, besides being one of the longest, is the most unblushingly didactic encyclopaedia of verse that was ever put forth as a poem. He had a very heavy hand, and he sowed with the whole sack. Our own Bishop Joseph Hall of Norwich, who called him ' some French angel, girt with bays ', described Du Bartas as—

The glorious Sallust, moral, true, divine,
Who, all inspirèd with a holy rage,
Makes Heaven his subject, and the earth his stage.

In his own time his myriad admirers preferred him above ' golden Homer and great Maro '. His earnest-ness and his cleverness—among other things he was the first man after the Renaissance to see that the obsession of the heathen gods was ridiculous in a Christian

literature—his abundance and his vehemence, made Du
Bartas a very formidable figure in the path of any
possible reform.

As an instance of the violence of fancy and gaudy
extravagance of language which had become prevalent
with the decline of the Pléiade, I will now present to
you what I select as a favourable, not a ridiculous,
example of the art of Du Bartas.   He wishes to paraphrase the simple statement in Genesis that, on the
fourth day, God set the stars in the firmament of heaven
to give light upon the earth.   This is how he does it:

> Even as a peacock, prickt with love's desire,
> To woo his mistress, strutting stately by her,
> Spreads round the rich pride of his pompous vail,
> His azure wings and starry-golden tail,
> With rattling pinions wheeling still about,
> The more to set his beauteous beauty out,—
> The Firmament, as feeling like above,
> Displays his pomp, pranceth about his love,
> Spreads his blue curtain, mixt with golden marks,
> Set with gilt spangles, sown with glistening sparks,
> Sprinkled with eyes, speckled with tapers bright,
> Powdered with stars streaming with glorious light,
> To inflame the Earth the more, with lover's grace
> To take the sweet fruit of his kind embrace.

Our first impression of such a passage as this is one of
admiration of its colour and of its ingenuity.   It is more
than rich, it is sumptuous; the picture of the wheeling
peacock is original and brilliantly observed.   But there
commendation must cease.   What could be meaner or
less appropriate than to compare the revolution of the
starry firmament as it proceeded from its Creator's
hands with the strut of a conceited bird in a poultry-
yard?   The works of Du Bartas are stuffed full with
these strained and fantastic similes, his surface sparkles
with the glitter of tinsel and pinchbeck.   At every turn

something majestic reminds him of an embroidery, of a false jewel, of something picturesque and mean. The planets, in their unison, are like the nails in a cart-wheel; when darkness comes on, heaven is playing at blind man's buff; the retreat of the armies of the King of Assyria reminds the poet of a gamekeeper drawing his ferret. He desires the snow to fall that it may 'perriwig with wool the bald-pate woods'. All is extravagant and false, all is offensive to the modesty of nature.

Du Bartas is stationed at the left wing of the army of poets. The right is held by Philippe Desportes, whose name has recently been made familiar to us by Sir Sidney Lee's investigations into the extraordinary way in which his works were pillaged in his lifetime by our Elizabethan sonneteers. Even Shakespeare seems to have read, and possibly imitated, Desportes's *Amours de Diane*. The producer in vast quantities of a kind of work which is exactly in the fashion of the moment is sure of a wide popular welcome, and the cleverness of Desportes was to see that after the death of Ronsard French taste went back on the severity of Du Bellay's classicism, and returned to the daintiness and artificial symmetry of the Petrarchists. It has been said that to the Italians of the sixteenth century Petrarch had become what Homer was to the Greeks and Virgil to the Latins. He was the unquestioned leader, the unchallenged exemplar. This infatuation, which spread through Europe, is of importance to us in our inquiry to-day, for Petrarch was really the worm, the crested and luminous worm, at the root of sixteenth-century poetry. It was extremely easy to imitate the amorous conceits of the Italian imitators of Petrarch, and of these imitators in France by far the most abundant, skilful, and unwearying was Philippe Desportes, to whom Petrarch's ingenious elocution appeared, as it appeared to all the critics of Europe, 'pure beauty itself'. By the close of the century it was no longer the greater Italians, such as Francesco Molza, who represented at its height the victorious heresy of Petrarchism, it was a Frenchman, of whom our own great lyrist, Lodge, in his *Margarite of America* in 1596, wrote 'few men are able to second the sweet conceits of Philippe Desportes, whose poetical writings are ordinarily in everybody's hand'. Desportes exercised over the whole of Europe an authority which surpassed that of Tennyson over the British Empire at the height of his reputation.

Here, then, was another and still more formidable lion couched at the gate of poetry to resist all possible reform. The career of Desportes had been one of unbroken prosperity. He had become, without an effort, the wealthiest and the most influential person of letters of his time. His courtly elegance had enabled him to be all things to all men, and although a priest of unblemished character, he had attended one Valois king after another without betraying his inward feelings by a single moral grimace. He had found no difficulty in celebrating the virtues of Henri III, and the anecdote about him that is best known is that he had been rewarded with an abbey for the homage of a single sonnet. He had exaggerated all the tricks of his predecessors with a certain sweetness and brilliance of his own, which had fascinated the polite world. The best that can be said of Desportes is that he was an artificer of excellent skill, who manufactured metrical jewellery by rearranging certain commonplaces, such as that teeth are pearls, that lips are roses, that cheeks are lilies, that hair is a golden network. But I will give you his own statement of his aim, not attempting to paraphrase his remarkable language. Desportes gives the following account of his ambition:

> I desire to build a temple to my chaste goddess. My eye shall be the lamp, and the immortal flame which ceaselessly consumes me shall serve as candle. My body shall be the altar, and my sighs the vows, and I will intone the service in thousands and thousands of verses.

What a ridiculous confusion of imagery! Here we have a man whose body is an altar, and whose eye—one of whose eyes—is a lamp, and whose passion is the candle in that lamp, and whose mouth and throat are detached from his body, and are preforming miracles in the vicinity. This is to take Desportes at his worst, and it is only fair to admit that the reader who winnows the vast floor of his work will find some grains of pure gold left. But the mass of these sonnets and odes and madrigals is extraordinarily insipid and cold, the similes are forced and grotesque, and everywhere pedantry takes the place of passion. When there is beauty it is artificial and affected, it is an Alexandrine beauty, it is the colour of the dying dolphin.

Such was the poetry which occupied the taste of France at the close of the sixteenth century, and whether its form was brief and amorous, as in the sonnets of Desportes, or long-winded and hortatory, as in the sacred epics of Du Bartas, it was uniformly exaggerated, lifeless, and incorrect. In all its expressions it was characterized by an abuse of language, and indeed, in the hands of the poets of the late Valois kings, the French tongue was hurrying down to ruin. One curious vice consisted in the fabrication of new phrases and freshly coined composite words. Of these latter, some one has counted no fewer than 300 in the writings of Du Bartas alone, and Professor Paul Morillot has observed that the licence which the poets of that age indulged in has been the cause of subsequent poverty in that direction, French having received and rejected such a glut of new and useless words as to have lost all appetite for additions of vocabulary. Another vice of the period was the ceaseless cultivation, in season and out of season, of a sort of antithetical wit. The sincerity of nature was offended at every turn by the monstrous cleverness of the writer, who evidently was thinking far more about himself than about his subject. Here is an example:

Weep on, mine eyes, weep much, ye have seen much,
And now in water let your penance be,
Since 'twas in fire that you committed sin,

and so on, with wearisome iteration of the hyperbole. We were to suffer from the same disease fifty years later, when a great English poet, capable of far nobler things, was to call the eyes of St. Mary Magdalene

Two walking baths, two weeping motions,
Portable and compendious oceans.

An excellent grammarian, M. Ferdinand Brunot, has remarked that at the end of the sixteenth century a lawless individualism—and in this term he sums up all the component parts of literature, style, grammar, treatment, and tone—had set in; that everybody had become a law to himself; and that the French language was suffering from the incessant disturbance caused by 'the fantastic individuality of writers' both in prose and verse.

This chaotic state of things, which threatened French literature with anarchy and French logic with bankruptcy, was brought to a stand-still and successfully confronted by the energy and determination of a single person. I recollect no other instance in the history of literature in which one individual has contrived to stem the whole flood of national taste. Of course, an instinct of French lucidity and reasonableness must have been ready to respond to the doctrine of the new critic, yet it is none the less certain that through the early years of the struggle there remains no evidence of his having been supported by any associate opinion. I dare say you recollect a famous Japanese print which represents a young lady standing on the edge of a cliff, and gazing calmly out to sea while she restrains the action of a great plunging horse by simply holding one of her feet down upon the reins. In the same way the runaway Pegasus of France was held, and was reduced to discipline, by the almost unparalleled resolution of a solitary man. This was François Malherbe, whose name, but perhaps very little else, will be familiar to you. I hope to show you that this poet, by the clearness of his vision and his rough independence, brought about a revolution in literature which was unparalleled. He cut a clear stroke, as with a hatchet, between the sixteenth century and all that came after it down to the romantic revival at the beginning of the nineteenth century, and he did this by sheer force of character. Malherbe was not a great poet, but he was a great man, and he is worthy of our close consideration.

Francois Malherbe was a Norman; there is a hint of the family having come from Suffolk, in which case the name may have been Mallerby, but we need not dwell on that. His parents were Calvinists, and he was born at Caen in 1555. This was, you observe, between the births of Spenser and Shakespeare; and Rabelais was just dead. Cervantes was eight years old, Lope de Vega was to be born seven years later. We ought to notice these dates : they give us a sense of what was preparing in Europe, and what was passing away ; a great period of transition was about to expand. Until he was thirty years of age Malherbe appears to have taken no interest whatever in poetry ; he was a soldier, a military secretary, a man of business. Then he went to live in Provence, where he read the Italian verse fashionable in his day, and began to imitate it. The kindest and most enthusiastic of his later disciples told Tallemant that Malherbe's early poems were 'pitiful'. We can judge for ourselves, since at the age of thirty-two he published a paraphrase, or rather a series of selections from Tansillo's *Lagrime di San Pietro*. The bad poets of the age were lachrymose to the last degree. Nothing but the honour of addressing you to-day would have induced me to read these 'Tears of St. Peter'. I have done so, and have even amused myself by paraphrasing some of them, but these I will not inflict upon you. It is sufficient to assure you that up to the age of forty the verses of Malherbe were not merely, as Racan put it, pitiful, but marred by all the ridiculous faults of the age. After all, I must give you a single example. This is translated literally from ' The Tears of St. Peter ' :

Aurora, in one hand, forth from her portals led,
Holds out a vase of flowers, all languishing and dead ;
And with the other hand empties a jar of tears ;
While through a shadowy veil, woven of mist and
        storm,
That hides her golden hair, she shows in mortal form
All that a soul can feel of cruel pains and fears.

At what moment Malherbe observed that this was a detestable way of writing, and conceived the project of a great reversal of opinion, we do not know. His

early life, and just that part of it on which we should like
light to be thrown, remains impenetrably obscure. But
we do know that when he arrived in Paris he had
formulated his doctrine and laid out his plan of campaign.
At Aix-en-Provence he had been admitted to the meet-
ings of a literary society, the chief ornament of which
was the celebrated orator and moralist Du Vair, who
ought perhaps to be considered as in some directions
the master of Malherbe. The ideas of Du Vair have
been traced in some of Malherbe's verses, and the poet
afterwards said, in his dictatorial way, 'There is no
better writer in our language than M. Du Vair.' It
was probably the dignity of the orator's attitude and the
severity of his taste in rhetoric which encouraged the
poet to adopt a similar lucidity and strenuousness in
verse. The two men, who were almost exactly of the
same age, may perhaps be most safely looked upon as
parallel reformers, the one of French verse, the other
of French prose.

Few things would be more interesting to us, in our
present mood, than to know how Malherbe, arriving in
Paris at the mature age of fifty, set about his revolution.
He found the polite world tired of frigid conceits and
extravagant sentimentality, above all tired of the licence
of the poets and the tricks which they were taking with
the French language. There was undoubtedly a longing for order and regularity, such as invariably follows
a period of revolutionary lawlessness, but no one was
giving this sentiment a voice. What was wanted after
such a glut of ornament and exuberance was an arbiter
and tyrant of taste who should bring poetry rigidly into
line with decency, plainness, and common sense, qualities
which had long been thought unnecessary to, and even
ridiculously incompatible with, literature of a high order.

All this we may divine, but what is very difficult to understand is the mode in which Malherbe became the recognized tyrant of taste. It was not by the production, and still less by the publication, of quantities of verse composed in accordance with his own new doctrine. Malherbe had hesitated long in the retirement of the country, waiting to be summoned to Court. Somehow, although he had published no book and can scarcely have been known to more than a handful of persons, he had a few powerful friends, and among them, strange to say, three poets whose work was characteristic of everything which it was to be Malherbe's mission to destroy. These were the Cardinal Du Perron, Bertaut, and Vauquelin de la Fresnaye. They formed the van of the poetical army of the moment, and it is a very curious thing that these three remarkable writers, each of whom remained faithful to the tradition of Ronsard, should have welcomed with open arms the rebel who was to cover Ronsard with ridicule. With a divine simplicity, they opened the wicket and let the wolf in among the sheep. They urged the King to invite Malherbe to Court, and, when His Majesty delayed, Malherbe very characteristically did not wait for a summons. He came to Paris of his own accord in 1605, was presented to Henri IV, and composed in September of that year the long ode called a ' Prayer for the King on his going to Limoges '. This is the first expression of classical verse in the French language.

In those days the intelligent favour of the King did more for a reputation than a dozen glowing reviews in the chief newspapers will do to-day. We must give credit to Henri IV for the promptitude with which he perceived that the cold new poetry, which must have sounded very strangely on his ears accustomed to the lute of Desportes and the trumpet of Du Bartas, was exactly what was wanted in France. He himself had laboured to bring back to this country, distracted as it had been in its late political disorders, the virtues of law, logic, and discipline. He recognized in this grim, middle-aged Norman gentleman the same desires, but directed to the unity and order of literature. A recent French historian has pointed out that ' the very nature of Malherbe's talent, its haughty, solemn, and majestic tone, rendered him peculiarly fitted to become the official and, as it were, the impersonal singer of the King's great exploits, and to engrave in letters of brass, as on a triumphal monument, the expression of public gratitude and admiration '. Malherbe, as has been said, was appointed ' the official poet of the Bourbon dynasty '.

The precious correspondence with his Provençal friend Peiresc, which Malherbe kept up from 1606 till his death in 1628, a correspondence which was still unknown a hundred years ago, throws a good deal of light upon the final years of the poet, and in particular on the favour with which he was entertained at court. There are more than 200 of these letters, which nevertheless, like most such collections at that age, succeed in concealing from us the very facts which we are most anxious to hear about. Thus, while Malherbe expatiates to Peiresc about queens and princes, he tells us nothing, or next to nothing, about the literary life in which we know that he made so disconcerting a figure. But that most enchanting of gossips, Tallemant des Réaux, has preserved for us an anecdote of a highly illuminating nature. We have seen that the supremacy in French poetry had been held for many years by Philippe Desportes, who was now approaching the close of a long life of sumptuous success. It could not be a matter

of indifference to the last and most magnificent of the
Ronsardists that an upstart, till now unheard of, should
suddenly be welcomed at court. He desired his nephew,
Mathurin Régnier—himself a man of genius, but not in
our picture to-day—he desired Régnier to bring this
M. de Malherbe to dinner. They arrived, but were
late, and dinner stood already on the table. The old
Desportes received Malherbe with all the politeness
conceivable, and said that he wished to give him a copy
of the new edition of his 'Psalms', in which he had
made many corrections and additions. Such a compliment from the acknowledged head of French poetry
was extreme, but Malherbe had already made up his
mind to bring down the reputation of Desportes with a
crash, as Samson destroyed the gates of Dagon in Gaza.
Desportes was starting to go upstairs to fetch the book,
when Malherbe in rough country fashion (*rustiquement*)
told him he had seen it already, that it was not worth
while to let his soup grow cold, for it was likely to be
better than his 'Psalms' were. Upon this they sat
down to dinner at once, but Malherbe said nothing more,
and when dinner was done he went away, leaving the
host heart-broken and young Régnier furious. This
must have been very soon after Malherbe's arrival in
Paris, for Desportes died in 1606.

All that has been recorded of the manners and conversation of Malherbe tends to explain this story. He
could be courtly and even magnificent, and he had a
bluff kind of concentrated politeness, when he chose to
exercise it, which was much appreciated by the royal
family. He was a tall, handsome man, with keen eyes,
authoritative and even domineering, generally silent in
society, but ready to break in with a brusque contradiction of what somebody else was saying. He was a

scorner of human frailty, believing himself to be above the reach of all emotional weakness. The violent force, which burned arrogantly in his spirit, comes out in everything which is preserved about him, in his verses, in his letters, in the anecdotes of friends and enemies. His retorts were like those of Dr. Samuel Johnson, but without the healing balsam of Johnson's tenderness. There was nothing tender about Malherbe, and we may admit that he could not have carried out his work if there had been. His intellectual conscience was implacable; he allowed nothing in the world to come between him and his inexorable doctrine. When he learned that the Vicomtesse d'Auchy (Charlotte des Ursins), the 'Caliste' of his own verses, had been encouraging a poet of the old school, he went to her house, pushed into her bedroom, and slapped her face as she lay upon her bed.

Tallemant tells us that 'meditation and art made a poet' of Malherbe, *non nascitur sed fit*. At no time did he learn to write with ease, and after so many years spent in the passionate cultivation of the Muse, his poetical writings are contained in as narrow a compass as those of Gray, who confessed that his 'works' were so small that they might be mistaken for those of a pismire. Malherbe had long pauses during which he seemed to do nothing at all except meditate and lay down the law. Balzac, who was one of those young men in whose company he delighted, declares that whenever Malherbe had written a thousand verses he rested for ten years. All this was part of a studied frugality. The Ronsardists and their followers had been lavish in everything; they had poured out floods of slack verse, loose in construction, faulty in grammar. If a slight difficulty presented itself to them, they evaded it, they leaped over it. Having no reverence for the French language, they invented hideous and reckless words, they stretched or curtailed syllables, in order to fit the scansion. There is recorded a saying of Malherbe which is infinitely characteristic. When he was asked what, in fact, was his object in all he was doing, he replied that he proposed 'to rescue French poetry from the hands of the little monsters who were dishonouring it '. The glorious Desportes, the sublime Du Bartas, the rest of the glittering and fashionable Petrarchists of Paris, what were they in the eyes of this implacable despot of the new intellectual order ? They were simply 'little monsters' who were 'dishonouring' what he worshipped with a fanatic zeal, the language of France.

When we turn to his own poetry, we see what there was in it which fascinated the opening seventeenth century. After all the tortures and the spasms, the quietude of it was delicious. If you go to Malherbe now, you must learn to put aside all your romantic pre-occupations. His verse is very largely concerned with negations : it is *not* ornamented, it is not preposterous, it is not pedantic. It swept away all the insincere imagery and all the violent oddities of the earlier school. For example, Bertaut had written, wishing to explain his tears :

> By the hydraulic of mine eyes
> The humid vapours of my grief are drawn
> Through vacuums of my sighs.

Desportes had talked of a lover who was 'intoxicated by the delectation of the concert of the divine harmony' of his mistress. All this preciousness, all this affectation of the use of scientific terms in describing simple emotions, was the object of Malherbe's ruthless disdain. Ronsard had said, 'The more words we have in our

language, the more perfect it will be '. Malherbe replied,
' No, certainly not, if they are useless and grotesque
words, dragged by the hair of their heads out of Greek
and Latin, an outrage on the purity of French grammar '.
He advised his disciples to eject the monstrous creations
of the neo-Hellenes, and to go down to the quays of
Paris and listen to the dock-labourers. They used
genuine French words which ought to be redeemed
from vulgar use, and brought back to literary service.

The existing poems of Malherbe, written at intervals
during the last twenty years of his life, are largely
pieces of circumstance. They are odes on public events,
such as the retaking of Marseilles, the official journeys
of the King, the regency of the Queen Mother, and the
alliance between France and Spain. They are elegies
on the deaths of private persons, a subject on which
Malherbe expatiates with the utmost dignity and
solemnity. They are sonnets, very unlike the glittering
rosy gimcracks of the preceding generation, but stiff
with stately compliment and colourless art. There is
no exact English analogue to the poetry of Malherbe,
because in the seventeenth century whenever English
verse, except in the hands of Milton, aimed at an effect
of rhetorical majesty, its stream became clouded. We
may observe the case of Cowley, who, I think, had
certainly read Malherbe and was influenced by him, in
spite of the diametrical views they nourished with regard
to the merit of Pindar. Cowley, at his rare and occasional best, has the same serious music, the same clear
roll of uplifted enthusiasm, the same absolute assurance
as Malherbe. He has the same felicity in his sudden
and effective openings. But there is too frequently
confusion, artifice, and negligence in Cowley. In
Malherbe all is perfectly translucent, nothing turbid is

allowed to confuse the vision, no abuse of wit is left to
dazzle the attention or trip up steadily advancing progress of thought. It is not easy to give an impression in
English of the movement of this clear and untrammelled
advance. But here are a couple of stanzas from the 1611
Ode to the Queen Regent on occasion of the King's
Mediterranean expedition :

> Ah! may beneath thy son's proud arm down fall
>   The bastions of the Memphian wall,
> And from Marseilles to Tyre itself extend
>   His empire without end.
>
> My wishes, p'rhaps, are wild; but—by your leave—
>   What cannot ardent prayer achieve?
> And if the gods reward your service so
>   They'll pay but what they owe.

By general consent the crown of Malherbe's poetic
genius is the famous 'Consolation to Monsieur Du
Perier on the death of his daughter'. It contains the
best-known line of Malherbe—

> Et, Rose, elle a vecu ce que vivent les roses,

about which I would merely say that it is one of those
accidental romantic verses which occur here and there
in all the great classical poets. There are several in
Pope, where they are no more characteristic of his
general style than is this of Malherbe's. So far from
being the chief line in the poem, it is, in spite of its
beauty, the least important to us in our present inquiry.
The 'Consolation' consists of twenty-one stanzas, written
long after the sad event of the death of the young lady,
whose name, by the way, was not Rose, but Marguerite.
The advice which the poet gives to the stricken father is
stoical and Roman. Weary yourself no more with
these useless and prolonged lamentations ; but hence-

forth be wise, and love a shadow as a shadow, and extinguish the memory of extinguished ashes. The instances of Priam and Alcides may seem to have little in them to cheer Du Perier, but we must remember that antiquity was held a more sacred authority three hundred years ago than it is now. Malherbe, with great decorum, recalls to Du Perier the fact that he himself has lost two beloved children. The poor man under his thatched roof is subject to the laws of death, nor can the guard on watch at the gates of the Louvre protect our kings against it. To complain of the inevitable sacrifice, and to lose patience with Providence, is to lack wisdom. The only philosophy which can bring repose to a heart bereaved is implicit submission to the will of God.

All this may not seem very original, but it is exquisitely phrased, and it is sensible, dignified, and wholesome. There is in it a complete absence of the ornament and circumstance of death which had taken so preposterous a place in the abundant elegiac poetry of the sixteenth century. We are familiar with the grotesque and sumptuous appeals to the *macabre* which we meet with in Raleigh, in Donne, in Quarles, all the dismal trappings of the tomb and embroideries of the winding-sheet. They are wholly set aside by Malherbe, whose sonnet on the death of his son is worthy of special study. This young man, who was the pride of the poet's life, was killed in a duel, or, as the father vociferously insisted, murdered by a treacherous ruffian. Malherbe made the courts ring with his appeals, but he also composed a sonnet, which is a typical example of his work. It is not what we should call 'poetical', but in clearness, in force, in full capacity to express exactly what the author had in mind to say, it is perfect. We seem to hear the very cry of the fierce old man shrieking for revenge on the slayer of his son. The sonnet was composed some time after the event, for the whole art of Malherbe was the opposite of improvisation. One amusing instance of his deliberate method is to be found in the history of his ode to console President Nicolas de Verdun on the death of his wife. Malherbe composed his poem so slowly, that while he was writing it the President widower not merely married a second time, but died. The poet, with consummate gravity, persisted in his task, and was able to present the widow with the consolation which her late husband should have received after the death of her predecessor.

During thirty years of growing celebrity, Malherbe fought for his doctrine. He had but slowly become a convert to his own laws, but when once they were clearly set out in his brain, he followed them scrupulously, and he insisted that the world should obey them too. It seems a strange thing that it was the young men who followed him first and with most enthusiasm, until the fashionable ladies of Paris began to compete with one another in support of the classical doctrine, and in repudiation of their old favourite Desportes, whose fame came down clattering in a single night, like Beckford's tower at Fonthill. Malherbe brought poetry into line with the Court and the Church, in a decent formality. Largely, as is always the case in the history of literature, the question was one more of language than of substance. Take, for example, the 'Stanzas to Alcandre on the Return of Oranthe to Fontainebleau', and you will find them as preposterous in sentiment, as pretentious and affected in conception, as any sonnet of Desportes, perhaps more so, but their diction is perfectly simple and graceful, and they are composed in faultless modern French. Long before Moliere was born Malherbe was in the habit of reading his verses to an old servant, and if there was a single phrase which gave her difficulty, he would scrupulously revise it.

He was supported by a sublime conviction of his own value. It was a commonplace in all the poetical literature of the sixteenth century to claim immortality. Desportes had told his mistress that she would live for ever like the Phoenix, in the flame of his sonnets. We all remember Shakespeare's boast that 'not marble, nor the gilded monuments of princes shall outlive this powerful rhyme'. But no one was ever more certain of leaving behind him a lasting monument than Malherbe. He said, addressing the King :

All pour their praise on you, but not with equal hand,
For while a common work survives one year or two,
What Malherbe writes is stamped with immortality.

The self-gratulation at the close of the noble ' Île de Ré' ode is quite disconcerting. In this case, also, he reminds the King that

The great Amphion, he whose voice was nonpareil,
    Amazed the universe by fanes it lifted high;
Yet he with all his art has builded not so well
        As by my verse have I.

His boast, extravagant as it sounds, was partly justified. Not in his own verse, but in that which his doctrine encouraged others to write—and not in verse only, but in prose, and in the very arrangement and attitude of the French intellect—Malherbe's influence was widespreading, was potent, and will never be wholly superseded. He found French, as a literary language, confused, chaotic, no longer in the stream of sound tradition. He cleared out the channel, he dredged away the mud and cut down the weeds ; and he brought the pure water back to its proper course. Let us not suppose that he did this completely, or that his authority was not challenged. It was, and Malherbe did not live to see the victory of his ideas. He did not survive long enough to found the Académie, or to welcome Vaugelas, the great grammarian who would have been the solace of his old age. There were still many men of talent, such as Pélisson and Agrippa d'Aubigne, who resisted his doctrine. But he had made his great appeal for order and regularity ; he had wound his slug-horn in the forest. He had poured his ideas into the fertile brain of Richelieu ; he had started the momentous discussions of the Hôtel Rambouillet. He had taught a new gene-ration to describe objects in general terms, to express natural ideas with simplicity, to select with scrupulous care such words as were purely French and no others, to eschew hiatus and inversion and to purify rhyme, to read the ancients with sympathetic attention but not to pillage them. His own limitations were marked. He seems to have had no sense whatever for external nature ; while he overvalued a mathematical exactitude of balance in versification and a grandiose severity in rhetoric.

But we are not attempting this afternoon to define the French Classic School, but merely to comprehend how and when it came into being. It preceded our own Classic School by the fifty years which divide Malherbe from Dryden, who, in like manner, but with far less originality, freed poetry from distortion, prolixity, and artifice. Whe Malherbe died no one could guess how prodigious would be the effect of his teaching. Indeed, at that moment, October 6, 1628, there might even seem to be a certain retrogression to the old methods, a certain neglect of the new doctrine, which seemed to have been faintly taken up.   But, looking back, we now see that at the moment of Malherbe's death, Corneille was on the point of appearing, while there were children in the nurseries who were to be La Fontaine, Pascal, Molière, Mme de Sevigné, Bossuet.   Boileau and Racine were not even born, for Malherbe sowed early and the harvest came late.

The ruling passion accompanied this resolute reformer to the very close of his career.   His faithful disciple, Racan, his Boswell, has drawn for us the last scene :

> One hour before he died, M. de Malherbe woke with a start out of a deep slumber, to rebuke his hostess, who was also his nurse, for using an expression which he did not consider to be correct French. When his confessor ventured to chide him, he replied that he could not help it, and that he wished to preserve up to the moment of his death the purity of the French language.

NOTE

The passage on p. 8 is quoted from Josuah Sylvister's version of ' Les Semaines'.   For all the other translations the lecturer is responsible.